REMARKABLE TREES

OF SOUTH AFRICA

REMARKABLE TREES
OF SOUTH AFRICA

Neels Esterhuyse
Jutta von Breitenbach
Hermien Söhnge
Izak van der Merwe

BRIZA

Published by
BRIZA PUBLICATIONS
CK 1990/011690/23

BRIZA
www.briza.co.za
PO Box 11050
Queenswood 0121
Pretoria
South Africa

Second edition, first impression 2016

Copyright © in text: The authors
Copyright © in photographs: The authors and individual photographers listed
Copyright © in published edition: Briza Publications

All rights reserved. No part of this publication may be reproduced or transmitted in any form or by any means without written permission of the copyright holders.

ISBN: 978-1-920217-66-2

Project manager: Reneé Ferreira
Cover design: Ronelle Oosthuizen
Page layout: Alicia Arntzen, The Purple Turtle Publishing CC
Reproduction: Resolution Colour, Cape Town
Printed and bound by ABC Press, Epping, Cape Town

FRONT COVER: Door-frame tree (*Ficus burkei*) at Modderfontein, Rustenburg, North West
BACK COVER: The late Ms Jutta von Breitenbach admiring the largest matumi tree in South Africa, Amorentia Estate, Limpopo
ENDPAPERS: Buffalo grazing in a fever tree forest, Pafuri area, Kruger National Park (Photo: René de Klerk)
HALF TITLE PAGE: The Sagole baobab seen through the eyes of Josua Nell, emeritus professor in Fine Arts, Rhodes University, Grahamstown
TITLE PAGE: A large-leaved rock fig with octopus-like branches clinging to a rock face in the Soutpansberg
DEDICATION: Forest officer with village children at the giant Ga-Ratjeke baobab
CONTENTS: The saligna gum avenue at the O'Connor memorial, Woodbush, Tzaneen

Photographic credits
The photographs that appear in this book are mainly by Enrico Liebenberg (www.championtrees.com); the Department of Agriculture, Forestry and Fisheries; Izak van der Merwe; Dr Friedrich von Breitenbach (deceased) and Neels Esterhuyse. Other photographers are acknowledged.

Shutterstock images: p. 101 (bottom); p. 108; p.138; p. 143 (bottom); p. 144; p. 145; p. 178; p. 183 (bottom); p. 215; p. 239 (bottom); p. 250 (top); p. 253 (bottom)

DEDICATION

In tribute to all foresters, conservationists and tree lovers of this country who contributed to the protection of our tree heritage.

The contributions, where applicable, of our indigenous people – those living off, and in the shade of, our trees were most valuable, and are highly esteemed. They, too, have contributed towards ensuring that their descendants will be able to enjoy our trees. To those future generations, then, this book is dedicated.

CONTENTS

Foreword 11
Acknowledgements 12
Preface to the Second Edition 13
Introduction 14
The Big Five trees of South Africa 21
Champion trees of South Africa 38
Trees as monuments and in gardens, parks and arboreta 62
Tree and forest conservation in South Africa 104
Trees and science 114
South Africa's forestry industry 118
Tree families 123

CYATHEACEAE
Tree Fern Family 124

ZAMIACEAE
The Cycad Family 125

PODOCARPACEAE
The Yellowwood Family 131

CUPRESSACEAE
The Cypress Family 134

ARECACEAE
The Palm Family 138

POACEAE
The Grass Family 146

LILIACEAE
The Lily Family 148

CANNABACEAE
The Hemp Family 152

MORACEAE
The Fig and Mulberry Family 154

PROTEACEAE
The Protea Family 161

FAGACEAE
The Beech Family 168

PORTULACACEAE
The Portulaca/Purslane Family 174

LAURACEAE
The Laurel or Avocado Family 175

ROSACEAE
The Rose Family 179

FABACEAE SUBFAMILY MIMOSOIDEAE
The Thorn Tree Family 182

FABACEAE SUBFAMILY CAESALPINIOIDEAE
The Flamboyant Family 195

FABACEAE SUBFAMILY PAPILIONOIDEAE
The Pea Family 200

PTAEROXYLACEAE
The Sneezewood Family 205

MELIACEAE
The Mahogany Family 207

EUPHORBIACEAE
The Milkbush Family 211

CACTACEAE
The Cactus or Prickly Pear Family 215

ANACARDIACEAE
The Mango Family 217

MYRTACEAE
The Myrtle or Eucalyptus and Guava Family 221

PINACEAE
The Pine Family 228

ARALIACEAE
The Cabbage Tree Family 232

VITACEAE
The Grape Family 233

BOMBACACEAE
The Kapok Family 234

SAPOTACEAE
The Milkwood Family 240

OLEACEAE
The Olive Family 243

GENTIANACEAE
The Gentian Family 246

COMBRETACEAE
The Bushwillow Family 247

APOCYNACEAE
The Oleander Family 249

BIGNONIACEAE
The Jacaranda Family 251

PEDALIACEAE
The Sesame Family 254

RUBIACEAE
The Gardenia Family 255

ASTERACEAE (COMPOSITAE)
The Daisy Family 256

Fallen Giants 258

Bibliography 260

Index 261

Sponsors

Special thanks to Nicky and Strilli Oppenheimer of E Oppenheimer & Son for their support of this book.

Strilli Oppenheimer in Brenthurst Garden, where indigenous and exotic trees complement each other. The eucalypt tree in the background is a remnant of the original Forest Town.

The generous contribution of Ms Joey van der Merwe is hereby recognised, made in memory of her late husband Mr Wilson van der Merwe, who contributed to forestry research and management during a long career spanning from 1946 to 1984. He became Director: Forestry Research, and ended his career as Deputy Director-General: Forestry. His career influenced his son (author Izak van der Merwe) to follow in his footsteps as forest scientist.

Pretoria Tree Seeds
For a greener world
mwesterhuyse@lantic.net

Non-financial contributors

agriculture, forestry & fisheries
Department:
Agriculture, Forestry and Fisheries
REPUBLIC OF SOUTH AFRICA

Champion Tree Project of South Africa

National Register of Big Trees of South Africa

bringing ideas to life

Adopt a Champion Tree Programme

Marching towards the future and the continued protection of our tree heritage (Photo: Department of Water Affairs and Forestry)

Foreword

"… Just thinking about trees and their indifferent majesty and our love for them teaches us…how observing of life we can be, when we can honour this beauty that owes us nothing."

– Elegance of the Hedgehog –

The beauty we observe in nature is no ordinary matter, and trees play an important part in shaping the landscape of a country. Given the rich diversity of indigenous and introduced trees in South Africa, coupled to a growing public interest in trees, books celebrating this heritage were bound to see the light. The first edition of this book, published in 2001 as a guide to our own remarkable trees, greatly contributed to the body of knowledge of local tree specimens that are of outstanding value owing to size, age and other factors. It can be said, without exaggeration, that this book is the ultimate reference work on the tree heritage of the country, given the wide scope and depth of information presented. The information was meticulously gathered over a long time by the authors, with the assistance of many knowledgeable people. The book strikes a balance between science and readability, and therefore presents facts, history, anecdotes and myths about our local trees in an informative and entertaining style accessible to the public.

The first publication of *Remarkable Trees of South Africa* sparked many new and exciting developments regarding the socialisation and conservation of trees in South Africa. It also gave publicity to the National Register of Big Trees of South Africa (NRBTSA©), initiated by the Dendrological Society of South Africa. Known as the Big Tree Register, its aim to identify and give recognition to the largest indigenous species, to measure and to register them. The list serves as a basis for, and is in certain aspects also congruent with, the Champion Tree Project of the Department of Agriculture, Forestry & Fisheries. This project was launched under the leadership of co-author Izak van der Merwe, supported by an enthusiastic and knowledgeable team. Both projects have contributed to the conservation of trees and to enhancing public awareness about trees. Furthermore, the long and ongoing debate on the real 'Big Five Trees' has finally been settled, while highlighting the tallest trees, both indigenous and alien, the most corpulent ones, the most curious and the most special forest trees in South Africa.

Readers are encouraged to look in awe at trees for their beauty, marvel, shape, cultural features, the trunks and branches, or the colour and texture of their leaves. While there is so much to be admired visually, it is no wonder that new 'professions' such as tree-climbing and canopy rides are fast becoming popular – not only worldwide but also locally, whilst at the same time supporting scientific tree management. A bird's eye view is given of the relationship between trees and science, with some reference to their important medicinal value. A captivating story is told – my personal favourite – of how a very valuable camel thorn forest in the Northern Cape was saved through the cooperation of a variety of concerned stakeholders.

Valuable contributions of the private sector are highlighted, from entrepreneurs utilising cocoons of moths breeding in trees and others putting the fruit of the marula tree to delicious use, to the tireless efforts of an amateur agriculturalist; all contributing in a very special way to a number of positive outcomes. Clearly these are all laudable examples of assisting in alleviating the great need for job creation, thereby enhancing the respectability of the livelihood of members of a largely rural community – that part of our nation whose lives are the most intimately intertwined with our scarce and valuable trees.

Naas Grové
President: Dendrological Society of South Africa

Acknowledgements

This book would not have been possible without the contribution of numerous persons over thousands of years. Starting with the Latin naturalist Pliny (the Elder), AD 23 to 79, a vast number of adventurers, sailors, writers, poets, botanists, businesspeople, government and other officials, foresters, farmers and plant enthusiasts could line up to receive due thanks. To them can be added the many contemporary contributors, known and unknown. To all of these people our sincere appreciation and thanks.

We also acknowledge those generations of indigenous people whose knowledge of plants and trees was passed on faithfully and meticulously by mouth to the next and the next – until today's generation, and those to come will join in expressing their thanks and appreciation.

More specifically we are indebted to a number of organisations and individual members of these organisations for information provided. They are, in alphabetical order:
- Agricultural Research Council
- APBCO Insurance Brokers
- Aurecon
- Bartolomeu Dias Museum Complex
- Botanical Society of South Africa
- Cycad Society of South Africa
- Dendrological Society of South Africa
- Department of Agriculture, Forestry and Fisheries
- Department of Environmental Affairs
- Department of Forest Science, University of Stellenbosch
- Department of Water Affairs
- E Oppenheimer and Son
- Forestry South Africa
- George Museum
- Hans Merensky Holdings Pty Ltd
- Institute for Commercial Forestry Research
- Institute for Parks and Recreation (Southern Africa)
- MONDI Ltd
- Nasionale Afrikaanse Letterkundige Museum en Navorsingsentrum (NALN, Bloemfontein)
- Nelson Mandela Bay University, Saasveld Campus
- SANBI (South African National Biodiversity Institute)
- SAPPI Ltd
- SA Forestry Company Ltd (SAFCOL)
- South African Heritage Resources Agency (formerly National Monuments Council)
- Tree Society of Southern Africa
- Voortrekker Museum, Pietermaritzburg
- Wildlife and Environment Society of South Africa
- York Timbers

Special mention must be made of the unflagging diligence of the late Ms Jutta and Dr Friedrich von Breitenbach. Dr Fried rendered unsurpassed service to the erstwhile Department of Forestry by developing a conservation-orientated management and utilisation system for indigenous forests. The couple founded the Dendrological Foundation, followed by the Dendrological Society of South Africa, with the aim of promoting the protection and preservation of trees and tree-dominated ecosystems. The *National Register of Big Trees of South Africa*, for which they devised the local tree-measuring formula and methodology, is the brainchild of this remarkable couple. They have also made a valuable contribution to literature on forest and tree flora, thereby promoting the serious study of trees in southern Africa. Dr Fried compiled the *National List of Indigenous Trees* and the *National List of Introduced Trees* (both illustrated by Jutta), and several lists of common tree names in the indigenous languages. A final monumental work by the Von Breitenbach couple is the *Tree Atlas of Southern Africa*, a bilingual encyclopaedic opus on the more than 1 300 indigenous species in southern Africa.

Preface to the second edition

The first edition of *Remarkable Trees of South Africa* seems to have filled a particular niche in the interest of not only tree-lovers, but also the layman, not necessarily keen on the intricacies of a specialised botanical study. The addition of historical snippets thrown in randomly must have attracted the lover of history, too.

This wide interest has resulted in valuable feedback, as had been requested in the first edition. Comments and suggestions, mostly positive, were received from many quarters. Specimens of trees qualifying as remarkable for various reasons were reported, while further information about existing features were brought to the attention of the authors.

The introduction of new measuring instruments has resulted in more accurate measurements, ensuring the veracity of our facts. In this respect, the assistance of knowledgeable tree climbers has been of great value, especially towards decisive information with regard to the National Register of Big Trees and of the Champion Tree Project (a project introduced two years after the first edition of this book was published). Several new trees were discovered that could be brought into consideration, and more accurate tree height measurements were made, with the result that it can be announced that the tallest tree in South Africa reaches up to an impressive 81,5 m.

Since the first edition of the book appeared, several new discoveries have been made. A new tree height record of 115,72 m has been set by a giant redwood tree (*Sequoiadendron giganteum*), found in the Redwood National Park in the United States. It has been found, too, that with regard to corpulence, South African baobabs (*Adansonia digitata*) do not have to stand back an inch to the world record holders. Several local baobabs have trunk diameters at breast height in excess of 10 m, closely behind the 11,62 m diameter of the Montezuma cypress (Mexican bald cypress) in Mexico, known as the Tule Tree. The 57,9 m circumference reported for that tree in the preface to the first edition, included the folds of the trunk and was seemingly done below breast height, while comparisons are made on straight measurements at breast height, or alternatively the diameter. In fact, dendrologists measured a baobab on the farm Glencoe near Hoedspruit with a trunk diameter of 15,9 m, exceeding that of the Tule tree (this discovery was reported on various websites). Measurement of that tree was exceedingly difficult due to the massive sagging branches and undulating trunk. Sadly, the crown of this tree collapsed in 2009, as often happens to very old baobabs, and although the tree is still living, its trunk is hidden by a tangle of gigantic collapsed branches and cannot be seen or measured in its entirety any more.

Since the appearance of the first edition, a widely reported request for an overall full-colour edition was received. This has prompted the publishers to commission the authors to do a revised edition, which necessitated co-option of an additional author. Izak's contributions, largely towards updating the existent text and introducing the latest developments on the forestry front, are greatly appreciated by the rest of the panel.

Readers are requested to take note that, as far as was possible, changes in the names of towns, streets, provinces, etc., have been accounted for. Finality can, however, not be guaranteed, as this is an ongoing process. This also applies to tree nomenclature. The *Acacia* name change has been a controversial matter. In this book, we follow the new taxonomic names for the subgenus, which was divided and transferred into the genus *Vachellia* (the former *Acacia* species with straight thorns and round flowers) and the genus *Senegalia* (the former *Acacia* species with hooked thorns). More information on the origin of this controversy can be found in in an article by J Carruthers and L Robbin titled: 'Taxonomic Imperialism in the battles for Acacia: Identity and science in South Africa and Australia'. This article appeared in Volume 65(1) of the *Transactions of the Royal Society of South Africa*, dated February 2010.

The authors
September 2016

Introduction

South Africa's indigenous trees are generally slow growers, mainly on account of the country's geological and climatic features, as described below. This accounts for our indigenous trees not competing with those of some other countries in respect of height or age. Furthermore, it is a scientific fact that certain trees do not achieve outstanding measurements, owing to their natural form and unique characteristics. To have achieved exceptional measurements regarding size or height, or to qualify as a remarkable tree for other reasons, therefore, would have taken many years, in most cases. Others did not survive the onslaught of time, leaving only stumps as silent witnesses of remarkable events having taken place in their shade. However, the country boasts the tallest and stoutest trees as yet annotated on the continent, with several trees among the top ten trees in the world, with trunk diameters of more than 10 m, and with many trees over a thousand years in age.

To appreciate South Africa's trees, remarkable or exceptional for whatever reason, some basic facts about the climatic and associated botanical features of the country should be kept in mind. South Africa is a relatively dry country (semi-arid), with an average rainfall of approximately 440 mm per annum: more than 50% of the country has an annual rainfall of less than 500 mm. South Africa is, however, singularly rich in woody plants, and plants in general, with about 25 000 species occurring naturally here (compared to some 15 000 in Australia and 6 000 in Canada). This comprises some 10% of the world's flora species on about 1% of the earth's land surface.

Ecosystems or biomes

Taking various factors into consideration (climate, soils, etc.), South Africa's land surface can be divided into the following ecosystems or biomes, each carrying its own number of the more than 1 300 tree and shrub species classified as trees:

Natural Forest, with which trees are mostly associated, occurs in scattered patches along the mountain chains from the Cape Peninsula south-eastwards, with the largest concentration in the southern Cape coastal areas in a strip of about 150 km (the Knysna-Tsitsikamma forests), following the eastern aspects of the mountains on the eastern coast to Mpumalanga (the Drakensberg range) and Limpopo Province (the Soutpansberg and the Blouberg). This biome covers less than half a million ha – less than a half per cent of the total surface area of South Africa.

Savannah, or **Bushveld** (natural woodlands), the most extensive forest resource, covers approximately 40 million hectares, mostly in the warmer regions. This biome contains a mixture of deciduous and shrub-like trees, with hardy grassy plants.

Albany or **Subtropical Thicket** (also known as **Valley Bushveld**) is a dense growth of trees and xerophytic plants such as spekboom (porkbush, *Portulacaria afra*) and many thorny plants. This biome covers about 3 million ha, mostly in the Eastern Cape.

Grassland, covering the central plateau with its summer rains and cold winters, is characterised by sour to sweet grasses, interspersed with patches of trees growing mainly on river banks, kopjes and in gullies.

More than a third of the land surface is covered by the **Karoo** (semi-desert) – which can be subdivided into the **Nama** and **Succulent Karoo** biomes – and the **Desert** areas, with very hot summers and very cold winters, and less than 300 mm rainfall per annum. Xerophytic (i.e. able to grow in dry conditions) vegetation dominates, with hardy trees and shrubs growing along dry river courses and on kopjes.

Specialised vegetation refers to halophytic (saline soil) vegetation, swamp vegetation and mangroves.

(Cape) Fynbos is found mainly in the winter rainfall region, from Vanrhynsdorp in the Western Cape in a sickle-shaped strip through the Western Cape, to Grahamstown in the Eastern Cape. This small biome forms a plant kingdom of its own, namely the **Cape Floristic Kingdom**, amazingly rich in plant species (more than 9 000 species), with a high degree of endemism (only found in a particular region). See box on pages 16–17.

The Big Tree Register

A tree may be regarded as exceptional or remarkable by the layman owing to its perceived size. Size is, however, relative, as it depends on the particular species in the first place, and may be determined subjectively in accordance with personal preferences: a tree may either be impressive in height, have a massive bole, or have a wide crown. To address this problem, a method was devised by the Dendrological Society of South Africa so that different trees can be compared to determine their size, and a register of South Africa's big trees is kept by the Society.

The Big Tree Register was conceived to:
- record big trees as impressive examples of tree growth, for their natural beauty and for scientific study
- preserve these trees as a valuable natural resource
- preserve these trees as inspiring symbols of conservation
- determine the largest specimen of every species so that it may be declared a national monument.

To enter a big tree in the register, the following particulars have to be supplied:
- botanical name and national tree number

OPPOSITE PAGE: Natural Forest: a closed canopy habitat dominated by trees, with emergent Outeniqua yellowwoods above the canopy

Measuring tree height with a hypsometer

- standard names
- size (if known)
- trunk diameter and girth
- tree height measured by hypsometer or tree climber
- mean crown spread ($2r$)
- circular crown cover ($r^2 \times 3{,}14$)
- size index ($\sqrt{D} \times H \times \sqrt{2x}$)
- name and locality of property
- date on which measurements were taken.

Each big tree registered receives a registration number as well as a grid reference number.

An amazing plant kingdom

The Cape Floristic Kingdom (resembling the Macchia vegetation of the Mediterranean regions) is the smallest of the six plant kingdoms of the world, covering only 0,04% of the earth's total land surface, but has an exceptionally large number of plant species. Having covered originally 67 000 km², which has dwindled to 42 000 km² through human intervention, this unique biome is currently endangered – a matter that needs urgent attention. The largest plant kingdom is the Boreal (42% of the earth's total land surface), followed by the Paleotropic (35%), the Neotropic (14%), the Australian (8%) and the Antarctic (1%).

The Cape Floristic Kingdom is rich in plant species but is under serious threat as a result of human intervention (Photo: Department of Water Affairs and Forestry)

The richness in plant species in the Cape Floristic Kingdom can be ascribed to the following factors:

The age of the flora: this area was not glaciated after flowering plants began to evolve some 110 million years ago. Botanists assume the Cape Floristic Kingdom to be one of the oldest surviving floras in the world.

A wide variety of habitats in the region: from 'young' coastal plains to 'ancient' mountain peaks occur here. The sea level fluctuated considerably in the past, and at one time the Cape Peninsula seems to have been an island – which accounts for the large number of endemic plants. The mountains throughout the Western Cape appear, for various reasons, to have been isolated in the past. On these 'islands' new species evolved, to produce the variety encountered today.

A large range of climates: from Mediterranean (winter rainfall) in the west, to constant on the south-eastern coastal (George-Knysna) area, to summer rainfall in the Port Elizabeth-Grahamstown area. Kirstenbosch, on the eastern slopes of Table Mountain, has an average annual rainfall of 1 400 mm, while Camps Bay, on the western slopes, receives 800 mm on average.

Three types of vegetation recognised by botanists: *true fynbos*, a heathland vegetation type that grows in the mountains in infertile sandstone soils, and two non-heathland shrublands, *renosterveld* and *strandveld*, with grasses and bulbous plants as the more common plant types.

The Kogelberg Biosphere Reserve, on the eastern side of False Bay, Western Cape, the first of its kind in southern Africa, is registered by UNESCO (the United Nations Education, Science and Culture Organisation) in recognition of this unique, pristine floristic kingdom.

The age of a tree

Age is a second important yardstick of the remarkability of a tree. It is generally accepted that the oldest trees in South Africa are about 1 000 to 2 000 years old. The age of the oldest bristlecone pine (*Pinus aristata* var. *longaeva*) on the Rocky Mountains in the United States has been established at some 5 000 years. One of the olive trees in a grove on the Mount of Olives in the Garden of Gethsemane outside Jerusalem is said to be 2 300 years old. Scientists of Tasmania maintain that the oldest trees in the world are a stand of Huon pine (*Lagarostrobos franklinii*) on the slopes of Mount Read, Western Tasmania.

The age of standing trees is determined scientifically through carbon dating, while that of a felled tree can be determined by counting the year rings – softwoods, in particular, have distinct annual rings.

Research and carbon dating by Dr S Woodbourne (iThemba Laboratories), and others, have indicated that most of the large baobabs (*Adansonia digitata*) in South Africa are about 1 000 years old; the oldest one dated at just over 1 800 years. The oldest yellowwoods (*Afrocarpus falcatus*) and leadwood trees (*Combretum imberbe*) dated so far are also about 1 000 years, and the camel thorn (*Vachellia erioloba*) about 600 years.

A fully grown yellowwood tree on its march to old age – the oldest specimens are believed to be about 1 000 years old

Historical and cultural significance of trees

Apart from size and age, trees may be regarded as remarkable for historical reasons, for the role that they played in the religious life of the peoples of the country, for their medicinal properties, or for their aesthetic importance, to name but a few criteria.

Two major problems have to be mentioned here. Although South Africa's relative wealth in trees indisputably belongs to the whole nation, and has been enjoyed and utilised as such since earliest times, the first written recordings can only be traced back to about the last quarter of the 17th century. At that time botanists from European countries started collecting specimens from South Africa's vegetation and had them classified and written up scientifically. In this respect names such as Linnaeus, Burchell, Le Vaillant, Thunberg, Baines, Lichtenstein, and places like Kew and other botanical gardens have become familiar among local plant lovers. Very little information is available about trees in pre-colonial times – the 'Post Office Tree' in Mossel Bay is virtually the only known example of the history of a tree dating back to that period.

In the second place, much valuable information has regrettably been lost about the various uses of trees by indigenous peoples – countless medicinal uses, for instance, which may have been handed down orally, but have become lost with time. Much energy is spent nowadays in search of these, and a number of books have already been published in this regard.

Conserving trees – the nation's heritage

The aim of this book is not to serve as a botanical handbook, but to make a contribution towards the preservation or protection of trees as such, and to provide information about trees, collected from a variety of sources, that should not be allowed to be lost. Knowledge should lead to appreciation, to protection, to care, and to the point where synergy between humankind and their beautiful environment is accomplished.

The South African National Heritage Resources

More than 20 trees and groups of trees of historical or cultural significance were declared National Monuments under the National Monuments Act of 1969. This Act was replaced by the National Heritage Resources Act of 1999, and these trees are now listed as National Heritage Resources, although the familiar National Monument plaques still remain at many of these sites. These trees are usually linked to important cultural or historical events or personalities. Well-known trees in this category include, for example, the famous 'Post Office Tree' at the Dias Museum in Mossel Bay, and an impressive row of camphor trees planted about three centuries ago by Governor Willem Adriaan van der Stel at Vergelegen Estate, Somerset West. (Detailed descriptions are given in the relevant chapters – see *Tree Families*.)

Some trees or groups of trees listed as National Heritage Resources are also declared Champion

Emblem of the former *National Monuments Council* (now the *National Heritage Resources Agency*) still in use at some protected sites, including trees of cultural and historic significance

Trees under the National Forests Act of 1998. Champion Tree criteria, however, determine that the trees must also have a significant size or landscape presence, therefore not all trees listed as National Heritage Resources will qualify as Champion Trees. The process of a tree to be declared a National Heritage Resource is onerous, because the immediate land area on which the tree stands also has to be surveyed and included in the declaration. This affords the trees a greater measure of protection than those protected under Section 12 of the National Forests Act (Champion Trees), for the latter only protects the trees and not any land area. Declaring Champion Trees, however, is by comparison fast and uncomplicated, and more responsive to situations where trees of national conservation importance are under threat and require protective action.

The National Heritage Resources Act protects all man-made structures or objects older than 60 years. By implication trees older than 60 years are also protected, but only if significant cultural importance can be proven. Legally this is a grey area that has yet to be tested in court.

South African National Heritage Resources should not be confused with Natural Heritage Sites, a number of which are referred to in the text (Kathu Forest, for instance). The South African Natural Heritage Programme was launched in 1984 as a co-operative venture between the then Department of Environmental Affairs and Tourism, Provincial Nature Conservation Agencies, Schneider Electric, the World Wildlife Fund South Africa, and private landowners. The project presented the opportunity to individuals to participate actively in preserving South Africa's rapidly disappearing natural areas.

Emblem of the former *South African Natural Heritage Programme*

A large number of the tree species described are being protected in one or more heritage sites, some of which are mentioned. (For further information readers are referred to the Bibliography.)

The Post Office milkwood tree at Mossel Bay, the first tree recorded in the history of South Africa

The Big Five Trees of South Africa

This section showcases the Big Five from the South African tree world – the largest or tallest trees, both indigenous and alien, the most corpulent ones and the most special forest trees in South Africa. The selections are based on size and accessibility and all the trees also appear in the Big Tree Register (see page 47) and/or the Champion Tree List (see page 51).

Tree size criteria

South African trees are grouped into six size classes according to the overall size index often attained by trees of a species, from exceptionally large trees with size indexes of 250 and more, to very small trees with size indexes of less than 15. Table 1 lists the different classes of tree sizes, as described by Johan Barnard in the book *Bushveld – Ecology and Management* (ed. Dr Peet van der Walt):

Table 1: Classes of tree sizes

Class	Description	Size index
1	Exceptionally large trees	>250
2	Very large trees	181–250
3	Large trees	121–180
4	Medium size trees	41–120
5	Small trees	16–40
6	Very small trees	1–15

Table 2 lists the size and age criteria developed by Dr Coert Geldenhuys for the evaluation and shortlisting of trees to be declared Champion Trees under the National Forests Act of 1998:

Table 2: Champion Tree size and age criteria

| Criteria | Value | | | |
	Low value	Moderate value	High value	Very high value
Height, m	<25 m	25–30 m	31–40 m	>40 m
Stem diameter, m	<1,0 m	1,00–1,50 m	1,51–2,50 m	>2,50 m
Crown spread, m	<15,0 m	15,0–25,0 m	25,1–35,0 m	>35,0 m
Size index, value	<120	120–180	181–250	>250
Age, years natural	<100 years	100–150 years	151–250 years	>250 years
Age, years planted	<60 years	60–100 years	101–150 years	>150 years

OPPOSITE PAGE: Tree climber scaling a saligna gum tree at the Woodbush State Forest, Limpopo – these are the tallest trees measured in Africa (Photo: Leon Visser)

A family joins in measuring a gigantic manna gum on the farm Familiehoek, Ermelo (Photo: Christine Joubert)

The Big Five Indigenous Trees

Among the exceptionally large trees the baobabs (*Adansonia digitata*) reign supreme. The largest indigenous tree according to size index is the **Sagole baobab** in Vendaland. During the shooting of a television programme on Champion Trees fifty-five local kids took hands around the enormous trunk of more than 33 m.

Various wild fig species attain great sizes in this country, especially cluster figs (*Ficus sycomorus*), Wonderboom figs (*Ficus salicifolia*) and the common wild fig (*Ficus burkei*). The most suitable candidate for the second place would definitely be the rarer **Wonderboom fig**, of which the most famous specimen at the Wonderboom Nature Reserve in Pretoria (City of Tshwane) attained great dimensions through unusual means. With a crown measuring 61 m from one side to the other at its widest point (average of 55 m from two measurements), this tree actually consists of three rings of daughter trees around a mother tree no longer existing, which propagated where branches touched the ground. It is argued that this tree is one organism (although the linked branches were severed some years ago), and it certainly has the appearance of a single tree with a rounded solid canopy. Some common wild figs attain trunk circumferences of more than 6 m, while cluster figs can grow impressive canopies of more than 40 m in diameter.

Indigenous trees rarely top 40 m in height, and matumi trees share that honour with the **Outeniqua yellowwoods** (*Afrocarpus* *falcatus*), which take third position. These yellowwood trees are the true monarchs of the natural forests, emerging above the canopies of the montane forest types from the southern Cape right up to the Soutpansberg in Limpopo. Most famous of these are the Big Trees of the Knysna and Tsitsikamma Forests, and the Eastern Cape Monarch standing in the Tyume Valley near the picturesque hamlet of Hogsback in the Amatola Mountains.

Fourth on the list of the local Big Five are the **matumi trees** (*Breonadia salicina*) that grow in the riverine forests of the Limpopo and Mpumalanga Provinces. Largest of these are the 'Three Queens' of Amorentia Estate in the Politsi Valley near Tzaneen, which all stand within earshot from one another.

Last of the Big Five is the **monkey thorn** (*Senegalia galpinii*), which occurs widespread in the Bushveld of the northern provinces of the country. These trees can attain great size indexes with some impressive crown dimensions of more than 40 m recorded, combined with trunk circumferences of over 6 m. One tree in the Marikana area (Bojanelo District in North West) actually approaches that magical 40 m height which seems so difficult to reach. The size measurements of the big trees may change over time; also as a result of new and more accurate measurements by tree climbers, but the ranking order of these trees seldom change as a result.

Whereas the choice of the first three positions should meet with general agreement, opinions regarding numbers four and five vary greatly among tree fundi. Alternative candidates in these positions could be species such as the ana tree (*Faidherbia albida*) or the nyala tree (*Xanthocercis zambesiaca*), of which some really magnificent specimens have been measured recently.

1 **Sagole baobab** near Sagole Spa, Limpopo

Height: 20,5 m
Stem size: 10,8 m dbh
Crown size: 40 m
Size index: 426

The impressive girth of the Sagole baobab, Limpopo – our largest indigenous tree

THE BIG FIVE TREES OF SOUTH AFRICA

2 Wonderboom fig, Pretoria (Tshwane), Gauteng

Height: 22 m
Stem size: 5,32 m dbh (multiple stems)
Crown size: 56 m
Size index: 380

ABOVE: The famous Wonderboom fig in the Tshwane metropolitan area, Gauteng

RIGHT: Giant Outeniqua yellowwoods, one of the most popular tourist attractions along the Garden Route, Western/Eastern Cape

3 Outeniqua yellowwood, Tsitsikamma, Garden Route National Park, Eastern Cape

Height: 39,3 m
Stem size: 2,8 m dbh
Crown size: 33,6 m
Size index: 379

THE BIG FIVE TREES OF SOUTH AFRICA

4 **Matumi**, Amorentia Estate, Modjadjiskloof, Limpopo

Height: 33 m
Stem size: 2,81 m dbh
Crown size: 37 m
Size index: 336

LEFT: Water-loving matumi trees mainly prefer the riverine areas of Limpopo and Mpumalanga
BELOW: An imposing monkey thorn tree, Rust De Winter, Limpopo

5 **Monkey thorn**, Rust de Winter, Bela Bela, Limpopo

Height: 30 m
Stem size: 3,01 m dbh
Crown size: 41,2 m
Size index: 334

The Alien Big Five

The Big Five tree list of exotic tree species in South Africa is impressive, with some outperforming indigenous trees by far in terms of height and size index. Tree sizes attained by a number of gum species locally and their extremely fast growth rates are held in awe by arborists from their native countries Australia and Tasmania. Heights of over 70 m are commonly reached, often within seven or eight decades of their planting. In applying these criteria, top honours would go to the **saligna gum** (*Eucalyptus saligna*), followed by the **river red gum** (*Eucalyptus camaldulensis*). A plantation block of saligna gum trees planted in 1906 at Woodbush State Forest has the distinction of being the tallest planted trees in Africa, with the tallest recently measured at 81,5 m. Although the river red gums do not attain similar heights, they compensate with enormous trunk circumferences of over 6 m and impressive crowns often exceeding 35 m.

Impressive examples of **Moreton Bay fig trees** (*Ficus macrophylla*) can be found in various parts of the country. Their massive trunks protrude above sturdy root buttresses and tangles of roots snaking in all directions. Such a tree in the Arderne Garden, Claremont, Cape Town, is described under the Fig Tree family. Several groves of **Californian redwood** (*Sequoia sempervirens*) were planted more than 80 years ago in the Western Cape, Eastern Cape, KwaZulu-Natal and Limpopo Provinces as experimental timber stands. Although not nearly as impressive as the centuries-old redwood monarchs in their native country, some of these stands now approach 60 m and are still growing strong. It is expected that these trees may challenge the gum species for top honours within a few decades. **Camphor trees** (*Cinnamomum camphora*) are also strong and hardy growers, and nowhere is this more clearly demonstrated than the awe-inspiring row of trees planted about three centuries ago at Vergelegen Estate near Somerset West.

Some local pine trees have attained world-class heights for their species. Most notable of these is a **taeda pine** (*Pinus taeda*) growing at Buffelsnek State Forest near Knysna in the Western Cape, measured at 60 m.

RIGHT: Redwood stand, Woodbush State Forest, Limpopo

BELOW: The giant Moreton Bay fig in Arderne Garden, Cape Town (Photo: Enrico Liebenberg)

BOTTOM: Lane of massive camphor trees planted three centuries ago at Vergelegen Estate, Somerset West, Western Cape (Photo: Mark Minter)

OPPOSITE PAGE:
TOP: Saligna gum trees, surpassing the height of all trees in South Africa, ultimately topping a breathtaking 80 m in this stand planted in 1906 by AK Eastwood at the Woodbush State Forest, Limpopo

BOTTOM: River red gum trees, although not competitive in terms of height, reach high overall size indexes due to impressive trunk and crown dimensions, Stellenbosch, Western Cape (Photo: Leon Visser)

The Corpulent Big Five

Baobab trees reign supreme among the indigenous trees for the sheer bulk of their trunks, and deserve a Big Five list of their own. The corpulent Montezuma cypress at Tule in Mexico has been publicised as the stoutest tree in the world, with a bewildering variety of trunk measurements, varying from 57 m to 36,2 m, depending on whether the trunk was measured at ground level or at breast height and whether it was measured straight or along the creases of the heavily buttressed trunk (see also page 239). The most reliable straight measurement at breast height appears to be a diameter of 11,62 m (the circumference measures over 42 m, which equates to over 14 m diameter, but the smoothed out trunk diameter is lower if the trunk buttresses are accounted for, as they should be). Yet the actual corpulent world champion remained hidden from the world in a lonely corner of the Bushveld, even long after its discovery and measurement by the late Dr Fried von Breitenbach. The trunk circumference of the **Glencoe baobab** near Hoedspruit in Mpumalanga measured at no less than 49,9 m (a very difficult measurement that had to be done below breast height). That was before the recent demise of the tree when most of its crown sagged to the ground. Even though the crown is alive and sprouts leaves, the massive branches that sagged to the ground do not make trunk measurements possible any more, and for all practical purposes the tree is not considered to be a contender for the local Corpulent Five. The **Sagole tree** in the far north of Limpopo holds top honours among the local baobabs with a size index of 426 and trunk circumference of just over 33 m, and is considered to be the largest indigenous tree in the country.

The **King of Ga-Ratjeke baobab**, recently discovered at the village of Ga-Ratjeke near Modjadjiskloof, takes second place on the basis of its size index of 383, even though the index formula for its combined trunk diameters of three stems are far below that of the **Platland baobab** (also known as the **Sunland baobab**). This tree, too, is located near Modjadjiskloof. The taller height and wider crown diameters of the first two contenders on the list of big baobabs give them the edge over the Platland baobab in their overall size index calculations. The trunk of the Platland tree appears as a coarse granite wall, belying the fact that it has a cavernous interior large enough to host a cosy bar. Part of this tree collapsed in August 2016, but the remaining tree is still impressive and in good health.

Another fibrous monster rises above the arid bushveld near Ellisras (Lephalale). This is the **Buffelsdrift baobab** near Lephalale – a worthy candidate to share the Corpulent Five podium. Last in line is the **Post Office baobab** near Leydsdorp, complete with steps into its interior and a ladder into its crown.

As far as size indexes go, trunk circumference and crown size work in favour of the baobabs, as much as their lack of height works against them. The measurement of a baobab trunk circumference could vary as much as a metre between very dry and very wet periods, for the fibrous mass serves as a sponge that can hold vast amounts of water.

At the time of writing, a new baobab has been brought to the attention of the authors, which could displace one of the Corpulent Five contenders on the list but has not been visited by experts yet. This tree grows in the Nature Reserve of Forever Resorts at Tshipise in Limpopo, reputed to have a trunk circumference of about 30 m at breast height.

OPPOSITE PAGE:
TOP: The Sagole baobab in Limpopo, the largest indigenous tree in South Africa
BOTTOM: An imposing baobab recently discovered by dendrologists at the rural village of Ga-Ratjeke, Limpopo, taking second place among the baobabs on overall size

The Big Five baobabs of South Africa (excluding the collapsed Glencoe baobab)

1

Sagole baobab near Sagole Spa, Limpopo

Height: 20,5 m
Stem size: 33,9 m circ (10,8 m dbh)
Crown size: 40 m
Size index: 426

2

King of Ga-Ratjeke at Ga-Ratjeke village, Limpopo

Height: 23,5 m
Stem size: 24,15 m circ; 7,85 m circ & 2,14 m circ (8,21 m dbh)
Crown size: 32,6 m
Size index: 383

The Big Five Trees of South Africa

3. Sunland baobab/Platland baobab, near Modjadjiskloof, Limpopo

Height: 19 m
Stem size: 33,6 m circ (10,7 m dbh)
Crown size: 36 m
Size index: 372

4. Buffelsdrift baobab near Lephalale (Ellisras), Limpopo

Height: 22 m
Stem size: 24,3 m circ (7,7 m dbh)
Crown size: 30,2 m
Size index: 336

THE BIG FIVE TREES OF SOUTH AFRICA

5 **Post Office baobab** near Leydsdorp, Limpopo

Height: 20 m
Stem size: 19 m circ (6,1 m dbh)
Crown size: 24,1 m
Size index: 242

ABOVE: The 'pub' and 'post office' baobab near the rural town of Leydsdorp, Limpopo. The ladder is a fairly recent addition
OPPOSITE PAGE:
TOP: The most visited baobab in the country – the Sunland or Platland baobab near Modjadjiskloof, Limpopo
BOTTOM: The Buffelsdrift baobab near Lephalale, Limpopo

The Forest Big Five

In the high forests of South Africa there are but a small number of tree species that can push their crowns above the forest canopy. These trees are known as forest emergents. The giant Outeniqua yellowwood (*Afrocarpus falcatus*) is such a tree. Yet the really large so-called Big Trees are scattered thinly in a handful of forests. The most prolific concentration of Big Trees occurs in the Knysna and Tsitsikamma Forests of the southern Cape. Of these the **Tsitsikamma Big Tree** takes top honours, not only for its size, but also for the number of visitors. The annual number of visitors along the well-worn boardwalk to this tree has at times exceeded the 90 000 mark, making it one of the largest attractions in the field of big tree tourism.

With its height of 39 m and bulky trunk of 8,6 m circumference the **Eastern Cape Monarch** near Hogsback weighs in at second place of the Forest Five. Though not visited by busloads of tourists, the popular Tyume trail takes a fair amount of recreational traffic past the tree during holidays. Most of the other Big Trees among the top five are all popular attractions, two of them within easy reach of the touristic town of Knysna, including the imposing **King Edward VIIth Tree** at Diepwalle State Forest. The **Blouberg Big Trees**, tall giants that grow high on the slopes of the Blouberg Mountains in Limpopo, are admired by hikers and mountaineers who trek up the mountain with local guides.

At Hoekwil near George grows a shorter but more corpulent giant, with a trunk circumference of 8,8 m. Due to visible crown dieback, the trunk of this tree was recently scanned with a tomograph (an instrument using radar to detect signs of cavities or wood rot), but was given a clean bill of health.

Other remarkable Outeniqua yellowwood trees include some tall giants growing in the Wonderwoud (Wonder Forest) in the Wolkberg Wilderness Area in Limpopo. These trees can be seen from afar, towering above the canopy, but can only be reached by a strenuous trek through wild and scenic landscapes. On the way to Goudveld State Forest past the hamlet of Rheenendal, a towering tree can be seen above the forest kilometres away. This is the **Dalene Matthee Tree**. A monument has been erected at the base of the tree in honour of the late Dalene Matthee, who brought the lives of 19th century woodcutters to life in her books, including the top seller *Circles in a Forest*.

A giant Outeniqua yellowwood, aptly named the Dalene Matthee Tree, gives shelter to a monument in memory of the author of the widely acclaimed *Circles in a Forest*, the first book of her forest trilogy

The Big Five Outeniqua yellowwoods of South Africa

1

Tsitsikamma Big Tree, along N2 near Storms River, Garden Route National Park, Eastern Cape

Height: 39,3 m
Stem size: 8,71 m circ (2,8 m dbh)
Crown size: 33,6 m
Size index: 379

LEFT: The imposing giant Tsitsikamma Big Tree on the Garden Route, attracting the largest number of tourists of any single tree in the country – up to 95 000 visitors in a year

BELOW: The Eastern Monarch, situated in the breathtakingly beautiful Tyume Valley at the edge of the rustic hamlet of Hogsback, Eastern Cape

2

Eastern Cape Monarch at Hogsback, Eastern Cape

Height: 39,4 m
Stem size: 8,65 m circ (2,75 m dbh)
Crown size: 29,6 m
Size index: 355

The Big Five Trees of South Africa

3 **Woodville Big Tree** at Bergplaas State Forest near George, Garden Route National Park, Western Cape

Height: 34 m
Stem size: 8,8 m circ (2,8 m dbh)
Crown size: 30,5 m
Size index: 314

4 **King Edward VIIth Tree** at Diepwalle State Forest near Knysna, Garden Route National Park, Western Cape

Height: 36,9 m
Stem size: 6,67 m circ (2,12 m dbh)
Crown size: 31,5 m
Size index: 301

TOP: The Woodville Big Tree near George, another popular and well-maintained Big Tree site managed by the South African National Parks

RIGHT: King Edward VII th Tree near Knysna, Western Cape, named after visiting royalty in the mid-nineteenth century

THE BIG FIVE TREES OF SOUTH AFRICA

5 **Blouberg Big Trees**, Blouberg, Limpopo

Height: 41 m
Stem size: 5,2 m circ
(1,65 m dbh)
Crown size: 31 m
Size index: 293

Outeniqua yellowwood trees in the Blouberg, Limpopo Province (Photo: Adam Harrower)

Tree climbing in South Africa

If rock climbing is held in awe by the general public and considered by some as a pastime of the lunatic fringe, then giant-tree climbing must be the mother of all fringe sports. That is how Mr Leon Visser of Stellenbosch sums up this small but growing worldwide craze that has infected South Africa as well. Arborists like Mr Visser are trained in tree climbing to inspect and care for trees, but giant-tree climbers come from all walks of life. Apart from their ambition to climb the biggest trees around the globe, these tree climbers assist in measuring tree heights of extremely tall trees in dense tree groves where height-measuring instruments like hypsometers are of little use. They also assist in monitoring and caring for Champion Trees, looking for signs of rot and disease high up in tree canopies, and occasionally prune dead or diseased branches. Tree climbers often contribute scientific knowledge about plant and animal life among the canopy.

Early in January 2013 an international team of tree climbers led by Mr David Wiles of the United Kingdom arrived in Cape Town to climb some of the largest Champion Trees in the country. This group of experienced climbers with some global tree climbs under their belt were attracted to South Africa owing to her reputation as probably the ultimate big tree country on the African continent. An important aim of this expedition was to raise awareness about the tree heritage of South Africa. The climb included the tallest known trees in Africa at the Woodbush State Forest, the largest baobabs in the country, and giant yellowwood trees in the Knysna and Tsitsikamma forests. The expedition was aptly named 'Climb the Ancient Trees of Africa'.

Members of an international tree-climbing expedition visiting South Africa, January 2013, to climb Champion Trees

The expedition ended on a high note. On 26 January 2013 the climbers scaled the tall saligna gum trees at Woodbush State Forest, famous for being the tallest measured trees in Africa. A new champion of champions was crowned when they measured a tree at 81,5 m, more than a metre taller than the previous record. The very last climb of tall rose gum trees at Satico plantation near Barberton discovered a tree of 72,3 m tall, and this stand of trees count among the five tallest tree groves in the country measured by tree climbers.

Modern tree climbers use safe climbing techniques that cause the minimum damage to trees. A lead weight attached to a line is shot over a sturdy branch high up with a crossbow or catapult. This line, attached to the climbing rope, is pulled over the branch, and the rope and branch are tested for strength. The climber then ascends the free-hanging rope with the aid of metal grips, although there are various techniques. Non-chafing ropes are usually used, and the unwritten ethics of tree climbing forbid the use of any apparatus that could damage the trees, such as spikes. Tree climbers, after all, are passionate about the trees they ascend. Wet and windy conditions considerably add to the risks of tree climbing, and climbs in bad weather are usually avoided. Fatal accidents are rare, owing to stringent safety precautions.

A tree climber scaling rose gum trees at Satico plantation, Mpumalanga

In the Knysna and Tsitsikamma forests a select group of forest workers are employed to fell senile or dying trees, most of which have traditionally been sold to the local furniture industry in the southern Cape by auction, but are now sold by tender. These forest workers are highly skilled in tree climbing, for they have to scale the forest giants to trim their branches before felling, in order to minimise damage to the forest. It says much for the skill of these professional climbers that no serious accidents have occurred during the scaling, trimming and felling of hundreds of large forest trees in the course of more than three decades.

Champion Trees of South Africa

Outstanding trees have attracted attention since time immemorial. Al Carder wrote in his book *Forest Giants of the World* that King Attalus of the ancient kingdom of Pergamum (located in present-day Turkey) had a giant pine tree on Mount Ida measured and recorded about two centuries BC.

Trees capture the imagination of people, who attach certain values to trees of outstanding size, beauty or historical value. These values are all embodied in both the Champion Tree project and the National Register of Big Trees of South Africa.

The human fascination with exceptional trees is universal, and Champion Tree projects or similar initiatives are found in many countries over the world. On the African continent, however, South Africa is the only country with a formal programme to protect individual trees and groups of trees for their intrinsic values.

A giant Lowveld cabbage tree at Kurisa Moya near Magoebaskloof (Photo: Enrico Liebenberg)

The Champion Tree project

The Champion Tree project was initiated in 2003 by the Forestry Branch of the then Department of Water Affairs and Forestry (the Forestry Branch is now seated in the Department of Agriculture, Forestry and Fisheries). Its aim is to identify and protect trees of national conservation significance.

Many trees of significance have been destroyed in the past, and the government endeavours to protect the most important trees proactively. This is done by declaring such individual trees or groups of trees protected in terms of Sections 12 (a) and (b) of the National Forests Act No 84 of 1998. Just as with protected tree species declared under Section 12 (d) of this Act, the cutting of Champion Trees without a licence is prohibited, and such a licence will only be issued in an emergency where a tree becomes unstable and threatens life or property. At the end of each year trees nominated by the public for Champion Tree status are evaluated by a panel of experts. The shortlist of trees compiled is then published in the Government Gazette and newspapers for comment, before their final declaration as protected.

At the Trevor Huddleston Memorial Centre, museum personnel and members of the Champion Tree evaluation team relax on the large stumps of the Sophiatown Oak – a tree that witnessed the forced removal of the Sophiatown community in the 1950s

The National Register of Big Trees of South Africa was initiated by the Dendrological Society of South Africa in 1980 (See Introduction: The Big Tree Register). Although the purpose of the register differs somewhat from that of the Champion Tree project and does not extend to exotic tree species introduced from overseas, it served as inspiration and a basis for the latter. The register endeavours to record the biggest specimens of the more common indigenous tree species, irrespective of whether these species attain large or small sizes.

The Champion Tree list, on the other hand, is dominated by exotic tree species, for it so happens that these species often grow much bigger or taller than indigenous trees. This has attracted much criticism from the purists, but the dilemma is: Where does one draw the line? Exotic trees are part of our tree heritage, and cannot be excluded. Award-winning writer Thomas Pakenham earned himself the wrath of indigenous tree lovers when he referred to them as the 'Taliban of the Trees', for few indigenous tree lovers are such extremists that they wish away the millions of exotic trees lining our streets and parks.

South Africa has an impressive array of trees of outstanding size and historical value, and many of these trees are introduced species brought to this country since the 17th century. The forestry industry, which provides in most of the country's timber needs, grew steadily from experimental plantings in arboreta in the late 19th century to a huge industry with more than 1,5 million ha under trees, mostly pine and eucalypt species. Our towns and cities also boast impressive urban forests consisting of street, park and garden trees, most of which are introduced tree species. Less than 5% of these exotic species have been listed as invasive, and the Category 1 species which are banned outright by regulations under the Conservation of Agricultural Resources Act of 1983, or Category 2 and 3 species occurring outside urban and plantation areas, are not eligible for Champion Tree status. An updated list of invasive species has recently been published under the National Environmental Management Biodiversity Act of 2004, which now also caters for prohibitions on the import of potential invader species not yet established locally.

Six main concentrations of Champion Trees are found in South Africa, with shared characteristics or histories, which may explain why almost a third of the Champion Trees are concentrated within less than 5% of the land surface. Magoebaskloof in the Limpopo Province has no less than seven declared trees and groups of trees, all within a radius of 30 km. These include large indigenous matumi trees (*Breonadia salicina*) at Amorentia Estate and several world-class planted compartments of various eucalypt species. The Knysna and Tsitsikamma forests of the southern Cape have four giant Outeniqua yellowwoods (*Afrocarpus falcatus*), and a karri gum (*Eucalyptus diversicolor*) compartment of 70 m tall just outside these forests. Both areas have a high and constant rainfall. The other four concentrations of Champion Trees occur in areas where early plantings took place by dedicated tree pioneers over the past three centuries in and around the Cape Town metropolitan area, in the Cradock and Stutterheim areas of the Eastern Cape, in the KwaZulu-Natal midlands and in the metropolitan areas of Gauteng. Tree-planting pioneers importing and planting seeds and seedlings, like Ralph Arderne and Joseph Storr Lister (Cape Town and surroundings), John Scanlen and David Hutchins (Cradock-Stutterheim area) as well as John Geekie and Joseph Baynes (KwaZulu-Natal midlands), greatly contributed to our heritage of exceptional trees. They were ably assisted by various individuals from indigenous communities, whose names have unfortunately not been handed down to us by the historic records.

Hence it can be said that natural conditions stimulating the growth of indigenous giants and early planting of introduced trees ensure that South Africa is one of the prime spots on the African continent to visit documented outstanding trees. Here one can find some of the tallest trees in Africa, the oldest and biggest oak trees on the continent (various *Quercus* species), baobab trees (*Adansonia digitata*) harbouring pubs and post offices, and a milkwood tree (*Sideroxylon inerme*) where Portuguese seafarers left messages five centuries ago. These trees are described throughout this book.

Two neighbouring countries are also host to some exceptional trees. A handful of indigenous trees measured in Botswana reach exceptional sizes, among which a sycamore fig (*Ficus sycomorus*) in the Tuli Block, with an overall size that tops all the indigenous Big Trees measured in southern Africa. Zimbabwe also boasts a rich tree heritage, partly due to forestry plantings from the early 20th century in high rainfall areas. Many impressive indigenous and exotic trees are described in the book *Historic Trees of Zimbabwe* by LJ Mullin, including a planted eucalypt compartment at Inodzi Estate in the east of that country that could be a close contender for the title of tallest trees in Africa, but has not been reliably measured in recent decades. One wonders how many giant trees still await discovery in the vast southern African wilderness to the north of our borders.

Rules of the game

In selecting Champion Trees, one is confronted by a fundamental problem. Beauty is in the eye of the beholder, as the saying goes, and the question is how big is big, and how old is old when trees are assessed? The criteria applied may also vary widely, but usually trees are revered for their size – their height, trunk and crown size. In South Africa these size criteria are applied with set benchmarks. Trees, for example, are considered to be exceptionally big if they are more than 40 m tall and/or have a crown spread of more than 35 m

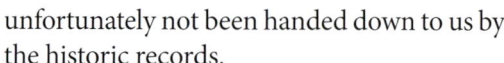

Headmaster Buks van Niekerk (second from left) proudly posing with his school grounds personnel and the Champion Tree evaluation team in the shadow of a large river red gum on the premises of the Waterkloof Primary School, Pretoria

and/or have a stem diameter of more than 2,5 m. Stem diameter as measured at breast height across the trunk with a calliper (dbh) is roughly a third of the trunk circumference, which is the measurement around the trunk at breast height.

Overall size is also considered, as determined by a mathematical equation combining all three size factors. Trees are considered to be exceptionally big if they score a size index of more than 250. Other criteria used locally are the highly subjective aesthetic and landscape image of a tree or group of trees, and their historical, cultural or tourism value.

The Big Tree Register is purely based on size measurements, but no threshold is set. The idea of this list is simply that the largest specimens of each tree species be recorded, regardless of its size. Yet the list does contain impressive trees of species of plant families such as the Bombaceae (including baobabs), Moraceae (including wild figs) and Rubiaceae (including matumi trees), which can attain great sizes. Many of the trees on this list therefore found their way into the list of Champion Trees.

Unlike the Big Tree Register, the Champion Tree project sets a minimum size regardless of the species. Basically the idea is that a tree should have a 'Wow!' factor, as Thomas Pakenham puts it in his book *Remarkable Trees of the World*. A tree is really exceptional if you stand in awe of its imposing size, but a relatively small or unimposing tree can also be awe-inspiring owing to another impressive factor such as its age or history. A good example is the gnarled and diminutive bristlecone pines of California in the United States, which can attain great ages of far more than 3 000 years.

Tree climber in the canopy of an Outeniqua yellowwood in the Knysna forests, Western Cape. (Photo: Drew Bristow)

The demise of a giant common wild fig at Eden Park, Umtentweni. Only healthy trees are considered for the Champion Tree Project, and dead or dying trees are delisted

Tree measurements are fairly straightforward, except when it comes to height. The trunk diameter or circumference and crown diameter can be measured easily with a measuring tape. Height measurement is more challenging, especially to a layman who has to use a simple trigonometric measurement technique with the aid of a ruler or stick. Hypsometers are used by foresters and tree specialists to obtain more accurate measurements, but these hand-held instruments can also be inaccurate for trees above 40 m in height located in dense tree stands. For that reason assistance is sometimes needed of land surveyors or professional tree climbers armed with climbing gear and long measuring tapes.

The Champion Tree project is a living programme, and new trees will be added to the list as time goes on. Sadly, some will die and fade from the list, but it is the inevitable fate that trees share with humans. Trees are fragile, and an axe or bulldozer can terminate the existence of a giant that grew for centuries at the wink of an eye. This has happened at the Commonwealth Plantation in the Magoebaskloof where six gigantic spotted gum trees (*Eucalyptus maculata*) were felled in 2010 by illegal loggers. Some Champion Trees have met a more natural fate, such as a collection of trees mostly consisting of deodar cedars (*Cedrus deodara*) planted more than a century ago by dignitaries at the old Government Buildings in Bloemfontein. These trees, adapted to occasional watering during dry seasons, apparently died when watering was interrupted by building renovation at the site.

Although the famous 'Slave Tree' of George in the Western Cape lost a huge part of its crown when a rotten branch sheared away, it is still an imposing landmark. The history of this English oak tree (*Quercus robur*) is recorded under the Beech family. At Glencoe farm near Hoedspruit (Maruleng) in Limpopo the crown of the second largest baobab measured in this country has sagged to the ground, yet most of the crown still sprouts greenery during summer. This tree was recently carbon-dated to about 1 840 years old, making it the oldest carbon-dated tree in the country. Trees such as the centuries-old camphor trees (*Cinnamomum camphora*) at Vergelegen Estate are well managed, cared for and monitored by arborists. Most of these venerable trees, however, are left to their own devices. They may fare well, until the day when a tree may suffer from too many visitors trampling the soil and carving graffiti. Boardwalks have been erected around some of these trees, like the Tsitsikamma Big Tree – an Outeniqua yellowwood receiving more than 90 000 visitors a year. Concern about another yellowwood giant at Hoekwil in the Western Cape has prompted the use of radar scans of the tree trunk with the aid of a tomograph, which can detect tree rot inside the trunk invisible to the eye. The scan gave a clean bill of health, but an increase of tourists flocking to the tree has necessitated the widening of the existing boardwalk.

The global company Aurecon launched the Adopt a Champion Tree programme locally in 2016 in partnership with the Department of Agriculture, Forestry and Fisheries. The aim of this programme is to raise funds for the care of Champion Trees, and to promote activities linked to these trees, including the monitoring of the trees, and related projects that will benefit communities. Within months of its launch the project has already contributed to the upgrading of picnic facilities at the Isidenge pine tree in the Eastern Cape, the erection of

The imposing camphor trees planted at Vergelegen Estate three centuries ago by governor WA van der Stel

several signboards at some Champion Trees, and the treatment of the Northcliff oak tree against mildew.

At the publication of this book more than 80 trees and groups of trees have been declared Champion Trees. But the criteria of national conservation significance are stringent, and many trees of regional or local conservation significance do not receive any form of protection. Few provincial or local authorities are up to the task, as factors like lack of capacity and the urgent demands of housing and services place tree conservation low on the list of priorities. There are exceptions, such as the Stellenbosch municipality, which dedicates staff and experts to look after the many historic trees in that town.

People can also make a difference. When the Trans African Road Concessions road construction agency planned to widen the N4 main road just outside Nelspruit (Mbombela) in 2011, a venerable old Wonderboom fig (*Ficus salicifolia*) was destined to bite the dust. That was until a group of determined protesters with placards posted themselves under the tree and attracted the attention of the media. Although this tree species is not rare and carbon dating found the tree to be less than 265 years old, it was saved by public pressure, and the road had to be diverted at a cost of more than a million rand.

The case above is a clear illustration that action by ordinary people can sometimes make a difference, and the basis for that action is a love for trees. The value of the Champion Tree project partly lies in instilling a love for trees – a love for trees that goes beyond the towering giants to those leafy friends in our streets and backyards.

The 'pancake' paperbark thorn tree of Karino near Nelspruit, which attracts tourists from far and wide (Photo: Richard Green). Inset: the impressive trunk of the tree from close up

Curious trees

Trees sometimes attract attention for strange reasons. In KwaZulu-Natal an exotic tree grew up the chimney of an abandoned factory (now demolished), and with some twist of humour was reputed to be the tallest pot plant in the world. The so-called 'pancake tree' near Karino on the N4 main road (Mpumalanga) attracts visitors due to its strange growth form (see *Thorn Tree family*). Trees like these have been nominated for Champion Tree status, but the criteria for the selection and shortlisting of Champion Trees exclude curiosity value. At a recent meeting of the Champion Tree Evaluation Panel a decision was taken to formulate a criterion on curiosity value, including impressive buttress roots, for consideration at its next meeting.

The longest tree roots ever recorded according to a website reference to the Guinness Book of Records belong to a wild fig (species not specified) on top of the mountains above the Echo Caves in Mpumalanga, with its roots appearing inside the cave 120 m down. Excavations in the Northern Cape have unearthed roots of a shepherd's tree (*Boscia albitrunca*) up to 65 m long. Trees sometimes propagate by strange means, such as the Wonderboom fig tree (*Ficus salicifolia*) in Pretoria (City of Tshwane), a now deceased mother tree that sprouted three rings of daughter trees over centuries. The widest crown width of 61 m of this tree is closely matched by that of a candle-pod thorn tree (*Vachellia hebeclada* subsp. *hebeclada*) which propagated in a similar manner, albeit in a more disorderly tangle. This tree near Nylstroom (Modimolle) is said to have served as encampment for Boer commandos during the Anglo-Boer War.

The Sunland baobab (*Adansonia digitata*) near Modjadjiskloof, also known as the Platland baobab, is famous not only due to its enormous size, but also for a bar inside the trunk. Many visitors, too, have entered the cavernous trunk of the Sagole baobab, which also houses a colony of rare mottled spine-tail swifts, unfazed by the popularity of their abode. Hollow trunks are not restricted to baobabs, however.

The crown of a three centuries-old English oak tree at Vergelegen Estate near Somerset West (Western Cape) is precariously supported by a massive hollow trunk of almost 11 m in circumference. It seems impossible for a tree of that size to survive when three-quarters of the trunk appear to be missing, yet hardly a dead branch is to be seen among the healthy greenery of the canopy. Top honours for a hollow trunk should go to the Ilembe Tree, a sycamore fig (*Ficus sycomorus*) near Kranskop in KwaZulu-Natal. Measuring 5,37 m in diameter at breast height according to a multi-stem formula for branches forking below breast height, but actually more than 23 m in circumference at its base, it is completely hollow and holds more than 10 head of cattle during bad weather.

The pub inside the Sunland baobab where tall tales about the age and size of trees are told

Most fig trees are fascinating, owing to the extraordinary root systems of some species, such as the flaring trunks and snaking roots of Moreton Bay figs (*Ficus macrophylla*). Another striking feature is the ability of certain wild fig species to grow precariously in rocky areas that hardly seem able to support any plant life, sending roots over bare rocks in an interlacing latticework of rock-breaking art. Similar phenomena, such as wild fig trees perching on old cattle kraal walls or embracing the lintel of a doorway of a house that disintegrated over time, are described under the Fig and Mulberry Tree Family.

A wild fig tree clinging precariously to a steep rock face

South Africa is home to a few species of underground trees, like the dwarf mobola (*Parinari capensis* subsp. *capensis*). Such phenomena are rare outside the African savannah. Of these underground trees (also referred to as *pyrogenic geoxylic suffrutices*), only the leaves of the crowns are visible, with the rest of the woody growth tucked away underground. According to some reports these trees may be thousands of years old, for they are virtually indestructible. The eminent tree fundi Professor Braam van Wyk calls these underground trees 'essentially immortal; nothing can kill them, except for habitat destruction. Grazers cannot kill them, fire cannot kill them, and they are drought resistant.' It could very well be that some of these plants have an underground biomass exceeding that of even the largest trees. Excavating them is exceedingly difficult, so this question could remain unsolved forever. The small deciduous shrub called 'plough-breaker' (*Erythrina zeyheri*) earned its name from its extensive underground root system that causes farmers headaches when preparing virgin land for crops.

The Top Thirty Indigenous Trees of South Africa

(National Register of Big Trees of South Africa – Dendrological Society of South Africa)

Tree measurements and rankings may change over time as trees are re-measured and new candidates are added to the list. A single diameter is also calculated for multiple stems according to a formula. Overall size index is calculated according to a formula including height, trunk and crown diameter.

Table 3: Top Thirty Indigenous Trees of South Africa   * dbh = diameter at breast height

	Tree Species	Height (m)	Stem dbh* (m)	Crown diam. (m)	Index figure	Location/site
1	*Adansonia digitata* Baobab/Kremetart	20,5	10,8	40	426	Sagole Village, Limpopo
2	*Adansonia digitata* Baobab/Kremetart (Crown partly collapsed)	17	15,9	37,05	413	Glencoe farm, Hoedspruit, Limpopo
3	*Adansonia digitata* Baobab/Kremetart	23,5	8,21 (multiple stems)	32,6	383	Ga-Ratjeke Village, Limpopo
4	*Ficus salicifolia* Wonderboom fig/Wonderboomvy	22	5,32 (multiple stems)	56	380	Pretoria (Tshwane), Gauteng
5	*Afrocarpus falcatus* Outeniqua yellowwood/Outeniekwageelhout	39,3	2,77	33,6	379	Tsitsikamma, Garden Route National Park, Eastern Cape
6	*Adansonia digitata* Baobab/Kremetart	19	10,7	36	372	Platland/Sunland, Modjadjiskloof, Limpopo
7	*Ficus burkei* Common wild fig/Gewone wildevy	25	5,09	41	361	University of Cape Town, Cape Town, Western Cape
8	*Afrocarpus falcatus* Outeniqua yellowwood/Outeniekwageelhout	39,4	2,75	29,69	355	Auckland Nature Reserve, Hogsback, Eastern Cape
9	*Adansonia digitata* Baobab/Kremetart	22	7,71	30,2	336	Buffelsdrift farm, Lephalale, Limpopo
10	*Ficus sycomorus* Common cluster fig/Gewone trosvy	25	3,94	45,7	336	Langkloof, Polokwane, Limpopo
11	*Ficus sycomorus* Common cluster fig/Gewone trosvy	31	3,34	35,1	336	Excellence farm, Mica, Limpopo

OPPOSITE PAGE: A rock-breaking fig draping its roots over a sandstone rock in Limpopo

Tree Species	Height (m)	Stem dbh* (m)	Crown diam. (m)	Index figure	Location/site
12 *Breonadia salicina* Matumi/Mingerhout	33	2,81	37	336	Amorentia Estate, Modjadjiskloof, Limpopo
13 *Senegalia galpinii* Monkey thorn/Apiesdoring	30	3,01	41,2	334	Rust de Winter, Bela Bela, Limpopo
14 *Ficus sycomorus* Common cluster fig/Gewone trosvy	23	5,37 (multiple stems)	35,7	318	Ilembe, KwaZulu-Natal
15 *Cussonia spicata* Common cabbage tree/ Gewone kiepersol	35	3,71	22	316	Kurisa Moya, Magoebaskloof, Limpopo
16 *Afrocarpus falcatus* Outeniqua yellowwood/ Outeniekwageelhout	34	2,8	30,55	314	Collin's Hoek, Hoekwil, Garden Route National Park, Western Cape
17 *Breonadia salicina* Matumi/Mingerhout	38	2,6	24,9	306	Amorentia Estate, Modjadjiskloof, Limpopo
18 *Afrocarpus falcatus* Outeniqua yellowwood/ Outeniekwageelhout	36,9	2,12	31,5	301	Diepwalle, Garden Route National Park, Western Cape
19 *Xanthocercis zambesiaca* Nyala tree/Njalaboom	35	2,15	33,5	297	Modena, Pontdrif, Limpopo
20 *Afrocarpus falcatus* Outeniqua yellowwood/ Outeniekwageelhout	41	1,65	31	293	Blouberg, near Polokwane, Limpopo (Politsi Valley)
21 *Prunus africana* Red stinkwood/Rooistinkhout	40	1,83	28,9	291	Straalhoek, Eastern Cape
22 *Faidherbia albida* Ana tree/Anaboom	36	1,78	36,2	289	Kruispad, Lephalale, Limpopo
23 *Ficus burkei* Common wild fig/Gewone wildevy	28	3,31	31,9	288	Eden Park, Umtentweni, KwaZulu-Natal
24 *Afrocarpus falcatus* Outeniqua yellowwood/ Outeniekwageelhout	36	1,88	33,6	286	Cyprus farm, Letaba, Limpopo
25 *Breonadia salicina* Matumi/Mingerhout	38,6	2,41	17,78	286	Amorentia Estate, Modjadjiskloof, Limpopo
26 *Senegalia galpinii* Monkey thorn/Apiesdoring	37	1,81	31	277	Veeplaas, Skuinsdrift, North West
27 *Faidherbia albida* Ana tree/Anaboom	32	2,08	29,9	252	Kruispad, Lephalale, Limpopo

	Tree Species	Height (m)	Stem dbh* (m)	Crown diam. (m)	Index figure	Location/site
28	*Afrocarpus falcatus* Outeniqua yellowwood/Outeniekwageelhout	35,4	1,72	28,35	247	Goudveld State Forest, Garden Route National Park, Western Cape
29	*Adansonia digitata* Baobab/Kremetart	20	6,11	24,1	242	Leydsdorp, Letaba District, Limpopo
30	*Ekebergia capensis* Cape ash/Kaapse essenhout	27	2,11	34,1	229	Hanglip State Forest, Makhado, Limpopo
	THESE TREES ARE ALSO BIG					
31	*Xanthocercis zambesiaca* Nyala tree/Njalaboom	22	3,54 (multi-stemmed)	29,8	226	Sagole Village, Limpopo
32	*Celtis africana* White stinkwood/Witstinkhout	39	1,6	19,7	220	Forest Hill, Tzaneen, Limpopo
33	*Ekebergia capensis* Cape ash/Kaapse essenhout	35	1,66	23,7	219	Lekgalameetse Nature Reserve, Limpopo
34	*Faidherbia albida* Ana tree/Anaboom	24	2,37	33,5	214	Rietfontein, Mokerong, Limpopo
35	*Ficus cordata* Namaqua Fig/Namakwavy	17	4,78	32,5	212	Abasas, Kgalagadi, Northern Cape
36	*Ficus natalensis* Natal Fig/Natalvy	22	3,02	30	210	Worcester, Western Cape
37	*Cussonia sphaerocephala* Forest cabbage tree/Boskiepersol	30	2,02	22,1	200	Berlin State Forest, Nelspruit (Mbombela), Mpumalanga
38	*Ekebergia capensis* Cape ash/Kaapse essenhout	39	1,24	20,7	198	Uitsoek State Forest, Lydenburg (Mashishing), Mpumalanga
39	*Ficus sansibarica* Knobbly fig/Knoppiesvy	22	2,02	32,2	178	Lekgalameetse Nature Reserve, Limpopo
40	*Faidherbia albida* Ana tree/Anaboom	33	1,11	23,12	167	Worcester farm, Limpopo
41	*Cordyla africana* Wild mango/Wildemango	19	2,01	37,4	165	Vlakbult, Barberton (Umjindi), Mpumalanga
42	*Anthocleista grandiflora* Forest fever tree/Boskoorsboom	30	1,27	22,6	161	Lekgalameetse Nature Reserve, Limpopo
43	*Ficus polita* Wild rubber fig/Wilderubbervy	27	3,9 (multiple stems)	26,8	156	Eden Park, Umtentweni, KwaZulu-Natal
44	*Combretum imberbe* Leadwood/Hardekool	21	5,46	30,3	152	Carthage, Tzaneen, Limpopo

Champion Trees of South Africa

(Individual Trees and Groups of Trees Declared as Protected Under Section 12 of the National Forests Act of 1998 by the Department of Agriculture, Forestry and Fisheries.)

Tree measurements and rankings may change over time as trees are re-measured and new candidates are added to the list. A single diameter is also calculated for multiple stems according to a formula. Overall size index is calculated according to a formula including height, trunk and crown diameter. In the case of tree groups, measurements are shown of the tallest or biggest trees. The numbering of trees is more or less in their order of declaration. (See also Table 2 on page 21 for Champion Tree size and age criteria.)

Table 4: Champion Trees of South Africa

* dbh = diameter at breast height

	Tree Species	Description	Height (m)	Stem dbh* (m)	Crown diam. (m)	Index figure	Location/site
1	*Adansonia digitata* (baobab) Sagole Tree, also known as Muvuyo wa Makhadzi	The largest indigenous tree of South Africa, and habitat for a rare colony of mottled spine-tail swifts	20,5	10,8	40	426	Sagole Village, Limpopo
2	*Adansonia digitata* (baobab) Glencoe Tree (Part of crown collapsed)	Second largest and oldest indigenous tree in South Africa, carbon dated to more than 1 800 years old	17	15,9	37,05	413	The farm Glencoe, Hoedspruit, Limpopo
3	*Ficus salicifolia* (Wonderboom fig) Wonderboom fig of Pretoria	Largest Wonderboom fig, carbon dated to more than 1 000 years old. Served as ox-wagon outspan area in earlier years, and there is a legend that the tree draws its growing power from a local chief buried under the tree	22	5,32 (multiple stems)	56	380	Wonderboom Nature Reserve, Pretoria (Tshwane), Gauteng
4	*Breonadia salicina* (matumi) One of a trio of trees called Three Queens	Largest matumi tree in South Africa	33	2,81	37	336	Amorentia Estate, near Modjadjiskloof, Limpopo
5	*Breonadia salicina* (matumi) One of a trio of trees called Three Queens	Second largest matumi tree in South Africa (forms part of a trio of large matumi trees)	38	2,6	24,9	306	Amorentia Estate, near Modjadjiskloof, Limpopo

OPPOSITE PAGE: The smooth, white bole of a giant lemon-scented gum, Paul Roos Gymnasium, Stellenbosch

	Tree Species	Description	Height (m)	Stem dbh* (m)	Crown diam. (m)	Index figure	Location/site
6	*Breonadia salicina* (matumi) One of a trio of trees called Three Queens	Third largest matumi tree in South Africa (forms part of a trio of large matumi trees)	38,6	2,41	17,78	286	Amorentia Estate, near Modjadjiskloof, Limpopo
7	*Adansonia digitata* (baobab) Platland Tree	Very large baobab and well-known tourist attraction with a bar inside	19	10,7	36	372	Platland/Sunland, near Modjadjiskloof, Limpopo
8	*Ficus sycomorus* (common cluster fig) Cluster Fig Giant	The largest cluster fig in South Africa	31	3,34	35,1	336	The farm Excellence, Mica, Limpopo
9	*Afrocarpus falcatus* (Outeniqua yellowwood) King Edward VIIth Tree	One of the well-visited Big Trees of the Knysna forests	36,9	2,12	31,5	301	Diepwalle, Garden Route National Park, Western Cape
10	*Eucalyptus saligna* (saligna gum) The O'Connor tree lane	Very tall landmark tree lane – planted in the 1930s by forestry pioneer AJ O'Connor. Situated next to O'Connor's memorial	71	1,36	32,1	469	Woodbush State Forest, Magoebaskloof, Limpopo
11	*Eucalyptus saligna* (saligna gum) The tallest trees in South Africa and Africa, with the tallest four known as the Magoebaskloof Giants (Measurement of tallest tree shown)	Stand of saligna gum trees planted in 1906 by forestry pioneer AK Eastwood, including the tallest trees in South Africa and Africa	81,5	1,04	10,7m	293	Woodbush State Forest, Magoebaskloof, Limpopo
12	*Sideroxylon inerme* (milkwood), Grandfather of Still Bay	Largest milkwood in South Africa, estimated to be about 1 000 years old	14	3,18	20	111	The farm Langebosch, Still Bay, Western Cape
13	*Sideroxylon inerme* (milkwood) Mossel Bay Post Office Tree	Historic tree believed to have been the tree at which an old shoe was placed for exchange of messages by Portuguese seafarers in the 16th century	8,5	1,1 (multiple stems)	32,9	51	Dias Museum, Mossel Bay, Western Cape

Tree Species	Description	Height (m)	Stem dbh* (m)	Crown diam. (m)	Index figure	Location/site
14 *Cinnamomum camphora* (camphor tree) The Vergelegen trees	Historic trees planted more than three centuries ago by Governor WA van der Stel – very large trees with a large landscape impact	26,3	4,01	31,4	295	Vergelegen Estate, Somerset West, Western Cape
15 *Quercus robur* (English oak) The Vergelegen Oak	Oak tree planted three centuries ago – largest and the oldest oak tree in the country	14	3,4	22,1	121	Vergelegen Estate, Somerset West, Western Cape
16 *Eucalyptus* species and a variety of other tree species (Tokai Arboretum – all mature trees)	Arboretum of historic significance with trees planted there since 1885. Laid out by Joseph Storr Lister at the beginning of the forestry industry	62	1,71	20,5	368	Table Mountain National Park, Cape Town, Western Cape
17 *Platanus acerifolia* (London plane) Tree avenue in KwaZulu-Natal National Botanical Garden known as Marriot's Lane	Tree avenue of exceptionally old plane trees – planted in 1908 by Mr WE Marriot (curator). This lane is a central landscape feature of the botanical garden	35	1,77	28,9	250	KwaZulu-Natal Botanical Gardens, Pietermaritzburg, KwaZulu-Natal
18 *Eucalyptus camaldulensis* (river red gum) The Irene Champion	Largest tree on an estate with a variety of trees planted since the late 19th century by a Mr Fuchs, employed by Alois Nellmapius	41	2,03	25,7	296	Irene Farm Estate, Centurion, Gauteng
19 *Eucalyptus paniculata* (grey ironbark), *E. maculata* (spotted gum) and *E. microrys* (tallow gum), Commonwealth Plantation	Arboretum or sample plot of large gum trees planted in the 1930s and protected to commemorate the Commonwealth Forestry Conference of 1935	80,1	1,18	20,5	394	Middelkop Plantation, Magoebaskloof, Limpopo
20 *Eucalyptus saligna* (saligna gum) Westfalia Show Block	Stand of tall gum trees planted in 1933 by the eminent Dr Hans Merensky	70	1,25	16,9	322	Westfalia Estate, near Modjadjiskloof, Limpopo

Tree Species	Description	Height (m)	Stem dbh* (m)	Crown diam. (m)	Index figure	Location/site
21 *Araucaria heterophylla* (Norfolk Island pine) Kweekskool Tree	Tallest Norfolk Island pine planted in 1826 by the wife of the last landdrost of Stellenbosch	46	1,9	21,21	292	Theological Seminary (Kweekskool), Stellenbosch, Western Cape
22 *Eucalyptus camaldulensis* (river red gum) Bergzicht Market Trees	Planted in 1880. Prominent trees providing shade for an entire informal market	34,5	2,32	35	311	Bergzicht Market, Stellenbosch, Western Cape
23 *Quercus robur* (English oak) Ryneveld Oaks	Planted in 1812. Five oak trees remaining of the previous generation of planted oak trees	29	1,48	17,6	148	Ryneveld Street, Stellenbosch, Western Cape
24 *Quercus robur* (English oak) Zandvliet Oak	Big oak tree planted in the 19th century at a historic farmhouse of an old wine estate	22	1,54	25,08	137	Solms Delta Estate, near Franschhoek, Western Cape
25 *Populus nigra* (Lombardy poplar) Ruth Fischer Tree	Historic tree serving as landmark for fugitives from the Apartheid security forces to find the safe house of Ruth Fischer, daughter of Bram Fischer	22	1,12	5,89	56	Lothbury Avenue, Auckland Park (Johannesburg), Gauteng
26 *Afrocarpus falcatus* (Outeniqua yellowwood) Tsitsikamma Big Tree	One of the most accessible Big Trees in Tsitsikamma forest. Visited by up to 95 000 tourists each year	39,3	2,77	33,6	379	Near Storms River, Garden Route National Park, Eastern Cape
27 *Afrocarpus falcatus* (Outeniqua yellowwood) Woodville Big Tree	One of the well-visited Big Trees of the Knysna Forests	34	2,8	30,55	314	Collin's Hoek, Garden Route National Park, Western Cape
28 *Afrocarpus falcatus* (Outeniqua yellowwood) Eastern Cape Monarch	Well-visited Big Tree known as the Eastern Monarch, along the Tyume Trail	39,4	2,75	29,69	355	Auckland Nature Reserve, Hogsback, Eastern Cape
29 *Afrocarpus falcatus* (Outeniqua yellowwood) The Dalene Matthee (Big) Tree	Landmark tree towering above the forest, and the site of a memorial to writer Dalene Matthee	35,4	1,72	28,35	247	Goudveld, Garden Route National Park, Western Cape

Tree Species	Description	Height (m)	Stem dbh* (m)	Crown diam. (m)	Index figure	Location/site
30 *Quercus robur* (English oak) The Slave Tree (Tree lost part of its crown)	Very large oak tree planted in 1811 – one of the biggest oak trees in the Southern Hemisphere	24	1,81	27,4	169	York Street, George, Western Cape
31 *Cedrus deodara* (deodar) Historic Bloemfontein trees (Almost all trees died)	Historic collection of trees of different species planted by visiting dignitaries since 1879	22	0,8	16,9	81	Old Government Buildings, Bloemfontein, Free State
32 *Quercus robur* (English oak) The Sophiatown Oak, also called The Hanging Tree (Tree died)	The tree was part of the history of Sophiatown and the struggle against the forced removal of the community in the 1950s	18	1,42	36	128	Bertha Street, Sophiatown, Johannesburg, Gauteng
33 *Eucalyptus (Corymbia) ficifolia* (red flowering gum) Ida's Valley Giant	Very large and attractive tree, estimated to be more than two centuries old. A landmark on an old historic farm	22,1	2,31 (multiple stems)	25,3	169	Ida's Valley Homestead, near Stellenbosch, Western Cape
34 *Quercus robur* (English oak) The Northcliff Oak	The largest and oldest measured oak tree in Gauteng	22	1,89	29,4	164	Northcliff, Johannesburg, Gauteng
35 *Ficus macrophylla* (Moreton Bay fig) Arderne Fig Tree	Landmark tree planted by tree pioneers Ralph and Henry Arderne	27,4	3,56	45,1	347	Arderne Garden, Claremont, Cape Town, Western Cape
36 *Auraucaria heterophylla* (Norfolk Island pine) The Arderne Pine	Landmark tree planted by tree pioneers Ralph and Henry Arderne	42,6	1,83	19,09	252	Arderne Garden, Claremont, Cape Town, Western Cape
37 *Quercus suber* (cork oak) Arderne Cork Oak	Landmark tree planted by tree pioneers Ralph and Henry Arderne	15,5	1,4	30,37	101	Arderne Garden, Claremont, Cape Town, Western Cape
38 *Quercis cerris* (Turkey oak) Arderne Turkey Oak	Landmark tree planted by tree pioneers Ralph and Henry Arderne	21,56	1,87	29,22	159	Arderne Garden, Claremont, Cape Town, Western Cape

Tree Species	Description	Height (m)	Stem dbh* (m)	Crown diam. (m)	Index figure	Location/site
39 *Pinus halepensis* (Aleppo pine) Arderne Aleppo Pine	Landmark tree planted by tree pioneers Ralph and Henry Arderne	32,9	1,74	30,95	241	Arderne Garden, Claremont, Cape Town, Western Cape
40 *Agathis robusta* (Queensland kauri) Arderne Kauri	Landmark tree planted by tree pioneers Ralph and Henry Arderne	27,7	1,57	26,45	179	Arderne Garden, Claremont, Cape Town, Western Cape
41 *Eucalyptus diversicolor* (karri gum) Brackenhill Gum Trees	Very tall landmark stand of karri gum, planted in 1922	70	1,46	25,77	429	Harkerville, near Knysna on the Garden Route, Western Cape
42 *Casuarina cunninghamia* (beefwood) Scanlen's Lane	Lane of large casuarinas planted in the 1860s by Charles Scanlen	27	1,68	23,12	168	Cradock, Eastern Cape
43 *Eucalyptus regnans* (mountain ash) The Benvie Trees	A trio of large trees situated on the scenic Benvie Arboretum, established by Scottish emigrant John Geekie more than a century ago	61	2,18	27,85	475	Benvie Arboretum, near New Hanover, KwaZulu-Natal
44 *Pinus radiata* (Monterey pine) The Eastern Cape Pine	Tallest pine tree in the Eastern Cape, planted in the late 1880s	51	1,5	15,5	246	Isidenge State Forest, near Stutterheim, Eastern Cape
45 *Eucalyptus citriodora* (lemon-scented gum) Paul Roos Trees	Scenic group of big trees on school grounds	39	0,76	22,1	160	Paul Roos Gymnasium, Stellenbosch, Western Cape
46 *Quercus robur* (English oak) Bonniemile Oak	Large oak tree on a farmyard next to the original wagon route linking Stellenbosch with Cape Town, planted by coachmen of Governor Simon van der Stel	24	1,64	33,5	178	The farm Bonniemile near Stellenbosch, Western Cape
47 *Eucalyptus camaldulensis* (river red gum) The Ruth Steer Tree	Prominent landmark tree in Stellenbosch, planted around 1880	33	2,5	33,15	301	Jonkershoek Avenue, Stellenbosch, Western Cape

Champion Trees of South Africa

	Tree Species	Description	Height (m)	Stem dbh* (m)	Crown diam. (m)	Index figure	Location/site
48	*Eucalyptus camaldulensis* (river red gum) Wits Campus Tree	Huge gum tree planted more than 80 years ago along a major road between Johannesburg and Rustenburg	34	2,37	37,55	321	University of Witwatersrand, Johannesburg, Gauteng
49	*Liriodendron tulipifera* (tulip tree) The Baynesfield Tulip Tree	Tree planted by Joseph Baynes in 1882 on the historic Baynesfield Estate	34	2,04	26,02	248	Baynesfield Estate, near Richmond, KwaZulu-Natal
50	*Sequoia sempervirens* (Californian redwood) The Grootvadersbos Redwood Grove	Stand of tall redwoods planted at Grootvadersbosch more than 90 years ago	58	1,38	12,2	238	Grootvadersbosch Nature Reserve, near Swellendam, Western Cape
51	*Eucalyptus saligna* (saligna gum) Herbert Baker Chapel Trees	Group of scenic trees standing next to a chapel designed by Sir Herbert Baker	45	1,89	27,25	322	Orpen Road, Cape Town, Western Cape
52	*Sequoia sempervirens* (Californian redwood) The Table Mountain Grove	Redwood trees planted in 1887 forming a landmark and recreation area for local residents	51	1,09	15,1	207	Tokai Plantation, Table Mountain National Park, Western Cape
53	*Senegalia galpinii* (monkey thorn) The Marico Tree	Tallest thorn tree measured in South Africa to date	37	1,81	31	277	The farm Veeplaas near Skuinsdrift, North West
54	*Ficus burkei* (common wild fig) Umtentweni Giant	Largest common wild fig in South Africa	28	3,31	31,9	288	Eden Park, Umtentweni, KwaZulu-Natal
55	*Eucalyptus camaldulensis* (river red gum) The Infruitec Gum Tree	Very large landmark tree planted about 130 years ago	38,2	3,08	37,05	409	Infruitec, Helshoogte Pass, Stellenbosch, Western Cape
56	*Eucalyptus camaldulensis* (river red gum) Wilgenhof Grandfather	Large tree planted about 130 years ago, and now a landmark	30,8	2,7	28,25	269	Victoria Street, Stellenbosch, Western Cape

Tree Species	Description	Height (m)	Stem dbh* (m)	Crown diam. (m)	Index figure	Location/site
57 *Adansonia digitata* (baobab) The King of Ga-Ratjeke	Third largest indigenous tree in South Africa	23,5	8,21 (multiple stems)	32,6	383	Ga-Ratjeke village, near Modjadjiskloof, Limpopo
58 *Quercus robur* (English oak) Akkerdraai Oak Tree	Large landmark oak tree, possibly older than 175 years	28	1,94	26	198	Annandale Road, Stellenbosch, Western Cape
59 *Eucalyptus grandis* (rose gum) Gum Tree Corner	Group of exceptionally large gum trees	59,1	1,33	16,89	279	KwaZulu-Natal Botanical Garden, Pietermaritzburg, KwaZulu-Natal
60 *Sequoia sempervirens* (Californian redwood) Misty Grove	A stand of tall sequoia trees planted about 90 years ago	59	1,08	18	260	Woodbush State Forest, Magoebaskloof, Limpopo
61 *Eucalyptus saligna* (saligna gum) Saasveld Sentinels	Large eucalypt landmark trees at the scenic Saasveld campus, more than 90 years old	39	1,47	34,2	276	Saasveld Campus, George, Western Cape
62 *Populus deltoides* (cottonwood tree) The Parktown Tree	The largest cottonwood tree measured locally, and a remnant of the semi-rural surroundings of Johannesburg which are now built up	35	1,66	28,07	238	Parktown North, Johannesburg, Gauteng
63 *Pinus pseudostrobus* (false Weymouth pine) The Three Matrons	The largest pine trees in Limpopo Province, planted in 1914	49,2	1,56	24,35	304	Woodbush State Forest, Magoebaskloof, Limpopo
64 *Ficus macrophylla* (Moreton Bay fig) The Zoo Giant	Large landmark tree near the entrance of the Pretoria National Zoological Gardens	27	3,8	41,4	339	National Zoological Garden, Pretoria (Tshwane), Gauteng
65 *Pinus taeda* (loblolly pine) The Buffelsnek Pine	Tallest pine tree measured in South Africa	60,1	1,2	18	279	Buffelsnek State Forest, Knysna, Western Cape

	Tree Species	Description	Height (m)	Stem dbh* (m)	Crown diam. (m)	Index figure	Location/site
66	*Ficus sycomorus* (common cluster fig) The Ilembe Tree	Very large tree in a rural landscape, known as a local landmark since a century ago	23	5,37 (multiple stems)	35,7	318	Ilembe, near Kranskop, KwaZulu-Natal
67	*Cussonia spicata* (Lowveld cabbage tree) The Kurisa Forest Giant	An imposing giant forest tree	35	3.71	22	316	Kurisa Moya, Magoebaskloof, Limpopo
68	*Eucalyptus camaldulensis* (river red gum) The Waterkloof Giant	Largest landmark tree of the eastern Pretoria suburbs. Remnant of a century-old tree plantation destroyed by suburban development	34	2,15	34,27	292	Waterkloof Primary School, Pretoria (Tshwane), Gauteng
69	*Adansonia digitata* (baobab) Buffelsdrift baobab/ Swartwater baobab	One of the five largest baobabs in the country	22	7,71	30,2	336	The farm Buffelsdrift, near Lephalale, Limpopo
70	*Afrocarpus falcatus* (Outeniqua yellowwood) The Blouberg Big Trees	Among the tallest indigenous forest trees in the country	41	1,65	31	293	Blouberg, near Polokwane, Limpopo
71	*Ficus burkei* (common wild fig) The Kindergarten Giant	Large landmark tree at the University of Cape Town campus	25	5,09	41	361	University of Cape Town, Cape Town, Western Cape
72	*Ficus thoningii* (common wild fig) The Vygekraal Trees	A scenic grove of large trees growing on the walls of a cattle kraal built in the late 19th century	23	1,6	28,6	155	The farm Vygekraal near Pretoria, Gauteng
73	*Eucalyptus grandis* (rose gum) The Satico Giants	Stand of third tallest trees in the country, planted in 1938	72,3	1,05	16,5	301	Satico Plantation, near Low's Creek, Mpumalanga
74	*Eucalyptus globulus* (blue gum) The Radyn Tree	Exceptionally large gum tree	40,2	4,75	27,5	459	The farm Radyn near Villliersdorp, Western Cape

	Tree Species	Description	Height (m)	Stem dbh* (m)	Crown diam. (m)	Index figure	Location/site
75	*Ficus macrophylla* (Moreton Bay fig) The Fernwood Trees	Landmark trees of the same vintage as the Arderne Garden trees (about 160 years old)	27,5	3,02	45,5	322	Fernwood Avenue, Newlands, Cape Town, Western Cape
76	*Cinnamomum camphora* (camphor tree) The Hohenort Grove	Grove of scenic camphor trees of about 250 years old growing behind cellars on a historic farmyard	24	2,1	18,9	151	Cellar Hohenort Hotel, Brommesvlei road, Constantia, Cape Town, Western Cape
77	*Eucalyptus globulus* (blue gum) The Welbedacht Tree	Landmark tree on a private nature reserve, planted in the 19th century	37,5	2,6	29,8	330	Welbedacht Reserve, Tulbagh, Western Cape
78	*Sequoia sempervirens* (Californian redwood) Hogsback Redwood Giants	Grove of large redwood trees planted almost a century ago	55	2,4	13,2	309	Hogsback, Eastern Cape
79	*Quercus suber* (cork oak) Ina Paarman Oak	Tree on the property of Mrs Ina Paarman, famous in the local food condiments industry. This scenic tree was planted in the mid-19th century	22,7	1,4	32,6	157	Constantia Main Road, Constantia, Western Cape
80	*Eucalyptus globulus* (blue gum) Houwhoek Inn Tree	Large tree planted in the mid-19th century at the oldest hotel in the country, which was a well-known railway stopover	27	3,2	26,8	250	Off the N2 road, Grabouw, Western Cape
81	*Eucalyptus saligna* (saligna gum) Merensky Lane	Scenic lane of trees planted by the eminent Dr Hans Merensky on the Westfalia Estate in the 1930s	69	1,65	21,5	411	Westfalia Estate, Modjadjiskloof, Limpopo
82	*Eucalyptus diversicolor* (karri) Boschendal	Lane of exceptionally large trees planted more than two centuries ago, among which is the largest measured tree in South Africa	50,4	2,7	33,6	483	Boschendal Estate, Helshoogte Road, Western Cape

Some global size comparisons

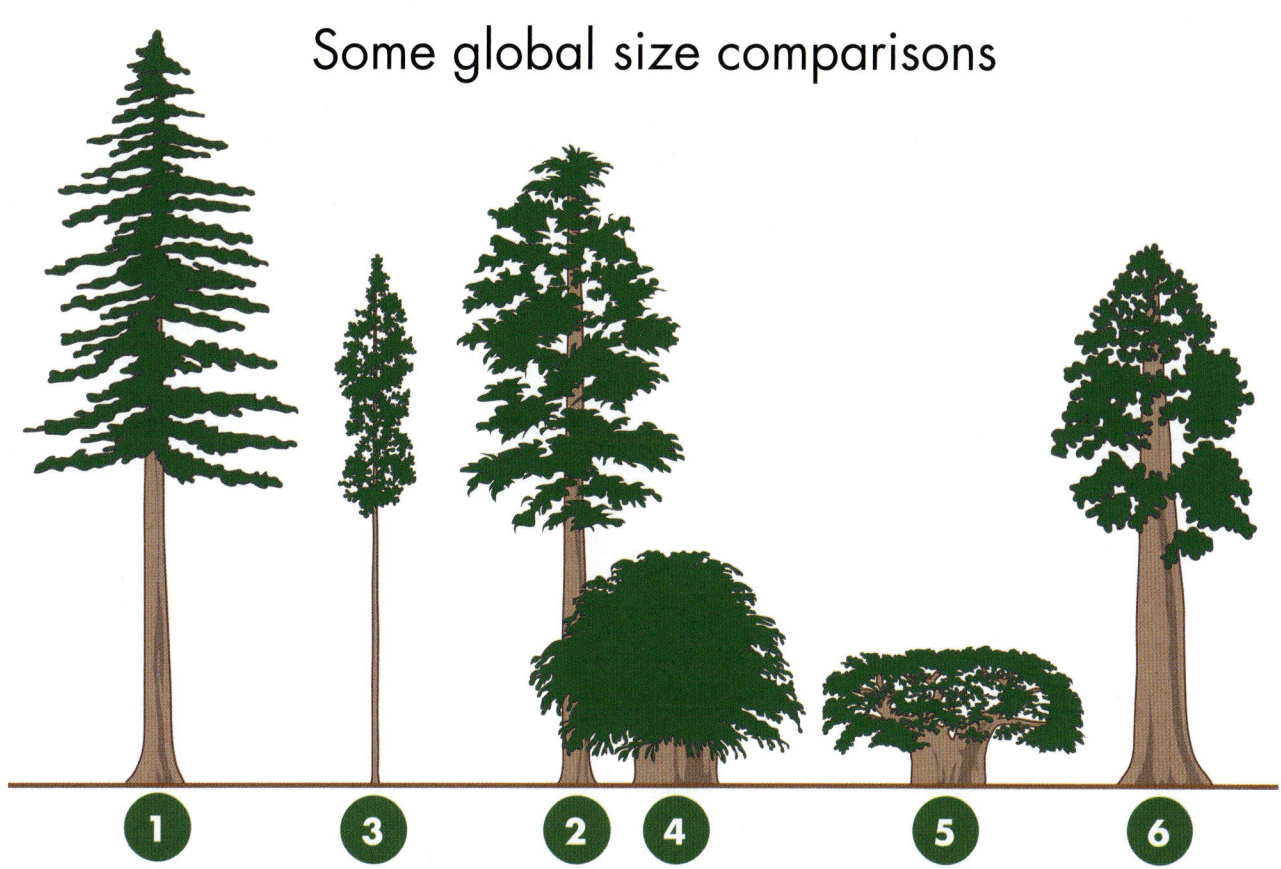

Tallest trees	Height (m)	Stem diameter at breast height (m)	Crown diameter (m)
1 *Sequoia sempervirens* **(coast redwood)** Hyperion tree, Redwoods National Park, USA	115,72	4,84	42
2 *Eucalyptus regnans* **(mountain ash)** The Centurion, Tasmania	99,6	4,05	35
3 *Eucalyptus saligna* **(saligna gum)** Magoebaskloof Giants, Limpopo Province, South Africa	81,5	1,04	10,7

Corpulent trees	Height (m)	Stem diameter at breast height (m)	Crown diameter (m)
4 *Taxodium mucronatum* **(Montezuma cypress)** Tule tree, Mexico	35,4	11,62	41
5 *Adansonia digitata* **(baobab)** Sagole tree, Limpopo Province, South Africa	20,5	10,8	40
6 *Sequoiadendron giganteum* **(giant redwood)** General Sherman tree, Sequoia National Park, USA	83,8	7,7	33

Trees as Monuments and in Gardens, Parks and Arboreta

Every city, town, village or farm in South Africa might well have its own remarkable tree, garden or park – remarkable for whatever reason. Details of many of these have been recorded. Unfortunately, however, even more are not documented. South Africa's vast rural stretches must have harboured many remarkable or rare trees of which the rural peoples, living closer to nature than their urban peers, would have had intimate knowledge. The histories of and tales about such trees will have been passed on orally from one generation to the next. Somehow, however, much of this has been lost with time – as have many of the trees themselves. The descriptions below can therefore in no possible way claim to be complete. Readers should feel free to add noteworthy facts and/or to bring them to the attention of persons or bodies concerned (see list under Acknowledgements).

Fortunately there is greater awareness nowadays about preserving this rich heritage. Officials and other individuals from cities, towns and other communities are becoming more knowledgeable about, and sensitive towards, trees in particular. The proclamation of a National Arbor Day, later National Arbor Week, with associated tree-planting campaigns aimed in particular at the youth, as well as the institution of the Arbor City Award, have borne fruit. Information about trees has become more easily obtainable through the various media, and there is a greater realisation of the value and importance of natural phenomena, in particular with respect to the protection and conservation of the environment and promoting tourism.

The number of declared national heritage resources (formerly national monuments) in South Africa runs into several hundreds. Most of these are buildings or structures, although single objects such as mountains, farms, streets and trees are also declared. In the case of buildings or streets, for instance, declaration includes the trees. (Add to this the more than 80 declared Champion Trees.)

National tree monuments and Champion Trees are described under the respective plant families, except those that for some reason or other fit in better under this chapter.

> Gardens and parks are not static entities, but are liable to change. A number of the parks and gardens described here have already undergone change, or will do so in future, or even cease to exist altogether, under new management and with altered circumstances and/or demands.
>
> The largely concise descriptions of the various gardens and parks might serve, so it is hoped, as a record of what was and what should be conserved for the benefit of future generations.
>
> A determined resolution towards this aim should prevent repeat of a case like the once worldwide renowned Ludwig's-burg Garden in Kloof Street, Cape Town – an incomparable and irretrievable treasure that has, within a mere 183 years' time, almost completely vanished and been obliterated from the minds of Capetonians, South Africans, horticulturists and nature lovers elsewhere.
>
> It should be emphasised that, apart from those described here, many more gardens of merit, not mentioned, should be prevented from undergoing a similar fate.

Western Cape

Table Mountain: declared a national monument in 1957

Sir Francis Drake, in his ship *Pelican*, sailed around the world in the years 1577 to 1580. In his account of the voyage he described the Cape of Good Hope as follows: 'This Cape is a most stately thing, and the fairest cape we saw in the whole circumference of the earth, and we passed by it on 18 June 1580'. Max O'Rell, a traveller-writer who visited Cape Town in 1893, wrote in his book titled *John Bull & Co* (1894): 'I do not know any town more picturesquely situated than Cape Town'. Looking from Adderley Street towards the Company's Garden and Table Mountain, he exclaimed 'I could never tire my eyes of this magnificent sight'.

The wonder of Table Mountain does not only lie in its beauty. It also symbolises the Cape Floristic Kingdom (the Fynbos Biome) with its vast richness in species, including trees. The endemic silver tree (*Leucadendron argenteum*) is one of Table Mountain's most glorious treasures, while the many gorges and kloofs abound with various high forest tree species. The lower slopes are graced by the exotic stone pine (*Pinus pinea*). Magnificent specimens of this tree give character to this beautiful mountain. On its south-eastern side Table Mountain is home to the Kirstenbosch National Botanical Garden with its glorious indigenous plant life.

Table Mountain – embodiment of the Cape Floristic Kingdom and a treasure chest of trees – the view that captured Sir Francis Drake's imagination?

Since 1998 Table Mountain is part of the Table Mountain National Park, managed by the South African National Parks (SANParks). The park was established to protect the environment of the Table Mountain chain on the Cape Peninsula, stretching from Signal Hill in the north to Cape Point in the south. After a lengthy international voting process, Table Mountain was declared one of the official 'New 7 Wonders of Nature' worldwide in 2012.

One of the many faces of Table Mountain: Lion's Head with a cluster of stone pines in the foreground

The Dutch East India Company's Garden (Kompanjiestuin): declared a national monument in 1962

Besides the Governor, Jan van Riebeeck, the most important person to set foot at the Cape in 1652 was his master gardener with the appropriate name of Hendrik Boom (*boom* = tree). The settlement began with a fort and a garden – the latter to provide fruit and vegetables to the crews of the ships sailing from Holland to India and back, and it was used exclusively for this purpose until 1679.

Scurvy was one of the enemies of early seafarers and, mindful of the role lemons play in combating the disease, it is no wonder that the lemon was chosen as one of the first fruit tree species to be planted in the Company's gardens (imported from the island of St Helena). It is reported that Maria van Riebeeck picked lemons on 15 July 1661.

The arrival of Governor Simon van der Stel brought about gradual change. The gardens of the free burghers and that of the Company at Newlands replaced the original garden to supply the necessary products. Consequently Governor van der Stel converted the first Company's garden into a botanical garden. Through the continued interest of his successors, among them WA van der Stel, Ryk Tulbagh and Van der Graaff, and their master gardeners, all botanists (Oldenland, Hartog and Auge, for instance), this garden became renowned for its beauty and the variety of plants. Much-travelled Francois Valentyn compared it with other famous gardens of the world, adding that '… none of the celebrated gardens of ancient times or of modern garden-lovers could be compared to this astonishing and beautiful garden in respect of the layout and the rare trees from the four corners of the earth'.

After the second British occupation of the Cape in 1806 the garden became neglected, with several encroachments, due to expansion of the city. In 1848 Sir Harry Smith appointed a Board of Commissioners to improve the condition of the neglected garden. One of the Commissioners was Ralph Arderne, founder of the Arderne Garden in Claremont.

The Company's Garden, Cape Town, with Table Mountain as backdrop

The declaration of the Company's Garden as a national monument in 1962 included Government Avenue on the eastern side of the garden, the two forming a unit. As early as 1685 Government Avenue was lined on both sides with orange trees, but these were later replaced by Governor Simon van der Stel with oak trees (*Quercus robur*). Although no longer the original ones, oak trees still line the lane.

The old Company's Garden, flanked by Government Avenue, with its interesting variety of indigenous and exotic plants and trees, is a green oasis in the Cape Town mid-city – one of the main visiting points in the 'Mother City'. This garden and avenue are a hive of activity in daytime – a meeting place for travellers from all points of the compass.

The Ludwig's-burg Garden, Kloof Street, Tamboerskloof

The only remnants of what was probably the most noteworthy of all gardens in South Africa are a fountain, a double garden wall and possibly a few trees.

Despite the fact that day-to-day passers-by are completely unaware of this superlative garden that once flourished along Kloof Street in Cape Town, the Ludwig's-burg Garden exercised an influence on practically every South African citizen, and still does so today. From this garden various magnificent specimens of trees and shrubs were made available to gardens all over the country, and it may even be that some of these became invasive plants in South Africa. Apart from the reputed jacaranda tree (*Jacaranda mimosifolia*), 1 660 exotic plants found their way to gardens from here.

Born in 1784 in the village of Sulz-am-Neckar, Württemberg, Germany, Carl Ferdinand Heinrich Ludwig arrived in Cape Town in 1805 as a pharmacist. He married a widow whose prospering snuff and beer selling business allowed him time to devote attention to his collections of *naturalia* consisting of birds, insects and plants.

A first consignment of such to Germany in 1826 earned him a baronetcy, and upon donation of an even larger collection to various German institutions, the University of Tübingen bestowed an Honorary Doctorate in Philosophy on the now Baron von Ludwig. In 1829 he bought three acres of land on Kloof Road, now Kloof Street, in the present-day Tamboerskloof. A further piece of land was obtained for the purpose of establishing a botanical garden, for which he imported plants from all over the world. Von Ludwig also maintained close relations with Kew Gardens staff and he became a prominent member of many Cape-based institutions. His collection of birds received favourable mention in the 1830 Annual Report of the South African Institution.

The name Ludwig's-burg was given to the garden around 1835. It had by then become world famous and was visited by every scientist or naturalist who travelled to Cape Town. In 1835 Volume 62 of *Curtis's Botanical Magazine* (Vol 9 of the new series) was dedicated to Baron von Ludwig by the editor, Sir William J Hooker, Director of Kew Gardens and professor of Botany at the Glasgow University. The dedication reads:

> *To CFH von Ludwig PhD,*
>
> *Knight of the Württemberg Civil Merit and Crown Orders,*
>
> *Friend and Patron of Botany at the Cape of Good Hope to whom our European gardens are indebted for many African plants of great rarity and beauty,*
>
> *the present volume is inscribed by his faithful and obliged friend and servant WJ Hooker.*
>
> *Glasgow, December 1835.*

Several plants were named after Von Ludwig, as well as a number of birds. In 1837 a second honorary doctorate was bestowed on him by the University of Tübingen, and he received the Freedom of the City of Stuttgart in Germany. Other tokens were a golden snuff box set with 34 diamonds given to him by King Wilhelm I of Württemberg, a marble bust of himself made by sculptor Theodore Wagner and a medal from the Grand Duke of Darmstadt. Von Ludwig achieved the unusual distinction of having a second book dedicated to him in 1838 with the publication of *The Genera of South African Plants* by William Harvey, then British Colonial Secretary.

Botanist friends of Von Ludwig who travelled to Voortrekker areas after the 1838 Great Trek took gifts of vegetable and wheat seed from Von Ludwig to Voortrekker leader Andries Pretorius. Whether he received any plant material in return, as he probably had hoped, is not known.

After Von Ludwig's death in 1847 his estate, including the acclaimed garden and its plants, went on public sale to various people and to the Company's Garden, which was upgraded soon after by a Board appointed for that purpose by Sir Harry Smith in 1848.

Eighty three years after his death his name was brought sensationally to the limelight. In 1930 the golden snuff box was found in the office of the Master of the Supreme Court in Cape Town, never

The fountain and a few trees are all that is left of the once famous Ludwig's-burg garden, Kloof Street, Tamboerskloof

having been claimed. After much publicity the judge ruled that the snuff box be sold and the proceeds distributed among the descendants. This was done in 1931, and it is said that Baron von Ludwig got more publicity from this case than when he was alive. His palatial residence at the corner of St George's and Longmarket Streets has been replaced by the Netherlands Bank. Traces of the renowned garden – the original walls, a fountain and a few trees – can be seen on the premises of the Villa Maria in Kloof Street. Clearly a case for timely intervention and conservation, now lost for ever.

Frank R Bradlow writes as follows about Baron von Ludwig:

> It is strange, and not a little sad, that a person who contributed so much to the life of Cape Town, and to horticulture's introduction in South Africa, is so little remembered by posterity. The name of the Baron is perpetuated in the land of his adoption by the scientific names of the three birds named in his honour, and of plants also named after him. There is also the singular distinction of having two scientific books dedicated to him; both now rare, and to the uninformed, obscure. These things, however, at least keep his name alive among a small circle of naturalists. But who remembers that he introduced the Jacaranda as well as some 1 660 other plants to South Africa, gave Cape Town gas light, was chairman of the first joint stock-mining company, and was above all, the father of the present Botanic Gardens?

The Arderne Garden, Main Street, Claremont: declared a national monument in 1979

Ralph Henry Arderne arrived in Cape Town in 1830. After a short stay in Grove Street, now Parliament Street, he moved to the 'country' on the Wynberg road, where he started a garden. His consultant was James Bowie, a plant collector from Kew Gardens, London, with which he exchanged plants and which he visited in 1892.

In 1845 Arderne bought a piece of land (5,6 ha) for £740, which was to become the present-day Arderne Garden. He named it 'The Hill' after the farm near Tarporly in Cheshire, England, where his ancestors had lived, and planned the garden with winding paths and to be as natural as possible. As an importer of timber, Arderne was in contact with many ships' captains through whose efforts he obtained plants for his garden from many countries, such as Australia, China, India, Lebanon, Spain and Chile. A small Norfolk Island pine (*Araucaria heterophylla*), which he bought for £5 that actually were intended to be spent on a dress for his wife, was planted with great care and developed into a huge tree 40 m high. Indigenous trees such as yellowwood species (*Afrocarpus* and *Podocarpus*), stinkwood (*Ocotea bullata*) and ironwood (*Olea capensis* subsp. *macrocarpa*) were also planted alongside tree ferns, bamboos and willows on the edge of ponds showing off exquisite water lilies. Azaleas, imported in vast numbers, soon became a feature of the garden.

Having been appointed to the Board of Commissioners for improvement of the Company's Garden, Ralph Arderne contributed much stock from his own garden. After his death in 1885 his son Henry Mathew moved into The Hill, spending all his spare time improving the garden. He imported rhododendrons, while the indigenous white watsonias (*Watsonia ardernei*) became a feature of the garden. On his return from the Barberton gold rush in the 1880s, he brought back Barberton daisy seeds for sowing.

The garden eventually became the setting for grand social occasions attended by well-known people, such as Rudyard Kipling, who reputedly said, 'This place ought to be an imperial possession for the botanists of the Empire ... it is a wonderful garden'.

After Henry's death in 1914 the big Norfolk Island pine tree also died, as had been predicted by the Claremont Malays.

The scenic Arderne Garden, Claremont, Cape Town (Photo: Marie Vrei/Friends of the Arderne Garden)

The Cape Town Municipality, realising the garden's beauty and scientific value, later bought the more valuable part. With many beautiful trees from all over the world, like the prominent Norfolk Island pines and a magnificent Australian *Ficus macrophylla*, the Arderne Garden now has the distinction of containing the densest concentration of Champion Trees in South Africa.

Leeuwenhof and Bo-Tuin, Oranjezicht

In 1850 Mr PJ Kotze, the father of Sir John Kotze, bought the old Dutch property Leeuwenhof, which dates back to 1694. Mr Kotze, by profession a farmer and businessman, became a member of the Cape Colonial Government and was twice the Mayor of Cape Town. He was a keen gardener, and imported rhododendrons to beautify his garden – an example followed by Ralph Arderne. To improve his knowledge, he bought a set of books on the subject of horticulture from Baron von Ludwig's estate. Leeuwenhof eventually became the official residence of the Administrators of the former Cape Province. Today it is the residence of the Western Cape Premier. Although the notorious 'black' south-easter (wind), or the 'Cape Doctor', does not allow trees to become extraordinarily large, Leeuwenhof does boast some splendid old Moreton Bay fig trees, yellowwoods, oaks and superb cycads. Leeuwenhof is still known for its magnificent garden, which contains a bougainvillea apparently dating back to 1850. Leeuwenhof and Bo-Tuin, two sections of the same property, were declared national monuments in 1966 and 1963 respectively.

De Waal Park, Camp Street, Oranjezicht

This park was laid out through the endeavours of David Christiaan de Waal, member of the Cape Colonial Government and Mayor of Cape Town in 1889/1890. It was opened to the general public in 1895 and declared a national monument in 1968.

De Waal Park features various kinds of trees, especially oak trees. It is situated in an old part of Cape Town and some magnificent stone pine (*Pinus pinea*) trees are to be seen in the vicinity.

Plantation show blocks

The South African Forestry Company Limited (SAFCOL), as well as a number of Forestry Agencies, manages a considerable number of arboreta on plantations countrywide, all of which are of great aesthetic and scientific importance. The age of these arboreta, or 'show blocks', varies from 50 years to more than 100 years. SAPPI, Mondi and Hans Merensky Holdings similarly manage several show blocks or areas of special interest in their plantations. Some of these are mentioned later in the book. Visits to these areas can be undertaken with the approval of the relevant organisations.

The Tokai Arboretum

It was at Tokai that Governor Simon van der Stel first planted oak trees and it is therefore fitting that the first serious attempts at practising commercial forestry took place there about two centuries later. Systematic tree planting for scientific purposes was started in 1885 in the Tokai arboretum by forestry pioneer Joseph Storr Lister – hence 'Lister's Place' tearoom in the Arboretum. Tokai Arboretum was declared a national monument 100 years later on National Arbor Day in 1985.

Exotic trees from many countries, especially those with climates similar to South Africa, such as Australia, India, the southern states of North America, and Mexico, have been established in the arboretum, as well as a great number of indigenous species and even small trees such as bottlebrushes – the latter to improve the ornamental aspect. The main feature of the arboretum comprises the lofty eucalypt trees, which display a variety of interesting and highly ornamental bark. Fine specimens are also to be seen of the smooth-barked apple gum (*Angophora costata*), near family of the eucalypts, with its decorative red-brown trunk.

The arboretum is frequently visited by botanists, horticulturists, forestry scientists and school groups. It is close to Tokai Manor House, also a declared national monument, where Storr Lister stayed while he was stationed in Cape Town as Conservator of the Western Conservancy of the Cape Colony.

Once described as 'a botanical garden devoted to trees', Tokai Arboretum is now managed and maintained by the Table Mountain National Park, part of the South African National Parks (SANParks). With the entire site declared a Champion Tree Arboretum, double protection of this site is ensured. It is current policy to systematically clear the pine and gum plantations on the slopes of Table Mountain, including those surrounding the arboretum, and to allow these areas to revert to fynbos. The arboretum itself has been retained, owing to its botanical and historic value, but it has become more prone to fires, partly as a result of the tree removal programme. A fire

swept through the area in 2015 and caused serious damage to the arboretum. By mid 2016, work was under way to restore at least part of the arboretum to its former glory.

Paarl Arboretum

In 1957 the Paarl Town Council set aside a site of about 31 ha for the creation of an arboretum. Some 225 municipalities and organisations throughout South Africa were requested to donate a tree. The arrangement of the tree specimens is geographical, with each section containing species from a different continent.

Babylonstoren Garden

The fruit and vegetable gardens on the farm Babylonstoren at the foot of Simonsberg were inspired by the Dutch East India's Company Gardens in Cape Town. This historic farm was founded around 1692 in the Drakenstein Valley to supply spice fleets sailing between the Netherlands and Asia. Designed by the French architect Patrice Taravella, the 3,5 hectare garden follows the Cartesian geometric patterns of the original gardens and houses over 300 varieties of edible or medicinal plants. Fruit and vegetables are harvested daily for two restaurants on the property, Babel and The Greenhouse. Specialist collections include some 7 000 clivia plants growing along a meandering stream and almost all varieties of indigenous cycads. Botanist Ernst van Jaarsveld is now establishing a large succulent collection.

Aerial view of the gardens at Babylonstoren (Photo: Courtesy Babylonstoren)

Botanical gardens

There are some 1 600 declared botanical gardens in the world. They are the laboratories of the plant world, including trees, which supply knowledge to the student and much pleasure to millions of people. South Africa's tree story would be incomplete without mentioning her botanical gardens. (Readers should note that the singular form *garden* is used throughout.)

SANBI, the South African National Biodiversity Institute, manages nine botanical gardens, some of which are declared national monuments: Kirstenbosch, the Harold Porter National Botanical Garden in Betty's Bay, the Karoo Desert National Botanical Garden in Worcester, the Free State National Botanical Garden in Bloemfontein, the KwaZulu-Natal National Botanical Garden in Pietermaritzburg, the Pretoria National Botanical Garden, the Walter Sisulu National Botanical Garden in Roodepoort, both in Gauteng, the Lowveld National Botanical Garden in Nelspruit (Mbombela), Mpumalanga, and the Hantam National Botanical Garden near Nieuwoudtville in the Northern Cape Province. Descriptions are provided under the relevant provinces.

OPPOSITE PAGE: Entering a 'tree cathedral' – Tokai Arboretum, Cape Town

Kirstenbosch National Botanical Garden

Undoubtedly the most famous of South Africa's botanical gardens is Kirstenbosch, of which it is said that at all times of the year it is one of the most beautiful gardens in the world. One reason for this is that Kirstenbosch is the habitat *par excellence* of fynbos, that unique floristic kingdom of the Cape.

Sir George Taylor, one of the former directors of Britain's Royal Botanic Gardens at Kew, wrote about his visit to Kirstenbosch: 'The impact of that visit has remained a cherished recollection over the years. With its superlative backcloth of mountain buttresses, for sheer grandeur the setting of Kirstenbosch is unsurpassed'.

Kirstenbosch is one of very few botanical gardens worldwide that came into existence to facilitate the study of a particular flora, and not for the introduction of economically useful plants or for the study of botany in general.

A few exotic trees do occur in Kirstenbosch, such as the English oak and the historic camphor and Moreton Bay fig trees, planted at the request of Cecil John Rhodes, as part of an avenue leading from the Groote Schuur manor to Hout Bay.

However, Kirstenbosch is not so much notable for its magnificent big trees as for the remarkable small silver trees and unique flowering Proteaceae, among which trees such as the wild almond tree hedge planted at the command of Jan van Riebeeck in 1660 are still to be seen.

Kirstenbosch, 528 ha in extent, of which 36 ha is cultivated area, has a long and interesting history. The garden has received many awards, among which that bestowed in 1999 by the International Society of Botanical Gardens, declaring this one of the seven outstanding botanical gardens in the world.

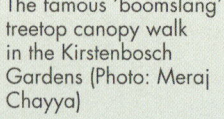

The famous 'boomslang' treetop canopy walk in the Kirstenbosch Gardens (Photo: Meraj Chayya)

It is a popular garden, even accessible to blind people by way of a trail where they can feel and smell some of South Africa's more interesting plants.

Kirstenbosch is one of the main tourist attractions of Cape Town, as part of the Table Mountain National Park, and with the distinction of being the first botanical garden to be included within a natural World Heritage Site. Ever since the arrival of Jan van Riebeeck at the Cape in 1652, South Africa has been renowned for gardens of world class. First it was the Company's Garden, then the Ludwig's-burg Garden, then again the Company's Garden as well as the Arderne Garden, and now Kirstenbosch.

The Harold Porter National Botanical Garden

This 200,5 ha garden, part of the Kogelberg Biosphere Reserve, displays the unique fynbos of the Betty's Bay area, among which are several *Mimetes* species. Interesting tree features of this garden are the forests in Disakloof and Luiperdkloof, both accessible by footpaths.

The Karoo Desert National Botanical Garden

Situated in Worcester, this garden displays plants of the dry and desert areas of South Africa and is renowned for its succulent plants (400 species occurring here naturally), and its glittering display of Mesembryantheaceae (vygies), in spring. Several *Aloe* and *Aloidendron* species can be observed here, such as the quiver tree, the giant quiver tree and the tree aloe. Other species include boer-bean trees, euphorbia, karee, wild olives and the camel thorn.

The Stellenbosch University Botanical Garden

The Stellenbosch University Botanical Garden is one of the smallest registered botanical gardens in the world and also the oldest of the university botanical gardens in Africa. The first curator, Dr Hans Herre, was appointed in 1925. With the help of his assistant, he collected the succulents for which this garden is renowned worldwide. Besides succulents, the garden boasts the largest collection of *Pelargonium* species in the world. It was also here that the *Welwitschia mirabilis*, the strange plant from the Namib Desert of Namibia and Angola, was cultivated from seed for the first time.

Indigenous as well as exotic trees grow in this garden, where examples of the mammoth tree (*Sequoiadendron giganteum*), Californian redwood (*Sequoia sempervirens*) and the dawn redwood (*Metasequoia glyptostroboides*) can be seen.

The Infruitec Heritage Garden, Stellenbosch (Garden of Remembrance)

This remarkable garden was initiated by Dr PG Marais, a previous Director of Infruitec, who said, 'What we plant is a precise replica of the parent stock and that in turn can be propagated from a bud. It is a monument that may last for 5 000 years or longer'.

From Jan van Riebeeck's *Daghregister* (diary) it was established that quince and medlar seeds were planted at the Cape on 24 August 1652. This date is rightfully considered by the fruit industry of South Africa as its date of birth. The date was celebrated for the first time 322 years later, on 24 August 1974, by the then Fruit Technology Institute, now ARC Infruitec-Nietvoorbij. The commemoration was fittingly marked with the planting of a wild almond tree (*Brabejum stellatifolium*), grown from a slip cut from the historic wild almond hedge in Kirstenbosch.

Other trees noteworthy for their scientific, historical or religious significance that were planted in this living monument are, *inter alia*:
- A Californian redwood (*Sequoia sempervirens*), planted in 1962 from seed brought from the Sequoia National Park, United States. These trees are renowned for being the tallest in the world.
- An Isaac Newton apple tree (Flower of Kent) planted in 1973. Although the original tree died in 1814, descendants were planted at various places, including Kew Gardens. The CSIR (Council for Scientific and Industrial Research) in Pretoria obtained material from these descendants in 1960 and Infruitec obtained material from the CSIR.
- A Hippocrates tree: London plane (*Platanus acerifolia*). The original Hippocrates tree on the island of Cos in the Aegean Sea is said to be more than 2 300 years old. (Hippocrates is known as the father of modern medicine and all medical doctors take the Oath of Hippocrates after qualifying.)
- Various vines are on view: vines deriving from the Graaff-Reinet vine which is one of the biggest in the world, planted in 1870; vines from Louis Pasteur's vineyard in France; from the Trinity vine in California, United States, which at one stage covered 930 m^2; and from the Dan-Ben-Hannah vine bred in Israel and released at Infruitec as the first virus-free vine. The Jewish breeder named the vine after his son and wife. Cuttings were also planted of the Hampton Court Palace vine, which is 250 years old, bears 1 000 bunches of grapes annually and is seen by hundreds of thousands of visitors each year. The last of the remarkable vines planted in the garden stems from the oldest vine in South Africa, planted in 1770, more than 200 years ago, at 90 Bree Street, Cape Town, and still bearing grapes every year. It is a vine of the cultivar 'Crystal', introduced from the United States. (Another remarkable vine grows at Infruitec, namely a 'Cabernet sauvignon' grafted on a 'Ramsey' rootstock, planted in 1980. Some time later its stem diameter was measured at approximately 25 cm, covering about 300 m^2, expected eventually to cover up to 400 m^2. At a stage it was producing some 6 000 bunches of grapes with a total weight of about three-quarters of a ton.)
- An orange tree from the farm Hexrivier, Citrusdal, planted around 1777.
- A sweet saffron pear from a tree growing in the Company's Garden in Cape Town and believed to have been planted during Jan van Riebeeck's tenure at the Cape.
- A milkwood tree grown from a cutting of the Post Office Tree, Mossel Bay.
- A Genadendal pear tree planted in 1738 by German missionary Georg Schmidt.
- A Gethsemane olive tree (the Rumi olive), the age of which was established through carbon dating at 2 400 years. It may be that Jesus walked in the shade of the parent tree, or even touched it.
- A marula (*Sclerocarya birrea* subsp. *caffra*), the fruit of which was used by many indigenous people to brew a drink. Today it is used to make a popular South African liqueur.
- A Koo apple tree from the Koo Valley near Montagu, Western Cape.
- A Canterbury mulberry tree from Canterbury Cathedral in England. Archbishop Thomas Becket was murdered there in 1170, and according to legend the four knights who murdered him hung their cloaks on the mulberry tree outside the cathedral. The nursery rhyme *Here we go round the mulberry tree* apparently refers to this incident.
- The Shakespeare mulberry which he reputedly planted at his home, New Place, in Stratford-on-Avon around 1597.
- The Napoleon willow, which was planted next to Napoleon's grave on the island of St Helena. When Deneys Reitz in later years visited the Boer Prisoners of War camp on St Helena (Anglo-Boer/South African War, 1899 to 1902), he brought cuttings of the Napoleon willow back to South Africa. Some of the cuttings were planted at the farm Roodeplaat

Trees as Monuments and in Gardens, Parks and Arboreta

The Gethsemane olive tree in the Infruitec Garden of Remembrance, Stellenbosch

near Pretoria, which later became the Roodeplaat Horticultural Research Institute, now the ARC Roodeplaat Vegetable and Ornamental Plant Institute (VOPI). A cutting from this tree was planted at Infruitec.
- A cutting derived from the Wonderboom fig (*Ficus salicifolia*) in Pretoria.
- A dawn redwood (*Metasequoia glyptostroboides*), from the Stellenbosch University Botanical Garden. This deciduous conifer was formerly only known from fossil remains dating back 70 million years and was thought to be extinct until some trees were discovered in China as recently as 1945. A Chinese forester, T Wang, came upon a tree near the village of Motoachi in Central China. The dawn redwood is closely related to the Californian redwoods and can nowadays be seen growing throughout the world in parks and gardens.
- The maidenhair tree (*Ginkgo biloba*), another conifer that dates from the age of the fossils. It is one of the most ancient of all living flowering plants. The tree occurred worldwide, and has not changed at all in a period of 150 million years. By the time humans came on the scene this species had retreated to a mountainous area in China. Its re-emergence is due to its being planted in temple gardens in China and Japan. The Western world only heard of the maidenhair tree when one Kaempfer wrote about his visit to Japan in the late 1600s. In 1730 the first plant arrived in Europe and in 1754 staff at Kew Gardens in England planted one tree, which is still thriving. The maidenhair tree is quite common in South Africa today and is seen in many towns and cities.
- Offspring of the oldest date palm (*Phoenix dactylifera*) trees in South Africa (see *Palm Family*).
- Carob (*Ceratonia siliqua*) trees from Israel. Also known as 'St John's bread', this name relates to the presumption that John the Baptist survived on the pods of this tree in the desert.
- A manatoka tree (*Myoporum laetum*) from Robben Island. Although an exotic, the repute of this tree is ascribed to the

fact that ex-President Nelson Mandela had spent 27 years in prison at Robben Island. This tree was in fact grown from a cutting of the tree closest to Mr Mandela's prison cell. (The list of trees relating to the late Madiba to be included in the Infruitec garden has not been closed and is still being updated.)

An informative brochure, with illustrations by the late Hannes Meiring, is available on the websites www.heritagegarden.co.za or www.heritagegarden-stellenbosch.com.

The Kweekskool Tree, Stellenbosch

Landdrost DJ van Ryneveld's wife planted a Norfolk Island pine (*Araucaria heterophylla*) in the Drostdy garden in upper Dorp Street, Stellenbosch, in 1826. It proved to be a deed of great foresight. A Norfolk Island pine not only resembles a church spire more than any other tree species, but since 1859 to this day the Drostdy remains in the service of God, as it accommodates a seminary (Afrikaans: 'kweekskool') by the Stellenbosch University.

The most serious mishap that has befallen this tree has been some damage to its crown. There are several theories as to how the crown 'came to a downfall'; one proclaiming that a supporter hoisted a Union Jack in the tree during the Anglo-Boer War, whereupon an opponent took it down, damaging the tree in the process.

Prof Brian Bredenkamp (emeritus) of the department of Forest Science at the University, however, established that the damage was caused by an enthusiast who hoisted the new flag of the Union of South Africa in the tree on 31 May 1928. The 'culprit' was one Morrison, a grandson of the Rev DS Botha, and the incident caused quite a stir in town.

With a height of 46 m the tree is the tallest in Stellenbosch, according to Prof Bredenkamp. Its diameter at breast height measures almost 2 m. This tree is now protected as a Champion Tree.

Stellenbosch's tallest tree: the Kweekskool (Theological Seminary) Tree – temptation to patriotic (and not so patriotic) students … (Photo: Enrico Liebenberg)

Stellenbosch – urban forest *par excellence*

When concern was voiced some time ago about the condition of trees on sidewalks and in open spaces in Stellenbosch, a Tree Advisory Committee was instituted to assist the municipality with the management of the trees within their boundaries.

Guided by the philosophy of its chairman, Prof Bredenkamp, viz. that trees are living organisms and have the right to live, and no one has the right to kill a tree unless he/she has planted it, the efforts of the Committee have met with remarkable success. This entails not only a marked decline in the number of requests for the felling of trees, but also the cooperation of developers in particular, who are now willing to go to great lengths to satisfy the guidelines set by the Committee, to the benefit of both the community and the investors.

This achievement has certainly succeeded in helping Stellenbosch retain its reputation both as 'urban forest' of the Boland and also as South Africa's first 'Oak City' (see *Beech Family*) – a veritable example of cooperation between the various role players within a community towards conservation of the environment!

Stellenbosch is famous for its leafy avenues of venerable oak trees. In 2012 the mayor of this tree-conscious town initiated a project to plant a million trees

The Eikenhof Arboretum, Grabouw

A remarkable arboretum was initiated in 1954 by Mr D Moodie and the late Mr HW Blackburn of the farm Eikenhof near Grabouw. Seedlings of 75 species were obtained, with the permission of the Department of Forestry, from the Knysna forests, among them trees such as yellowwoods, stinkwood, assegai and elder. Both the Outeniqua yellowwood and the elder were reported to have grown exceptionally well.

The Hexrivier orange tree, district of Citrusdal

A historic orange tree on the farm Hexrivier (Hex River) was declared a national monument in 1979. Hendrik Swellengrebel, the son of Cape Governor Swellengrebel, confirmed in his journals that orange trees grew in the Citrusdal area as early as 1777. Among these was the historic tree of Hexrivier. In 1925 the tree was damaged by fire when a snake had to be driven out of it. Dr RH Marloth, respected botanist, investigated the tree in 1939 and declared that it must be at least 160 years old.

Plettenberg Bay timber storehouse

Eerie monument from the heyday of timber export: Governor Joachim van Plettenberg's timber store, Plettenberg Bay

This timber store at Plettenberg Bay, declared a national monument in 1936, was built in 1787 during Dutch East India Company rule by order of Governor Joachim van Plettenberg, with the intention of exporting timber from the southern Cape forests from this bay. Johan Jacob Jerling, a burgher living on the eastern bank of the Keurbooms River, was commissioned to build the storehouse. The building is 61 m long and 6,7 m wide. The walls are of packed sandstone, 610 mm thick, and the building has ten windows and two doors.

The first load of wood was taken from the store by Captain Francois Duminy in his ship *De Meermin*. From 1817 exports declined, when the Knysna lagoon was opened as a harbour.

A clause in Jerling's contract stipulated the use of yellowwood for the roof beams, lintels, windows and door-frames. As yellowwood is not naturally durable, it could not withstand prolonged exposure to the elements. The woodwork and thatch soon rotted away, leaving only the stone walls. The lintels also rotted, resulting in the collapse of the overhead walls. The lintels were replaced with well-treated timber around 1983.

Old George–Knysna road, including the Kaaimans and Silver River bridges, and the Knysna-Tsitsikamma forests

This road, declared a national monument in 1981, warrants mentioning because it runs through part of the southern Cape natural or rain forests – a veritable wonder world of trees.

The southern Cape natural forests (the Knysna-Tsitsikamma forests) are a broken forest belt occurring along the coastal plateau and the lower slopes of the Outeniqua and Tsitsikamma Mountains. It is South Africa's largest forest complex, although only about 60 500 ha in extent, and therefore an asset that should be protected with fervour, as the total area covered by natural forest in South Africa covers only some 500 000 ha. The natural forests occur in scattered patches along the southern and eastern coast and mountain ranges of South Africa, where they are restricted to the most suitable sites.

These forests can be regarded as an expansion of tropical forests southwards from central Africa, although they are not true tropical forests any more, because many species have not survived the colder and drier periods of the long climatic cycles, with more tropical species dropping out the further south one goes. The Eastern Cape forests of the Amatola Mountains contain 250 species, only 125 of which have reached the southern Cape region, with a species like red stinkwood (*Prunus africana*) petering out to but a few trees in the southern Cape and none occurring in the forests closer to Cape Town.

The natural forests of South Africa, although limited in extent, played an important role in the development of the country, and in spite of the many trees that were removed over the centuries, the magnificence of these forests could not be ruined completely. A large percentage of the natural forests in South Africa has been protected for many years now. In the southern Cape, forestry scientists of SANParks manage 35 800 ha in accordance with a Senility Criteria Harvesting Yield Regulation System, where only trees with visible signs of dieback and which are within the last ten years of their life cycle are harvested.

The most renowned trees of South Africa's indigenous rainforests are the yellowwoods, of which both the Outeniqua yellowwood and common yellowwood reach giant proportions, and the black stinkwood, known for its precious and beautiful wood.

The southern Cape forests were a refuge to some 500 elephants in 1876. Their number dwindled rapidly to 20 in 1908, 11 in 1970, three in 1980 and, in 2000, a single cow roamed the forests. On the basis of sightings the presence of only one is upheld, although well-known zoologist Gareth Patterson alleges that, according to DNA sampling, there could be more. This assumption has, however, not reliably been established. (An earlier attempt to establish a viable breeding population by introducing young animals from the Kruger National Park was not successful.)

A 'forest' trilogy written in the 1980s by the South African author Dalene Matthee, and translated into several languages from the original Afrikaans, literally opened up the forests to visitors from all over the world. The English titles of these books are *Circles in a Forest*, *Fiela's Child* and *The Mulberry Bush*, and they were followed afterwards by a fourth title: *Magic Forest*.

Commenting on her experience of the forest, Ms Matthee stated: 'The mind is overwhelmed by the complexity of this wonder world. Schauberger once said each green leaf is in reality a tiny factory – the forest in its entirety is a powerhouse that radiates its energy far beyond the limits of its margins'.

Ms Matthee was honoured specially for this achievement by the South African Institute of Forestry, while one of the Forest Five Big Trees at Goudveld State Forest near Knysna was named after her with a monument erected at its base.

Fairy-tale beauty of the Knysna-Tsitsikamma forests

Eastern Cape

The parks of Port Elizabeth (Nelson Mandela Bay)

Best known of the Port Elizabeth parks is St George's Park, because of its location near the cricket field, swimming pool and bowling-green.

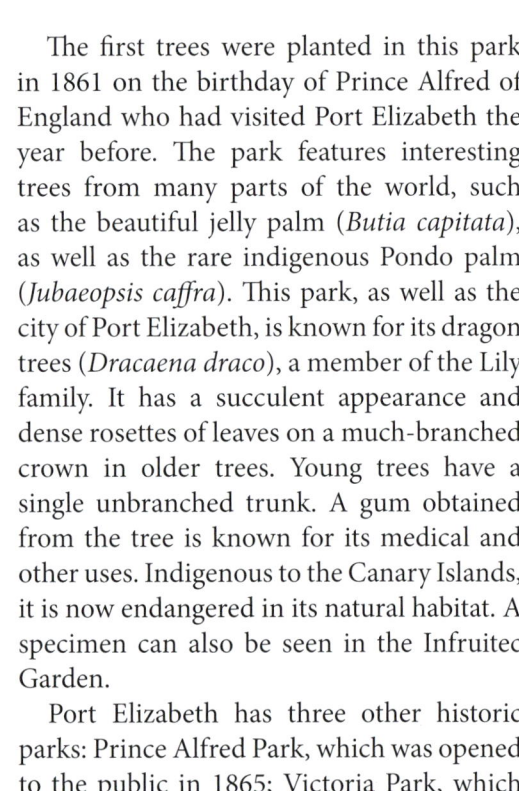

Magnificent dragon trees garnishing St George's Park, Port Elizabeth

The first trees were planted in this park in 1861 on the birthday of Prince Alfred of England who had visited Port Elizabeth the year before. The park features interesting trees from many parts of the world, such as the beautiful jelly palm (*Butia capitata*), as well as the rare indigenous Pondo palm (*Jubaeopsis caffra*). This park, as well as the city of Port Elizabeth, is known for its dragon trees (*Dracaena draco*), a member of the Lily family. It has a succulent appearance and dense rosettes of leaves on a much-branched crown in older trees. Young trees have a single unbranched trunk. A gum obtained from the tree is known for its medical and other uses. Indigenous to the Canary Islands, it is now endangered in its natural habitat. A specimen can also be seen in the Infruitec Garden.

Port Elizabeth has three other historic parks: Prince Alfred Park, which was opened to the public in 1865; Victoria Park, which was laid out in 1891/92 and served as the venue for a garden party during the British Royal visit to South Africa in 1947; and Settlers Park in the Baakens River Valley, a nature reserve set aside in 1932.

Grahamstown Botanical Garden

The land on which the botanical garden was established was granted to the Albany Botanical Society by the then Governor of the Cape Colony, Sir George Cathcart, in 1853. It is one of the oldest gardens in the country and the cottage on the grounds, dating back to 1830, was erected in the romantic country style known as *cottage orné*, with peaked Gothic windows and a Georgian chimney. The most outstanding feature of this garden is the fine specimens of *Araucaria* (monkey puzzle) trees from Australia.

The Reinet House vine, Graaff-Reinet

Normally vines are not regarded as trees, but this vine in Murray Street, Graaff-Reinet, which was declared a national monument in 1950, is remarkable. Its story begins with a parsonage in the town of Graaff-Reinet (named after Governor Jacob de Graaff and his wife Reinet), nestling against Spandau Kop and framed by the Tandjiesberg and the Ribboksberg with its eerie Valley of Desolation.

Around 1800 it became necessary to build a new parsonage for the Dutch Reformed Church. A stately Cape Dutch building in an H-form was erected. The third parson who occupied this house was the Reverend Andrew Murray, who stayed there with his wife for 45 years and where their six sons and five daughters were born. All of the sons, among them the illustrious Dr Andrew Murray, became Dutch Reformed ministers. Not only did the Reverend Murray serve his vast, outstretched congregation as far as the (later) Transvaal from there, but he received many visitors, including Dr David Livingstone and Robert Moffat, whose names are also connected with remarkable trees.

Andrew Murray was succeeded by one of his sons, Charles, who lived in the parsonage until 1904. Charles Murray was greatly interested in gardening and he planted a variety of plants from all over the world in the parsonage garden. In 1870 he planted a vine of the 'Black Acorn' variety, which was destined to become one of the biggest vines in the world. At one stage it had shoots over a distance of 120 m and the stem diameter measured 76 cm. A cutting of this vine was included in the grapevine pergola at the Infruitec Garden. When a new parsonage was built in 1904, the old one with its mammoth vine was converted into a girls' hostel which Ellen Murray, sister of Charles, named Reinet House after Reinet de Graaff. (Through the interest of the Rupert family Reinet House has been turned into a museum.)

Planted in 1870, this vine of the 'Black Acorn' variety is one of the biggest vines in the world (Photo: Wikimedia Commons)

Queens Park, East London (Buffalo City)

This tranquil 35 ha park that includes an indigenous forest was established in 1883 and is now a declared national monument.

Magennis Park, Uitenhage

Author Nancy Gardiner describes this park, which was established in the 19th century, as pleasantly mature and well shaded. Like most of the public gardens in South Africa, this garden played an important part in the social life of the town's inhabitants.

Free State

Historical trees in front of the old Government Buildings in President Brand Street, Bloemfontein (Mangaung)

These trees, declared a national monument in 1972, serve as monuments to those people who planted them. They represent an important chain of events in the erstwhile Orange Free State. The first two trees were planted in 1879 by President JH Brand to commemorate the first 25 years of the existence of the Republic of the Orange Free State. These trees were replaced in 1932 because the original ones died.

In 1890 the first steam train was welcomed in Bloemfontein. A garden party was held at the Government Buildings and on this occasion representatives of the four South African states each planted a tree in the garden. They were President FW Reitz of the Orange Free State, Sir Henry Lock, Governor of the Cape Colony, Sir Charles Mitchell, Governor of Natal and Dr WJ Leyds, representing President Paul Kruger of the Zuid-Afrikaansche Republiek.

In 1903 Mrs M Chamberlain, the wife of Joseph Chamberlain, British Secretary of Colonies, planted two hawthorn shrubs to commemorate their visit to Bloemfontein. These trees were replaced by two others in 1930. In 1905 Lord Alfred Milner, British High Commissioner and Governor of the Transvaal and Orange River Colonies, planted a tree in the garden.

Other dignitaries who planted trees in this remarkable garden on different occasions were Lord Selborne, British High Commissioner; Sir Hamilton J Goold-Adams, Governor of the Orange River Colony; the Duke and Duchess of Connaught and Princess Patricia; the Duke of Braganza, Crown Prince of Portugal, and Sir Matthew Nathan, Governor of Natal.

In 1979, one hundred years after the planting of the first two trees, the Honourable AC van Wyk, then Administrator of the Orange Free State, planted a wild olive in the garden – the tree emblem of the Free State Province.

The trees planted over the years were replaced when they died. Each tree was clearly marked with a name plate. The main species, with the exception of the wild olive, were deodar cedars and cypresses. Almost all died recently, however, apparently due to lack of watering during renovation work on the buildings.

The Free State National Botanical Garden, Bloemfontein

This garden was established in 1967 and declared a national monument in 1982. It is of particular scientific and environmental importance because it contains the only remaining Karoo vegetation in the region.

Senekal Church Square with Dutch Reformed Church garden

The cornerstone of this church, built from local rough-hewn stone, was laid in 1895. The site is enclosed by low rough-plastered walls to enable passers-by to enjoy the sight of the well-kept gardens. The walls are ornamented with fossilised trees, some of which measure 20 m. Today Senekal is situated in a grassland veld type with a few small trees – a far cry from the landscape some 250 million years ago.

Another interesting feature of this national monument site is that the trees and other plants in the surrounding garden carry the message of the Bible. The trees and other plants are marked by small plaques bearing the botanical name, a note indicating their use and where they are referred to in the Bible.

The historic trees in front of the old Government Buildings, President Brand Street, Bloemfontein - now dead, apparently because of negligence during nearby building renovations

KwaZulu-Natal

The Beachwood mangrove swamp

This mangrove swamp at the Mgeni River estuary in the Beachwood Mangrove Nature Reserve was declared a national monument in 1980 because of its scientific, educational and historical value.

The mangrove environment is extremely fragile and liable to destruction by development. The Beachwood mangroves, which are of the species *Avicennia marina* (white mangrove), were damaged when a bridge was built across the main channel of the estuary. This not only killed the trees, but also resulted in the disappearance of all associated animals. The bridge was later removed and rehabilitation commenced.

The term 'mangrove' refers to plants, not necessarily related, that grow in the mud and silt of tidal estuaries and lagoons. Nine genera from seven different families constitute South Africa's mangrove forests. They are: *Xylocarpus* (family Meliaceae), *Heritiera* (Sterculiaceae), *Sonnertia* (Sonneratiaceae), *Barringtonia* (Lecythidaceae), *Bruguiera*, *Ceriops* and *Rhizophora* (Rhizophoraceae), *Lumnitzera* (Combretaceae) and *Avicenna* (Verbenaceae).

Canoeing along a dense mangrove forest with the stilt roots clearly showing

In South Africa, mangroves occur sporadically in small areas along the KwaZulu-Natal coast and the northern parts of the Eastern Cape coast. Many of these forests are deteriorating as a result of silting caused by economic development and environmentally unfriendly land-use practices. For instance, the Bay Head Natural Heritage Site in Durban, containing three mangrove species, now covers a mere 10 ha. This mangrove forest previously stretched over an area of 100 ha.

Denizens of the intertidal zone

A mangrove swamp consists of trees and shrubs growing between the high springtide level and mean sea level. These plants require tropical conditions and grow only on sheltered shores and in river estuaries where salt water penetrates. Because of the low oxygen content of the salt water, strangely shaped roots are produced, namely elbow-shaped or pencil- and snake-like. Members of the genus *Rhizophora* have stilt roots and at high tide the plants seem to be floating while at low tide they perch on the spreading stilt roots.

Plants growing in mangrove swamps have to cope with salinities that would kill most others. Many of these plants therefore have salt-excluding mechanisms in the roots while others have glands that excrete a concentrated salty solution on the lower surface of the leaves. Some of the fruits are also specially adapted to this swamp environment. In certain species the seed germinates while still on the tree. The hypocotyl region of the embryo develops in an extraordinary way to form a dart-shaped seedling up to 40 cm long. When this seedling drops, it penetrates the mud like a dart and the roots develop within a few hours. Parent trees of these species are usually surrounded by a ring of young trees. Some species have seeds with resistant seed coats that allow them to remain viable after floating for long periods in sea water.

Mangrove trees have thick, leathery leaves which prevent excessive water loss. This is necessary because, when the mud starts to dry, the salt concentration becomes so high that the plants cannot take in more water and may even start drying out. Mangrove trees are therefore actually xerophytes (plants able to grow in dry conditions) growing in swamps.

Besides being interesting from a botanical viewpoint, a mangrove forest is also most interesting because of its microflora and animal life. The latter include oysters, periwinkles, whelks, barnacles and crabs.

The KwaZulu-Natal National Botanical Garden, Pietermaritzburg

The KwaZulu-Natal National Botanical Garden, established in 1870, was declared a national monument in 1984. It consists of an indigenous and an exotic section. The most renowned feature of this garden is the magnificent London plane avenue (*Platanus acerifolia*) of approximately 300 m, planted in 1908 by Mr WE Marriot, then curator of the botanical garden. The avenue was planted at a suggestion of the last Governor of Natal. In 2008 a regiment marched down the lane, led by Scottish pipers, as part of its centenary celebrations.

The indigenous garden area, started in 1970, contains KwaZulu-Natal vegetation. A stand of huge rose gum trees towers above the gardens in an area now known as Gum Tree Corner. The garden also boasts a large collection of cycads, including some rare and endangered species.

Durban Botanical Garden

The Durban Botanical Garden displays a large collection of exotic trees. The garden was originally developed in 1848 for the introduction of subtropical agricultural crops. After the original site proved unsuitable, it was moved to the present site. The first agricultural show was held here in 1851 and various subtropical products were exhibited on rough tables of yellowwood. Several curators were in charge of the garden; John Medley Wood having been the best known. During his term of office the agricultural aspect of the garden fell away and he concentrated on the botanical aspect. He collected Natal plants extensively, and 62 different species are named after him. His most dramatic discovery was that of *Encephalartos woodii*, of which only one male plant with several stems was found. A number of these stems were brought to the Botanical Garden by ox-wagon, and two fine specimens can still be viewed there today. They are extinct in nature, with only male plants available – indeed one of the rarest plants in the world. (Propagation is possible through vegetative material.)

Besides a collection of 240 different species of palms, the garden boasts an extensive orchid collection, a pond full of lotus plants and a garden for the blind where plants are labelled in Braille. A giant jacaranda was planted in 1885; at one stage this was thought to be the first introduction of this species to South Africa. A large number of rare trees occur: an Indian banyan fig on stilt-like, 'sculptured' aerial roots; a huge jackfruit (*Artocarpus heterophyllus*), also from India, with large coarse-skinned fruit borne on stout branches and on the stem; a cannonball tree (*Couroupita guianensis*) with big round fruit and beautiful waxy flowers hanging from string-like branches attached to the trunk; false flamboyant (*Colvillea racemosa*) from Madagascar, with magnificent orange trusses of flowers and, even more beautiful in flower, a *Triplaris americana* from Central America. Besides trees, many other beautiful plants grow in this garden, like bromeliads and a *Mucuna novo-guineensis* vine with its dazzling racemes of orange-red flowers.

OPPOSITE PAGE: The magnificent London plane tree avenue, KwaZulu-Natal National Botanical Garden, Pietermaritzburg
TOP RIGHT: Wood's cycad in Durban Botanical Garden: extinct in the wild, this is one of the rarest plants in the world (Photo: M. Purves: Wikimedia Commons)
BOTTOM RIGHT: Walking on stilts – a banyan fig 'marching on' in the Durban Botanical Garden

Mitchell and Jameson Parks, Durban (Ethekwini)

These two parks lie adjacent to each other at the higher end of Musgrave Street.

Mitchell Park is named after Sir Charles Bullen Hugh Mitchell, a former Colonial Secretary and Governor of Natal. The park was once an ostrich farm that proved to be unprofitable. In 1902 the bush was cleared, leaving the best specimens of indigenous trees to form the framework of the park. Several animals were introduced, of which Nellie, the Indian elephant, was the most valuable, being a gift of the Maharajah of Mysore in 1928. This gentle giant gave rides and amused the public for 21 years before retiring to Tarango Zoo in Sydney, Australia. In the 1940s the main flower walk was established, and with time Mitchell Park became renowned for its year-round display of flowers and its animals rather than its trees. However, a giant forest mahogany (*Trichilia dregeana*) can be seen very near to the Park. Some of the branches of this tree have become so heavy that they touch the ground and a number of them have been removed to prevent vagrants from living in its shelter.

Jameson Park was once a pineapple plantation owned by Robert Jameson. He started to farm there in 1856 and his preserve of pineapple jams became famous in South Africa and overseas. Jameson served on the Durban City Council and was responsible for the planting of many trees in the city. Jameson Park featured colourful annuals until the early 1950s, when roses were introduced, for which it became renowned.

The Butcher Arboretum, Kloof, Durban

An exceptional collection of indigenous trees was established by the late Mr RR Butcher on his property in Kloof. Since 1932 more than 150 different species of trees and shrubs have been planted. Until the 2000s the owner, Mrs Lissack, was, fortunately, also keen on preserving the arboretum for its scientific and aesthetic value.

Spring Grove Arboretum, Nottingham Road

This arboretum was established a century ago by Colonel Greene, Minister of Railways in the old Natal Government. It displays 70 species of trees, among which are beech, lime, horse chestnut and oak.

Skyline Arboretum, Margate

This arboretum of 14 ha was established around 1963 by Mr HB Nicholson, who retired to Margate after a career as a businessman in Johannesburg. He was a keen lover of trees and an active member of the Tree Society of South Africa. He introduced many indigenous and exotic trees to the Skyline Arboretum and some beautiful specimens can be seen here.

Twin Streams, Mtunzini

The name Ian Garland and conservation are synonymous. At Twin Streams Ian established an arboretum containing more than 80 000 northern KwaZulu-Natal trees, and initiated a conservation project in which he planted indigenous trees along stream banks, to reduce erosion where the original trees were removed due to sugar-farming practices. Parts of these plantings will be affected by the controversial planned Fairbreeze mine that will extract strategic minerals from sand, and which will be compensated for by the establishment of protected areas and the rehabilitation of forests as part of a so-called biodiversity offset. The forestry company Mondi, which purchased the farm from Dr Garland, continued with his project and has greatly increased the biodiversity. Twin Streams is a declared Natural Heritage Site.

Benvie Arboretum, New Hanover

Benvie Arboretum is situated high up in the folds of the Blinkwater Mountain, 50 km north-west of Pietermaritzburg. It enjoys a rainfall of 1 500 mm per annum. The arboretum covers 14 ha, and an excellent record of all the work done is available.

Mr John Geekie, an immigrant from Scotland, was the founder of this interesting arboretum. He established a business in Pietermaritzburg in 1860 and purchased the farm Benvie in 1883, where he retired in 1890.

An interesting feature of this arboretum is the huge Japanese cedar (*Cryptomeria japonica*) trees, some 42 m high with stem diameters of up to 1,06 m. These trees are under-planted by rhododendrons, azaleas and grass trees (*Xanthorrhoea hastilis*) from Western Australia. Other trees are Himalayan spruce (*Picea smithiana*); Spanish fir (*Abies pinsapo*); the mountain ash (*Eucalyptus regnans*), with a height of 70 m; and the rough-barked ribbon gum (*Eucalyptus viminalis* × *huberiana*), with heights of 40 m and diameters exceeding 2 m. A trio of high mountain ash trees survives, all topped back to just over 60 m in height by a severe storm, standing on stout flaring trunks measuring over 2 m in diameter at breast height. These are now protected as Champion Trees.

Apart from these exotic trees, Benvie farm has 256 ha of well-preserved indigenous forest. When Mr Geekie bought the farm, woodcutters were at work and a sawmill was in operation there. He closed all these operations to protect the indigenous forest. Benvie farm is still in Geekie hands, proudly managing the monumental work of their ancestor John.

A cluster of Japanese cedar trees in the Benvie Arboretum, New Hanover

The peerless Australian grass tree, Benvie Arboretum, New Hanover (Photo: Enrico Liebenberg)

Tree garden, Voortrekker Museum, Pietermaritzburg

Twelve trees were planted at the historic church museum site in Pietermaritzburg on the Day of the Covenant, currently the Day of Reconciliation, 16 December 1912, when black and white people assembled together. Among the dignitaries who planted trees was a Matabele woman named Jana, who planted a bushveld mahogany (*Trichilia emetica*) tree. Jana had been left an orphan at the battle of Vegkop and when she was seven years old she was severely wounded in the Bloukrans massacre of 1838. A small girl, Hester Maré, found her among the corpses. She had seven assegai wounds. Jana grew up with the Maré family and got her name from the family name Adriana. When she died in 1924 on the farm Umvotipoort at the age of 93 she was buried in the family churchyard. (Several legends exist about the origin of the popular Afrikaans song *Sarie Marais;* one of them is connected to this Maré family.)

Nine of the trees planted in 1912 had to be removed to allow for expansion of the buildings. Their stumps are preserved in the museum. Other trees planted there were a carob (*Ceratonia siliqua*) planted by Prof GM Pellissier, who was responsible for acquiring and restoring the Voortrekker Church built in 1839, and which was put to other uses from 1861, a maidenhair tree (*Ginkgo biloba*) planted by one JL de Jager, a Voortrekker descendant, and an Australian chestnut (*Castanospermum australe*), planted by another Voortrekker descendant, JG Hattingh.

In mentioning Prof GM Pellissier it is fitting to tell the story of another Pellissier tree. In 1912 the brother of Prof Pellissier, Dr HS Pellissier, attended a summer school in Nääs, Sweden. Every night the students gathered to join in folk dancing. This made a great impression on the young Pellissier and on his return to South Africa he devoted himself to the encouragement and preservation of folk-song and dancing back home. In 1952 Dr Pellissier returned to Nääs with 100 South African folk dancers. He planted a young birch tree (*Betula* species) with inscriptions in Swedish and Afrikaans saying that he was inspired in Nääs to found the Suid-Afrikaanse Volkspelebeweging (South African Folk-dancing Movement).

Hazeldene farm, Himeville

In 1937 Ken and Mona Lund bought a piece of land in Himeville which was reputedly infertile. Contrary to this surmise, Hazeldene has become renowned for its stately avenues and windbreaks and its spectacular display of autumn colours.

In spring the great number of trees burst into a variety of greens, and the cherries and other flowering trees add colour to the landscape. The third generation of the Lund family today still expand on the tree-planting efforts of their forebears.

Baynesfield Estate

Joseph Baynes purchased land near Richmond, where he became known as a progressive farmer contributing to the advancement of agricultural techniques. He built a house for his second wife, Sarah, in 1882, and planted a variety of exotic trees on the grounds of the estate surrounding this manor. These trees include two massive Outeniqua yellowwoods and a magnificent specimen of a tulip tree (*Liriodendron tulipifera*), standing 34 m tall and with a huge trunk of over 6 m in circumference.

Joseph died in 1925, leaving his farm in trust for the benefit of all South Africans. Today the estate hosts a museum, which includes vintage engines and tractors.

Giant tulip tree, Baynesfield

Gauteng

Pretoria National Botanical Garden

This garden was founded in 1946 and today contains one of the most important and comprehensive collections of indigenous flora in the country. It consists of landscaped and natural areas and was declared a national monument in 1979. Special features of this garden are the avenue of tree wistaria (*Bolusanthus speciosus*) along Cussonia Avenue and the striking iron entrance gates, one depicting aloes and the other different grasses.

In addition to an interesting collection of cycads and many other trees and plants to be viewed in this garden, some outstanding examples of the feared *Intovane*, the rainbow leaf or pynbos, are prospering there. Almost all of the 43 different South African species of *Acacia* (now transferred into the genera *Vachellia* and *Senegalia*) grow in this garden.

Apart from interesting plants, the Pretoria National Botanical Garden houses the South African National Biodiversity Institute (SANBI) Head Office and the National Herbarium, the fourth largest in the Southern Hemisphere, with approximately one million specimens, as well as the eighth international Peace Garden. Established in 1997, the form is a stylised combination of a tulip and a dove of peace.

The current botanical garden layout reflects different biomes of the country, including grassland, savannah and natural forest.

Pretoria National Botanical Garden – popular retreat to the nature-lover

The Manie van der Schijff Botanical Garden, University of Pretoria

This interesting botanical garden contains about 3 000 indigenous and exotic plant species within an area of 3,5 ha. Among them are some rare plants, such as a Modjadji cycad of 5 m donated by Queen Modjadji III in 1920, and a *Ficus religiosa*, grown from a cutting by Professor Manie himself. According to the curator, Jason Sampson, this is a true Bohdi. Although there are many of these trees in the world, to be a real Bohdi it has to originate from the Buddha Tree in India. Prof Manie's small cutting has developed over the years into a large tree of champion size.

The primary aim of the garden is to raise awareness of southern Africa's indigenous flora. The garden provides plant material for educational and research purposes, the collection and propagation of rare and endangered species, as well as research into indigenous species with horticultural potential.

Many fascinating plants, each with its unique history, interesting to investigate, are found here. For sheer beauty, too, when in early spring a profusion of the bright red flowers of *Erythrina falcata* burst into a stunning floral display, a visit to this garden is a must.

Springbok and Jan Celliers Parks, Pretoria (Tshwane)

Two Pretoria parks have indigenous plants as a theme, namely Springbok Park in Hatfield and Jan Celliers Park in Groenkloof. The latter park is the more recent one, established in 1962, and features a great variety of native trees, shrubs and other plants. It is also known as Protea Park, because of the many proteas growing there.

Springbok Park had its origin in 1905 when the suburb of Hatfield was developed. A street block then known as Grosvenor Square was reserved as a park. Because only indigenous trees occurred on this piece of land it was renamed Springbok Park. A special feature of the park is the white stinkwood trees (*Celtis africana*) that were planted in 1930 in groups of threes. After a few years they unfortunately overshadowed the sweet thorn trees (*Vachellia karroo*) that had occurred naturally there, causing them to die. Originally, Namaqualand daisies were planted among the trees, providing a profusion of colour in spring. In 1947 and 1948 the trees were thinned and other indigenous trees were added. As the trees grew bigger the sun-loving flowers were replaced by *Agapanthus*, the blue lily. The white stinkwood and other indigenous trees, together with the informal layout, make this park a peaceful place to visit. Springbok Park was declared a national monument in 1979.

White stinkwood trees, Springbok Park, Pretoria – an iconic garden tree

The Austin Roberts Bird Sanctuary

This park in Groenkloof, Pretoria, was declared a national monument in 1980. While it does not feature exceptional trees, but rather an assortment of indigenous and exotic trees, grasses and shrubs, the park is remarkable in that it provides a roosting place and breeding ground for thousands of birds within the boundary of a big city. More than 170 different bird species have been recorded there.

Melrose House, Pretoria

Melrose House and its grounds, in Jeff Masemola (formerly Jacob Maré) Street, were declared a national monument in 1971. This elegant house was erected in 1886 by George Jesse Heys, co-owner of the mail coach service between Pretoria and Kimberley. Heys named the house after Melrose Abbey in Scotland.

During the Anglo-Boer War Melrose House served as the British headquarters, with both Lords Roberts and Kitchener among the dignitaries who resided there. The treaty ending the war, known as the Peace Treaty of Vereeniging, was signed in the dining room of Melrose House on 31 May 1902.

Peace negotiations had taken place at a site near Vereeniging offered to the Boer and British generals by the pioneer mining magnate and millionaire industrialist Sammy Marks. After the negotiations the delegates travelled to Pretoria for the signing of the treaty. For many years afterwards the Brick and Tile Recreation Club at Vereeniging conserved the stump of an oak tree near which the peace negotiations took place.

Melrose House is one of the best examples of a late Victorian mansion in South Africa and it is one of Pretoria's most charming attractions. Little is known about the garden, where a few trees attract attention, among which is a magnificent Moreton Bay fig (*Ficus macrophylla*), planted in the corner of the property.

Burgers Park, Pretoria

Burgers Park, in Jeff Masemola (formerly Jacob Maré) Street, was declared a national monument in 1979. An important Victorian unit is formed by the park, with its formal layout, wrought-iron bandstand, kiosk and interesting caretaker's cottage, together with Melrose House opposite the street. In 1874 President TF Burgers submitted a motion to reserve a complete street block in Pretoria to establish a botanical garden. The garden was to be divided into four parts, representing the Northern and Southern Hemispheres, the Americas and the East. This plan did not realise due to a lack of funds. Nearly 15 years later an 'equestrian and pedestrian' (a 'rij en wandel') park was laid out. The contractor was George Heys, owner of Melrose House.

Special attractions of Burgers Park are the Moreton Bay fig (*Ficus macrophylla*) trees planted in 1913. The largest of these

Canary palms, Burgers Park, Pretoria

trees has, however, died. The beautiful Canary palms (*Phoenix canariensis*), were planted in 1910.

Another tree of interest in this park is an orange tree, the emblem of the Netherlands, planted in honour of Queen Wilhelmina when she ascended the Dutch throne in 1898. In 1923 the Pretoria Municipality presented her with a crate of oranges from this tree on the occasion of her silver jubilee. This tree has been replanted several times through the years. On one such occasion it had to be moved to an open spot because it suffered in the shade of the surrounding trees. Simultaneous to the planting of the orange tree in Burgers Park, another two orange trees were also planted in South Africa, one at the Springs Station, East Rand, which also had to be replanted several times. The second one, planted at the Johannesburg Zoo, apparently does not exist any more.

In 1906 an English oak (*Quercus robur*) was planted in Burgers Park as a symbol of the British Empire. In 1932 a white stinkwood (*Celtis africana*) was planted on the anniversary of the birth of George Washington two centuries before. Another white stinkwood was planted by the Chairman of the International Rotary Organisation as a token of friendship.

Several receptions took place in the early days in Burgers Park. In 1911 General Louis Botha was welcomed back here from England where he had attended the crowning of King George V. In 1954 a statue of President Burgers made by Moses Kottler was erected in Burgers Park. (The Rev TF Burgers served as President of the Zuid-Afrikaansche Republiek from 1872–1877.)

Pretoria National Zoological Garden of South Africa

In addition to animals from all over the world, the Pretoria Zoo boasts a number of magnificent trees, such as palms, Moreton Bay fig trees and a wide-spreading tipu (*Tipuana tipu*), originally from South America. The giant Moreton Bay fig tree near the entrance has been declared a Champion Tree.

A giant gum tree – one of the veritable tree monuments to the farsightedness of tree-lovers, planted by Forester Fuchs on behalf of industrialist Alois Nellmapius on Irene Estate in the late 1800s, enhanced by the efforts of Bertie van der Byl, later owner of the estate, in the early 1900s and today by Adrian van der Byl who already planted 3 000 trees

Irene Estate

Magnificent specimens of white stinkwood, eucalypts, English oak, casuarina and other species are found on Irene Estate, now part of the Centurion suburb Irene south of Pretoria. This property, part of the farm Doornkloof, was bought in 1889 by Alois Hugo Nellmapius, a Hungarian engineer who, after his arrival in South Africa in the early 1870s, became a prosperous industrialist. He named it after his daughter Irene.

Nellmapius employed a German forester named Fuchs to do the layout of his estate and in particular to plant trees, many of which have now reached impressive dimensions. After Nellmapius's death the property was bought by two other industrialists, Eckstein and Marks, both known for their tree-planting efforts elsewhere. As general manager they appointed Johannes Albertus van der Byl, who eventually bought the estate and continued to enhance it by further establishing trees. The fourth generation of the Van der Byl family is still caring for this tree heritage.

In 1908 General Jan Christiaan Smuts, who was later to become Prime Minister of the Union of South Africa, also bought a part of Doornkloof, which he preserved in its natural state. Smuts House, well known on account of the General's international stature, is a declared national monument.

Johannesburg – a man-made forest?

The early pioneers who settled on the treeless Highveld experienced a fuel and timber shortage, which compelled them to start planting trees. Many of these immigrants from tree-rich Northern Hemisphere countries were instrumental in transforming a bleak, inhospitable area into one of parks, streets and tree-filled gardens.

It is reported that Johannesburg held its first Arbor Day on 1 February 1890, when trees were planted in a new park near Doornfontein Club. In June 1893 it was estimated that some 25 to 30 million trees had been planted on the Rand. Tree-planting syndicates and companies flourished in the 1890s. The biggest afforestation scheme was that of Hermann Eckstein & Co, who bought the farm Braamfontein, employed the German forester Genth, and planted 300 ha to pine and mainly eucalypt trees. This area was named *Sachsenwald* – today's Saxonwold. What is today known as Zoo Lake (Park), officially the Hermann Eckstein Park, was established in 1904 and handed over to the Town Council by Eckstein on the condition that it be a 'park for all people, for all time'.

At a stage almost all of Johannesburg could be described as a virtual forest. Millions of trees lined the streets and graced the yards of homes in what was reputedly one of the largest man-grown urban woodlands in the world. 'Greater Johannesburg' boasted 1 750 different park areas (open spaces), of which The Wilds, Melville Koppies, Joubert Park, the Hermann Eckstein Park, Rhodes Park in Kensington, Bezuidenhout Valley Park, Pioneer Park and Delta Park were some of the oldest and most important. By 2001 the Johannesburg City Parks was taking care of 22 278 ha of open spaces and green areas, including 1,6 million street trees and 6 603,3 ha of developed parks. More open space has been added since, some forming part of the rivers and ridges network. Three parks are described below.

Panoramic view of an urban forest from the Melville Koppies, Johannesburg (Photo: Ozma Mcithwa)

The Wilds, Houghton Estate

The Johannesburg Consolidated Investment Company, Ltd (JCI) was founded in 1889 by Barney Barnato, and it is therefore almost as old as Johannesburg itself. In 1924 JCI donated 17,5 ha in Houghton Estate to the Johannesburg Municipality because of their long association. One of the conditions of the donation was that the land should be kept in its natural state as an open space for the recreation of the public. It was decided to call the park 'The Wilds'. In 1938 JCI donated another 1,2 ha to the City Council for extension of the park.

Development of the park commenced in 1937 and it has been intensively planted to showcase indigenous species. The Wilds is not only aesthetically pleasing but is of scientific and educational importance. The park was declared a national monument in 1981.

Melville Koppies Nature Reserve

Melville Koppies, covering an area of approximately 70 ha, was declared a nature reserve in 1959 and a national monument in 1968. It is not a reserve with extraordinary trees but here one may observe about a hundred tree and shrub species and many smaller plant species, as well as vegetation and geological formations that have existed in the area for thousands of years. Melville Koppies provides a valuable introduction to the study of ecology, botany, zoology and geology. This reserve also has a display of an iron furnace used by late Iron Age people in the area. The remains of stone walls can be seen, built by these inhabitants, who were displaced by the Difaquane wars that originated far away in the Zulu kingdom of King Shaka in the mid-19th century, and which swept through the central and northern parts of the country.

Joubert Park

Although overshadowed by other city parks in terms of the number and variety of trees, Joubert Park used to be the park most frequently visited in Johannesburg. The oldest of Johannesburg's parks, it was laid out in 1892, being graced by the adjoining Johannesburg/Joubert Park Art Museum, now the Johannesburg Art Gallery. Various exotic tree species were planted in the park.

Walter Sisulu National Botanical Garden, Roodepoort

Situated against the backdrop of the Roodekrantz ridge and the Witpoortjie waterfall, this garden covers almost 300 ha of both landscaped and natural veld. It contains only indigenous plants. Not only does it border on the Witwatersrand ridge, but the Crocodile River runs through the garden, providing a unique water-and-tree feature. Founded in 1982, the botanical garden's waterfall site has been a popular venue for picnic outings since the late 1800's. Almost 90% of the garden is made up of the Gold

The Walter Sisulu National Botanical Garden situated against the backdrop of the Roodekrantz ridge, Roodepoort

Reef Mountain Bushveld type. More than 600 plant species occur here, including over 60 tree species, and some 220 bird species. A pair of breeding black eagles add to the attraction of the dramatic scenery of the waterfall and krantzes, which are the focal point of the garden.

Brenthurst Garden

Brenthurst garden, with its high forest atmosphere, is regarded as Johannesburg's most splendid garden and it can be placed among the great gardens of the world. It covers an area of almost 20 ha and is part of the Brenthurst Estate, owned by the well-known Oppenheimer family since 1922. The eco-friendly garden is the responsibility of Strilli, wife of Mr Nicky Oppenheimer, who adopted a philosophy of natural gardening. No artificial fertilisers or pesticides are used, and the garden is teeming with wildlife. It consists of a pelargonium garden, children's terrace, grass garden, Japanese garden and a vegetable garden.

Many of the plants in the garden are indigenous, but introductions from Europe, Australia, New Zealand, South America and Japan add to its beauty and interest.

Besides the remarkable collection of indigenous and exotic trees and other plants, the garden is enhanced by a striking collection of sculptures, some of them carved out of wood of fallen trees. Two giant sculptures called 'Man and Woman' by the South African sculptor Louis Le Sueur are the tallest, with the standing figure of the male more than 6 m.

The history of the garden dates back to 1890, when eucalypt trees were planted to meet the demand for mining timber and building material for a booming Johannesburg. The plantation was part of the original Forest Town and Sachsenwald, now Saxonwold. (See insert: *Johannesburg – a man-made forest?* on page 95.) Brenthurst Garden nowadays provides a livelihood to 25 dedicated gardeners.

'Man and Woman', two giant sculptures by South African artist Louis Le Sueur, overlook the verdant growth of the Brenthurst garden

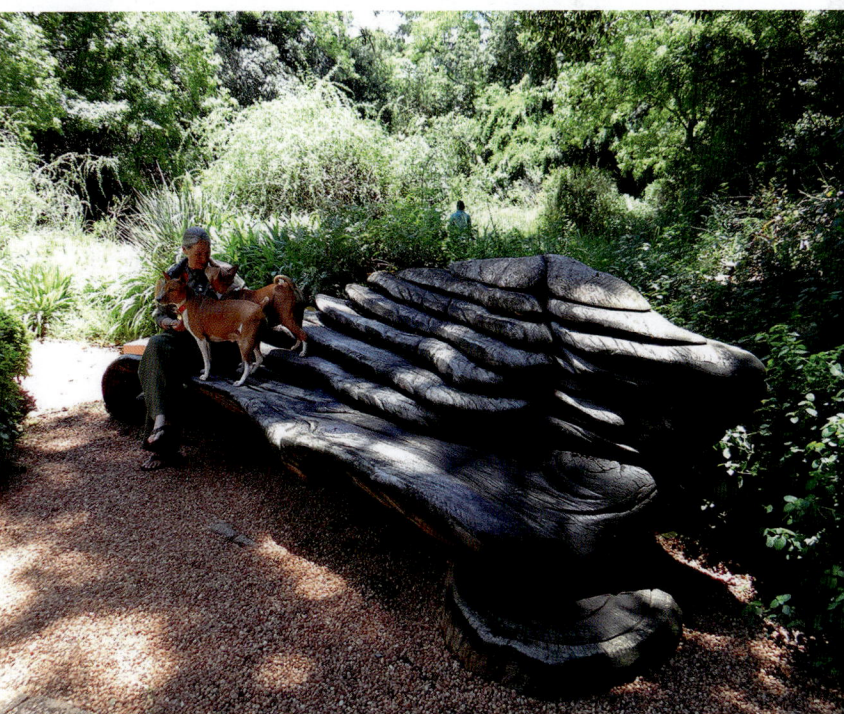

Strilli Oppenheimer and her African breed dogs relaxing on a wooden bench by Geoffrey Armstrong. True to her philosophy of natural gardening, she often uses fallen trees in one way or another as a point of interest to enhance the beauty of Brenthurst garden

Mpumalanga

The Lowveld National Botanical Garden, Nelspruit (Mbombela)

Kosi palm trees arch over a pathway in the Lowveld Botanical Gardens in Nelspruit

This garden originated in 1969 with grants of land from the town council of Nelspruit as well as the large farming enterprise HL Hall and Sons. It covers an area of 165 ha and includes the Nels River waterfall at the confluence with the Crocodile River.

Striking features of this garden are the collection of cycads (91 in total), a tropical African rainforest and a typical South African forest. A cycad gene bank has also been established at the garden, crucial to the conservation of the species. Besides the African baobab, all the species of baobab from Madagascar have been planted in this garden.

Nelspruit, declared Arbor City in 1992, is one of the places where existing indigenous trees have been incorporated successfully in the layout of the city.

Limpopo

City Square Park, Polokwane (Pietersburg)

City Square Park, which was developed for the town's centenary celebrations in 1986, is the most important park in Polokwane. It is an interestingly landscaped park with indigenous and some exotic trees. A number of sculptures can be seen there, including one of a donkey, to acknowledge the role played by this humble animal in the development of the Limpopo Province.

Tzaneen and Modjadjiskloof (Duiwelskloof)

These two Lowveld towns are blessed with excellent soil and good rainfall and are known for their forest-like residential areas, where people live in the shade of huge indigenous and exotic trees. Large forest fever trees (*Anthocleista grandiflora*), known for their huge leaves, grow in abundance in and around these towns. The **Louis Botha Park** in Modjadjiskloof, named after a local medical doctor, was established in 1990. As it is situated in an area with many indigenous trees, it already boasts big trees.

JDM Keet Arboretum, Westfalia Estate, Modjadjiskloof

One of the last projects initiated by Dr Hans Merensky, eminent geologist and nature conservationist, was the establishment of the JDM Keet Arboretum at Westfalia in 1952. Dr Keet, Secretary of Forestry from 1934 to 1942, was appointed to oversee the forestry interests of the Merensky Foundation after his retirement. The arboretum, containing mainly indigenous trees, is well maintained and serves as a source of interest and information both to school groups and other visitors.

The imposing Merensky lane on Westfalia Estate, formed by Saligna gum trees planted in the 1930s

Cheerio farm, Haenertsburg

Situated in the cool, misty heights of the northern Drakensberg, this farm is known not so much for its large trees, but for its spectacularly colourful ones – flowering cherry blossom trees (*Prunus* species), which, in early spring every year, transform the farm into a fairyland experience. This spectacle of colour from different cultivars of cherry blossoms in flower is enhanced by various crab-apple species and masses of azalea and rhododendron, with stately 'prehistoric' tree ferns watching over this 'English country garden'.

Eleven species of flowering cherries were propagated by the first owner of the farm, Ms Sheila Thompson, from a number of cuttings from trees grown by a Lady Bourne at Elgin, Western Cape.

Palm and tree parks, Louis Trichardt (Makhado)

These two parks alongside the main road to the north are relatively young, having been established in the early 1980s. A combination of good soil and a relatively high rainfall is conducive to tree growth and the parks should eventually develop into scenic areas with big trees. For more than three decades indigenous trees were planted at the main tree park in Louis Trichardt. In about 2003 the future of the park was threatened by plans for a shopping mall on that land, but public resistance and negotiation with the local authority saved the park, and the mall had to move to a new location.

A spectacle of colour created by mass plantings of azalea and rhododendron at Cheerio farm near Haenertsburg in Limpopo Province

North West

Lost City Botanical Garden

This remarkable garden surrounding the Palace Hotel at the Sun City complex in the Pilanesberg was established in 1990. Specimens from 3 400 different plant species were planted, 80% of which indigenous to South Africa and 20% exotic.

Full-grown large wild fig, baobab, palm and jacaranda trees were transplanted to create an instant tree garden (forest) of great beauty and interest. (The largest of the baobabs weighed 45 tons.) The garden was classified as a botanical garden in 2000 by the Botanical Society of South Africa.

Camel thorn trees – a common sight in certain areas of the northern provinces

The Botanical Garden at the Lost City in the Pilanesberg, where exotic plants mingle happily with indigenous species of the African bush

Northern Cape

The Hantam National Botanical Garden

The Hantam National Botanical Garden near Nieuwoudtville has been kept in its natural state, being the ideal site to represent the Succulent Karoo Biome. Trees are largely absent, with the rocky outcrops mainly covered with shrubs. This latest addition to SANBI's botanical gardens is described as 'a fascinating treasure trove of biodiversity'.

Kimberley parks

The city of Kimberley boasts two well-kept and tree-rich parks: **Queens Park**, established in 1876, and the **Ernest Oppenheimer Garden**, established in 1962. Besides trees, the latter park features the Diggers fountain – five men holding a digger's sieve over a fountain.

Jan Kempdorp poplar avenue

When the Vaalharts irrigation scheme was laid out in the 1930s, each plot was demarcated by lanes of Fremont cottonwood (*Populus fremontii*) trees. A row of these trees was also planted along the main road from Jan Kempdorp to Vaalharts, a distance of approximately 30 km. The trees around the plots had to be removed when they matured. The avenue along the road, however, remained, providing an aesthetically uplifting experience to the traveller. Some of the trees have unfortunately died off due to the bark being removed for firewood purposes. At the time of writing the trees were under threat from plans to remove them for a security fence.

Arbor Cities and Towns

A project of the Forestry Branch of the erstwhile Department of Environment Affairs which had far-reaching results as far as general tree planting is concerned was the Arbor City/Town Award, instituted in 1984 and concluded in 1994.

The Institute of Parks and Recreation named a city or town each year that qualified for the award, in accordance with the broadly applied criteria of promotion of vegetation, tree richness of streets and parks, and environmental conservation.

It was a one-time award that could be retracted. Only one award was made per year, with the erstwhile four provinces rotating. The award was made by the Minister and consisted of a signboard with a specially designed emblem and appropriate wording. The emblem could

The emblem of the Arbor City/Town Award, an initiative that ran between 1984 and 1994

be duplicated by the recipient town at will. Signboards were erected at the main entrances and in many cases the emblem was used on official letters, either in the letterheads or as a shadow print on the paper.

The cities and towns that received the Arbor award were Pretoria, 1984; Cape Town, 1985; Durban, 1986; Bloemfontein, 1987; Roodepoort, 1988; Port Elizabeth, 1989; Eshowe, 1990; Sasolburg, 1991; Nelspruit, 1992; Somerset West, 1993, and Grahamstown, 1994.

In all the abovementioned cities and towns trees abounded. The climate in some cases is conducive to tree planting, while early sketches and photographs of others such as Bloemfontein, Roodepoort and Sasolburg, show hardly any trees, because factors such as altitude and severe winter frosts make it difficult for trees to survive. The dedication of many far-seeing tree lovers and horticulturists is acknowledged by these awards.

The Project was revived in 2002 and is currently managed by the Department of Agriculture, Forestry and Fisheries in partnership with Total and the Institute of Environment and Recreation Management. Recent recipients of the award are: Stellenbosch Metropolitan Municipality (Western Cape) and eThekwini Local Municipality (KwaZulu-Natal) in 2014; and Johannesburg Metropolitan Municipality (Gauteng) and Hessequa Local Municipality (Western Cape) in 2015. The 2016 recipients were the Cape Town Metropolitan Municipality (Western Cape) and the Alfred Duma Local Municipality and the Endumeni Local Municipality, both KwaZulu-Natal.

The Union Gardens in Pretoria, which was crowned Arbor City in 1984

Tree and Forest Conservation in South Africa

South Africa is noted for her remarkable tree heritage, not only because of her status as a mega-diverse country that includes a large variety of indigenous woody species, but also for the richness of her trees of outstanding size or historic significance. The diversity of more than 1 300 indigenous tree and shrub species is enhanced by more than a thousand introduced tree and shrub species, many of which are closely associated with the history and sense of place of towns, cities and rural landscapes. Stellenbosch is noted for its leafy lanes of English oak trees (*Quercus robur*), Pretoria for its jacaranda trees (*Jacaranda mimosifolia*) covered in purple during late spring, and the eastern Free State for its yellowing Lombardy poplars (*Populus nigra*) in autumn. Indigenous trees also give a sense of place, such as the camel thorn (*Vachellia erioloba*) of the Kalahari region and the stately baobabs (*Adansonia digitata*) of the northern Bushveld.

Yet trees are emotional subjects wherever they stand. Alien invasive species are eradicated countrywide through the internationally acclaimed Working for Water programme, sometimes evoking the ire of members of the public who have become attached to trees in their environment, irrespective of whether they are invasive or not. Trees are the subject of legal battles and countless feuds between neighbours. Unlike tree protection orders that safeguard trees in many European countries, exotic or indigenous trees on private property are not protected in South Africa, except for listed indigenous tree species and a handful of individual trees and groups of trees proclaimed as protected, with some legal provisions relating to natural forests. Trees older than 60 years can also be considered protected by the National Heritage Resources Act of 1999, but only if proven to be of significant cultural value (including historical value).

A Wonderboom fig near Mbombela, saved from destruction for road building by placard-wielding activists, stands victorious next to the very road that threatened its existence

Protecting our tree heritage

Trees play a vital role in the ecology of many veld types, providing food, shade and shelter to a host of animal species, binding the soil and moderating temperature. We all depend on their products in our daily lives, from paper to furniture and medicines based on root, leave or bark extracts. Several million rural households still depend on trees for firewood, for construction materials and traditional medicinal products. Human pressures such as bark harvesting threaten tree populations in some areas, driving some species such as the pepperbark tree (*Warburgia salutaris*) closer to extinction in the wild. Studies indicate that on average rural households in the erstwhile homeland areas use over five tons of wild plant matter per year per household, of which over four tons comprise firewood.

Vast progress has been made in the conservation of natural forests and other woody biomes during the past century. Millions of hectares have been added to protected areas in that time. Modern technology such as satellite images, Lidar radar scans from aircraft that map vegetation structure, and computer programs that process data to determine the biodiversity values of vegetation types are but a few of the many powerful tools used to aid conservation planning and the monitoring of the environment. A plethora of environmental legislation now regulates environmental management. Land use and development control has tightened with the introduction of environmental impact assessments, lists of proclaimed protected tree species have been compiled, and all natural forests are now protected under the National Forests Act of 1998. More than a hundred individual trees and groups of trees of national importance have been proclaimed either to be National Monuments (now National Heritage Resources) or Champion Trees. South Africa's international obligations in this respect have also increased with the signing and ratification of various conventions such as the Convention on Biological Diversity.

A tree planting ceremony at the Pretoria Botanical Gardens captured on television during Arbor Week. Such events greatly promote the public awareness of the country's tree heritage

Despite this progress, the country's tree heritage and wider environment have come under increasing pressure. The population has increased tenfold to just over 50 million people during the past century, demanding ever more living space and resources and creating ever increasing volumes of waste and pollutants. Urban areas, mines, agriculture and infrastructure have swallowed and fragmented vast areas of natural habitat. Increasing the land area under protected areas has become all the more important, also for the woody biomes, seeing that lists of protected tree species are not sufficient to safeguard our tree heritage and their habitat settings.

Millions of rural households still depend on firewood to provide in their domestic energy need

Elephants destroying fever trees in the Mapungubwe National Park (Photo: Beate Holscher)

The woody biomes

Three woody biomes (broad vegetation types dominated by trees) are prevalent in South Africa, namely the Savannah or Bushveld biome, which covers about 40 million ha of the land surface, the Albany Thicket biome (also known as Subtropical Thicket), which covers about 3 million ha, and the small and fragmented Natural Forest biome, which covers less than half a million ha. These biomes are varied. Some 87 savannah woodland types, 13 thicket types and 26 natural forest types have been identified, each with a unique combination of plant and animal life and unique vegetation structures. This variation is the product of many factors such as climate, topography, geology and soils. It is also an indication of the huge plant and animal diversity in this landscape mosaic – a diversity topped only by two other mega-diverse countries in the world – for the country holds about 10% of the world's plant and animal species on just 1% of its land surface. The aim of the government's National Protected Area Expansion Strategy is to ensure that all vegetation types are properly represented in protected areas, which is a cornerstone of the aim to protect as much of our biodiversity as possible.

The savannah boasts about 5 700 plant species, second only to the Fynbos biome. A larger variety of species of mammals (167), birds (532) and reptiles (161) is found here than in any other biome in the country. The decline in flagship species such as wild dogs (*Lycaon pictus*), ground hornbill (*Bucorvis leadbeateri*) and Cape vulture (*Gyps coprotheres*) is an indication that parts of the savannah are under pressure, especially due to land use change. It is estimated that more than 50 000 ha of savannah disappear under mines, agricultural lands, urban areas and infrastructure annually. Part of the national conservation strategy is to get as much of each woodland type in formal protected areas as possible. By 2008 about 9% of the biome was under formal protection, close to the biodiversity conservation target of 10% that was set in the National Protected Area Expansion Strategy. Yet many of the savannah vegetation types are under-represented in protected areas. This target had to be adapted upwards after a new minimum global protected area target of 17% of all veld types was set at a Conference of the Parties in 2011 by countries who signed and ratified the Convention on Biological Diversity. Yet informal protected areas and game farms also contribute to conservation of the Bushveld, and cover more land area than the formally protected areas, even though their contribution is not accounted for in the national and international targets.

Scientific monitoring and studies over several decades indicate that bush encroachment affects almost a third of the savannah in southern Africa, and that savannah is extending at the expense of grasslands. Higher levels of carbon dioxide, mostly due to increased pollution, are often cited as a contributing factor to woodland densification, as increased carbon favours the growth of woody species. A number of local indigenous tree species, such as black thorn (*Senegalia mellifera*), have been declared bush encroachers. Although encroachment reduces the carrying capacity of the veld, eradication through poisoning or mechanical means proves to be an expensive undertaking and requires long-term intervention.

Savannah is a dynamic ecosystem adapted to fire as well as grazing or browsing by wildlife or cattle. Over-grazing, however, leads to changes such as bush encroachment, while concentrated numbers of mega-fauna like elephants (*Loxodonta africana*) in a few protected areas like the Kruger National Park may cause so much damage to trees that the tree cover of some savannah landscapes become visibly reduced. A study of tree damage and mortality in the Greefswald Forest in the Mapungubwe National Park indicates that the bark of several tree species is favoured by elephants, especially marula trees (*Sclerocarya birrea* subsp. *caffra*). Almost half of these trees sustained damage, with more than 12% of these being completely ringbarked. Research has furthermore shown that the frequency and intensity of fires also play a significant role in the survival of trees, especially seedlings, and that elephant damage to mature trees make them more susceptible to fires. Models developed on the basis of such research assist with the understanding or prediction of tree demography (e.g. the mix of tree species occurring in an area, the percentages of seedlings, sub-adult and mature trees occurring, and mortality rates of trees). Such research and modelling are necessary for proper management, which needs to be adaptive to environmental change.

Samango monkey – a rare tree-living inhabitant of natural forests, now listed as a red data species

The Albany Thicket biome is a closed canopy shrubland-like vegetation with much succulent and thorny vegetation that occurs in the Eastern Cape, up to 300 km inland from the coast. More than 1 550 plant species occur in this vegetation, of which almost 67% are endemic. Some scientists consider thicket to be a xerophytic form of forest because thickets actually have more affinities to forest than to savannah woodlands. An estimated 42% of the thicket area is moderately to severely degraded, mostly due to overgrazing by goats and cattle. By 2008 about 7% of the thicket biome fell in formal protected areas, and this protection has recently been boosted by the expansion of the Addo Elephant National Park. As in the savannah, many farmers within the thicket biome have converted to game farms and private reserves, adding significantly to protection outside formal reserves.

Albany thicket is particularly susceptible to degradation. A substantial percentage of the thicket types have the porkbush or spekboom (*Portulacaria afra*) as canopy dominant or major component of the plant biomass. The Subtropical Thicket Rehabilitation Programme was launched in 2004 to restore degraded thicket areas and to use porkbush and other thicket species to sequester carbon (carbon taken up during photosynthesis, which helps to reduce the amount of this greenhouse gas in the air). Porkbush in particular has a phenomenal rate of carbon sequestration. Such projects qualify for carbon credits under the Kyoto Protocol, whereby polluting industries (mostly in developed countries) pay for projects that will offset

The natural habitat of the ground hornbill is under threat as a result of human activities

the pollution they create above the agreed emission standards.

An interesting inhabitant of the thickets and forests of the Eastern Cape is the tree hyrax (*Dendrohyrax arboreus*) – a nocturnal browser living in trees. Increased grazing and disturbance of thickets have led to a steep decline in tree hyrax populations. As in the case of savannah woodlands, thicket is also vulnerable to destructive browsing by elephants, but in the thicket biome these mammals are limited to a few protected areas like the Addo Elephant Park.

Natural forests are vulnerable due to the fragmented nature of this biome, occurring scattered in thousands of small pockets in the higher rainfall regions in the east of the country, from the Soutpansberg in Limpopo to the Cape Peninsula. A few larger forest complexes do exist, like the Knysna and Tsitsikamma forests that boast several well-visited Outeniqua yellowwood Big Trees (*Afrocarpus falcatus*) along the Garden Route. Natural Forest has the highest plant species diversity per hectare of all the biomes of South Africa (418 species per ha on average for the total biome compared to 98 species per ha for the species-rich fynbos, which is similar to the macchia veld type of the Mediterranean region). This, of course, takes nothing away from the high conservation importance of the fynbos, which is much more expansive in area but outstrips all biomes in terms of overall number of plant species (many endemic), but with relatively few tree species, such as the silver tree (*Leucadendron argenteum*).

Natural forests usually grow in layers, with a ground layer (herbaceous stratum), a shrub layer and a canopy layer, but can also include intermediate trees below the canopy and emergent trees above the canopy. Canopy trees form the bulk of a forest, where 90% of the photosynthesis takes place. These are self-contained ecosystems growing in relatively nutrient-poor soils and depending on the constant recycling of nutrients. Forests are fringed by belts of hardy pioneer plants, forming transitional zones (ecotones) between the forest and surrounding veld types like grassland, fynbos or woodland.

Healthy restored thicket dotted with spekboom contrasts with degraded and denuded thicket (Photo: Lee Ezzy)

Short-lived pioneer trees usually occur in these forest margins, like the blossom tree (*Virgilia oroboides*), that protect the adjacent mature forest from fires and the drying effects of the sun, and are able to regenerate rapidly after a fire.

Gap dynamics play an important part in forest ecology. Old trees die standing, or topple over to create gaps, causing the shade-tolerant plants inside these gaps to make way for sun-loving pioneers. Tree seedlings or intermediate trees under the canopy then race to the top, to close up the canopy within a decade or more. Natural disturbances such as these actually contribute to plant and animal diversity for they create mosaics of gaps and forest areas in various stages of regrowth with different species compositions, unless such disturbances reach catastrophic proportions due to deforestation by humans or natural events such as cyclones.

Mangrove forest is a rare and curious forest type, growing on the tidal mud-flats of estuaries. Trees such as white mangrove (*Avicennia marina*) grow pencil roots protruding above the mud, while black mangrove trees (*Bruguiera gymnorrhiza*) perch on knee roots and red mangrove (*Rhizophora mucronata*) on stilt roots that literally keep the tree trunks above the tidal high-water marks.

Although deforestation of the natural forest happens not nearly on the scale of savannah woodland or thicket, the one to two thousand hectares lost per year is a serious matter in respect of such a small biome, especially when rare forest types like mangrove are affected. Forest degradation without loss of forest cover is a rather more serious threat, for pressures such as cattle grazing in the forest understorey, bark harvesting and the cutting of understorey pole-sized trees have greatly increased in some rural areas, to the extent that more than a third of the natural forests are already moderately or seriously degraded. Fortunately about 37% of the natural forest biome is represented in formal protected areas, which far exceeds the national target of 23%, yet some forest types are seriously under-protected and are prioritised for inclusion in future protected areas. In traditional rural areas some of these protected areas are under pressure from surrounding communities.

A thin green line

Environmental degradation in South Africa reflects the socio-economic divisions of society. On the one hand the degradation is driven by largely poor households who often invade sensitive habitats and use the resources to survive, and on the other hand habitats are destroyed and resources consumed or replaced on a large scale to support affluent households using manifold more of these resources per capita than their poorer rural neighbours. To affluent households this harsh reality, if reduced to the basics, is not so apparent, for the trade-offs with nature happen piecemeal through economic transactions on a daily basis far removed from the points of impact. The papers we read come from commercial plantation trees that have replaced natural habitats, the chocolate we eat may contain cocoa from plantations that have replaced forests in the tropics, and so the list goes on. Environmentalist Dave Pepler once said that the umbilical cord between modern human beings and the earth has been severed, for unlike older generations who had to plant their own food, slaughter animals and cut their own fuelwood, people do not see the environmental impacts of their actions any more.

What happens locally is but a mirror of the global environmental crisis with divisions between the consumptive developed countries and the underdeveloped countries seeking to use their resources to develop and uplift the poor. In essence the driving forces of environmental degradation are population growth coupled to growing resource needs per capita. Add to that modern technology that empowers humans to change their environment rapidly – and nature has to pay the price. Since humans are dependent on healthy ecosystems, they too pay the price if these systems are pressured. Yet such very basic and obvious observations are often omitted from important development and economic policies, from the national to the local levels, where nature is relegated to the backseat. For that reason environmentalists locally and globally are attempting to put a price on nature through the science of environmental economics, calculating the value of environmental services such as carbon sequestration, soil conservation and flood attenuation. These services amount to billions of rand annually, to which our trees and forests contribute greatly.

The ecological footprints of countries and cities are complex and reach all over the globe, due to the international trade. A Chinese contractor decorating offices in

Illegal deforestation of natural forests has become an increasing challenge despite excellent environmental laws

Tree and Forest Conservation in South Africa

Shanghai with wood veneer does not give a second thought to the tropical forests felled in Gabon to supply that commodity, just as an average Capetonian may not be aware that the little camel thorn wood or charcoal used for his weekend braai affects the ecology of a distant woodland in the Northern Cape or Namibia, and how this adds up to the thousands of tons of braaiwood used monthly. Such resources are often illegally harvested, especially in the tropical timber trade. South Africa has become a transit country for tropical timber from Africa, but the monitoring of cross-border timber movement in southern Africa from tree species requiring controlled harvesting and permits under the Convention on International Trade in Endangered Species (CITES) is woefully inadequate.

South Africa is often mentioned as a country with some of the best environmental legislation in the world, but the country seriously lacks capacity to implement this legislation adequately. Various provincial ordinances and national acts provide direct and indirect protection for trees and woody biomes dominated by trees, foremost among these being the National Forests Act of 1998. This Act protects all natural forests, and no forest trees may be cut, destroyed or damaged without a licence. The same applies to a list of 47 indigenous tree species that were proclaimed as protected. Several other tree species occur on lists of protected fauna and flora, proclaimed under ordinances of the various provinces. The National Forests Act also provides for the protection of individual trees (see *Champion Trees of South Africa*) and specific woodlands (see *Saving a Camel Thorn Forest* on page 186).

The Department of Agriculture, Forestry and Fisheries employs forest officers at national and regional level to manage State forests, to enforce the National Forests Act and to provide technical support by monitoring, mapping and obtaining scientific information on natural forests, woodlands and trees. The Department of Environmental Affairs and Tourism, provincial authorities and some local authorities also employ environmental officers with similar functions, but their environmental conservation focus reaches much wider than forests and trees. To these official conservation organs can be added several non-government organisations that either focus primarily on tree conservation and awareness, or indirectly contribute to the protection of trees and woody biomes.

LEFT: Harvesting bark for medicinal purposes, most of which end up in informal muti markets in cities and towns
RIGHT: Forest guards on patrol in a State forest

To many, trees and forests are merely commodities to be used, whether for household needs or commercial gain. The pepperbark tree (*Warburgia salutaris*) is facing extinction due to the harvesting of its products for household or commercial medicinal use. SAPPI is currently promoting the propagation of thousands of pepperbark seedlings to be planted back in the wild. Bushman's tea (*Catha edulis*) is under severe pressure for the harvesting of leaves of the drug called khat, while matumi trees (*Breonadia salicina*) are increasingly targeted by crime syndicates and farmers for its highly prized timber. A few cycad species face extinction due to the high prices fetched from collectors. Sometimes trees and forests are in the way of property owners or developers seeking ways to make profit, whether from mining or development. Such mining and development is considered necessary for progress, of course, but it all too often happens illegally, or in sensitive areas that should have been earmarked for protection.

In this country hundreds of people are involved with forest and tree protection in one way or another, in many different professions, from forest scientists to arborists. Yet they face an unprecedented scale of environmental pressures, especially habitat change and resource use. The manpower and resources allocated to this daunting task is unfortunately inadequate, but without this thin green line much more of the forests and tree heritage of the country would have been a memory of the past. Officials employed at the sharp end of environmental protection harbour no doubt that we have entered a phase of lawlessness and disrespect for the environment that will gradually undermine the ability of ecosystems to support human wellbeing, unless our society wakes up to this reality and takes action.

Working for Water – combating the invaders

Over a long period of time about 9 000 exotic plant species were introduced to South Africa, of which more than a thousand tree species. These foreign trees have undeniably brought about many advantages. They can be summarised as follows (some products are mentioned in the text):

- Contributing significantly to saving the country's indigenous heritage (commercial tree plantations, for example, gradually replaced natural forest trees as the main source of timber)
- Stabilisation of vast stretches of driftsands along the Western and Eastern Cape coasts
- Animal fodder
- Various products for human consumption, including most fruit products
- Protection of crops (windbreaks) and livestock (shade and shelter)
- Mine props to the mining industry
- Paper pulp to the paper industry
- Tanning materials to the leather industry
- Rayon and viscose to the clothing industry
- Rafters, poles and boards to the building and furniture industries
- Fencing, firewood and building materials to farms
- Landscape and ornamental values.

Exotic species spread naturally, and in some areas in South Africa very fast, on account of a more favourable climate, for instance. Hardy pioneer tree species generate rapidly in disturbed veld, especially after fires, like black wattle (*Acacia mearnsii*). A mature black wattle tree can produce millions of viable seeds. Tree species that spread rapidly and change the landscape are also known as 'transformer species' because they can transform the ecosystems in which they are placed. Dense infestations of exotic trees may withdraw so much groundwater through transpiration that they reduce the water flow of streams to a mere trickle and dry up wetlands.

When exotic species are introduced, their natural enemies are as a rule not introduced initially as well. Biological control as a method of combating the spread of exotic species has been applied in South Africa since the 1930s with success (see the *Cactus Family*). Unfortunately, this had proved to be slow and costly, so other methods of eradicating harmful, dangerous or noxious exotics were introduced.

Exotic tree species are found to be a threat to:
- The existence or productive growth of indigenous species
- Water catchments and water security
- The productive use of land
- The conservation of biological diversity
- The natural ecological functions of ecosystems, as well as an increase in the frequency and extent of fires and flooding in some instances.

Legislation to control invasive plants was introduced as early as 1860, when spiny cocklebur (*Xanthium spinosum*) was declared a noxious weed in the Cape Peninsula. Thereafter various Provincial Administrations enforced legislation on the eradication of weeds. In 1937 the Noxious Weeds Act, No 42 of 1937 was promulgated, and then in 1999 regulations were published under the Conservation of Agricultural Resources Act, 1983 (Act No 43 of 1983) (CARA) to combat invasive plants (amended in 2001). The increasingly restrictive legislation was necessitated through the accelerated deterioration of natural ecosystems by the rampant spread of invasive plants. In 2011 Dr Christo Marais of the Working for Water Programme released monitoring data, which puts the land area invaded by such plants at about 20 million hectares, much more than was previously believed.

Established in 1995, the Working for Water programme is a nationwide programme launched by government to address the serious problem posed by invader plants. It is currently administered by the Department of Environmental Affairs and Tourism, operates on an annual budget of more than a billion rand and employs more than 20 000 people, although this number fluctuates annually. This internationally acclaimed programme meets environmental and social needs at a scale and in a manner matched by few other projects worldwide, and has received some prized environmental awards as a result. Apart from providing jobs and incomes to many jobless people, the short-term benefits have been assessed as water saving, enhancing tourism, better control over fires, preventing soil erosion, providing an additional source of fuelwood and woodworking timber, and entrepreneurial enterprises such as charcoal production and wood-pulping.

The long-term advantages have already become visible in the creation of permanent jobs and small businesses, increased water conservation awareness, and awareness of the value of trees. Hundreds of projects are run countrywide, and a range of methods are used to control invasive plants. These include mechanical methods such as tree-poppers, ring-barking and tree felling; chemical methods such as applying environment-friendly herbicides, and biological control agents, or a combination of these methods. South Africa is regarded as one of the world leaders in the biological control of invader plants, which involves the introduction of natural enemies to these plants such as insects and pathogens. These are tested by the Department of Agriculture, Forestry and Fisheries under controlled conditions before release. More than 200 plant species were originally declared weeds and invader plants in 1999, of which more than 120 were woody species. These were listed under the following three categories:

Eradicating invasive plants is labour intensive, and follow-up treatment of areas cleared of invasive plants is vital to prevent their regeneration

Category 1: Weeds that must be eradicated wherever they occur, and no trading is allowed. Trees in this category include the rock hakea (*Hakea gibbosa*).

Category 2: Invader plants of commercial value that are allowed to be grown under controlled conditions such as a commercial tree plantation. Trading of these plants and their products are allowed. Tree examples are wattle, eucalypt, pine and poplar species.

Category 3: Invader plants mainly used for ornamental purposes in demarcated areas, mostly urban areas. Street and garden trees like jacaranda, tipuana, syringa and guava are popular examples.

In 2014 new regulations and an updated list of invader species were published in terms of the National Environmental Management Biodiversity Act of 2004. Some 559 plant and animal species were listed as invasive, with a further 560 species not yet occurring locally, but prohibited from import.

Authors' Note

Some of the tree species regarded as weeds in South Africa have been described in this publication. While it is acknowledged that these species rightfully played, and still play, an important role in the development and history and economy of South Africa, the aim is not to promote the planting of these species. They are mentioned to complete the picture, because they are usually aggressive growers and some of them flower in profusion, placing them among the most conspicuous and remarkable vegetation species in the country.

Trees and Science

The science of trees is varied, with many specialist fields helping us to understand and manage trees. Some research helps us to get a handle on management problems relating to the use and conservation of trees and woodlands. This chapter gives a bird's eye view of a few tree research fields.

Ecology and utilisation of indigenous trees

Camel thorn (*Vachellia erioloba*) and leadwood (*Combretum imberbe*) are both protected tree species facing threats from a huge braaiwood industry. The Department of Agriculture, Forestry and Fisheries (and its forerunner), responsible for issuing licences to cut protected tree species, has had to collate the results of existing research on the ecology and use of these tree species, and has initiated research to fill the gaps. This research has enabled the government to determine the extent and nature of the braaiwood market and the role of these tree species in the woodland ecology, which was translated into guidelines on where, when and how to allow the harvesting of these two tree species.

The braaiwood market is substantial, amounting to more than two hundred tons of wood consumed monthly in Gauteng alone, of which leadwood makes up a small percentage. In Cape Town the market is different, where most of the wood consumed is the alien invasive species rooikrans (*Acacia cyclops*), while more than a quarter of the braaiwood used is camel thorn. The majority of this indigenous wood, however, is imported by road from Namibia.

Monitoring firewood sold at a filling station to determine the volumes of licensed and unlicensed wood sold from protected species like leadwood and camel thorn

Research on the ecology of camel thorn shows a direct link between the diversity of bird and other animal life and the size or age of trees, where larger trees play an important role in the ecology, *inter alia* providing shade, browsing and nesting sites. Nutrient and moisture levels in the soil are higher under the large trees than in their surroundings, thereby stimulating the growth of a variety of herbaceous plants under these trees. Further research by the Nelson Mandela Metropolitan University has found that even dead camel thorn trees fulfil an ecological function, as the variety of lizards found in an area is directly related to the occurrence of dead trees in an advanced stage of decay, which of course harbours more insects serving as food. The outcome of such research is that no live camel thorn trees may be harvested and that the guidelines prescribe a minimum number of dead trees to be left per hectare.

Camel thorn is one of the most researched indigenous tree species in South Africa, not only because of its important ecological role as a keystone species, but also because of the threats it faces. An urgent research focus at this stage is the significant numbers of camel thorn dying in groups throughout southern Africa. In some cases this appears to be caused by the lowering of the water table through land uses such as mining, while in other instances the research results are inconclusive. The Tree Protection Cooperative Programme of the Forestry and Agricultural Biotechnology Institute at the University of Pretoria is trying to determine whether the *Ceroplesus* species, a pest insect occurring on many of the trees, is a primary cause of tree death, or merely a secondary pest responding to trees already weakened by other stress factors.

Indigenous tree species and water use

The Council for Scientific and Industrial Research has long been a leader in research on the water use of exotic commercial tree species, but is currently also studying the water use of indigenous tree species, with assistance from the Water Research Commission. Through sap flow and transpiration rate measurements useful information has been gained, enabling a comparison of the tree growth and water use efficiency of various indigenous species, and also between indigenous and exotic commercial trees like pine and gum species. This information is necessary to determine whether indigenous trees could be introduced in commercial plantings closer to streams, where exotic species would have disastrous impacts on stream flow. Such techniques could also be adapted to determine whether certain tree populations experience water stress, and thus explain one possible cause of inexplicable tree deaths in certain areas.

RIGHT: Instrument measuring the sap flow of trees in the Southern Cape forests (Photo: Johan Bester)

BELOW: Verdant forest in an advanced stage of succession now grows on sand dunes rehabilitated by Richards Bay Minerals on the north coast of KwaZulu-Natal. This particular forest was the scene of mining for minerals a mere four decades ago

Medicinal uses of indigenous plants

Many studies have been conducted locally on the medicinal properties of trees, often with a commercial motive. Certain studies focus on the chemical properties of the bark, leaves or roots of trees targeted for traditional medicinal uses, such as the pepperbark (*Warburgia salutaris*) and bushman's tea (*Catha edulis*), which could benefit the pharmaceutical industry. Some traditional healers or rural communities possess extensive knowledge of the medicinal properties of plant products that has been transferred from generation to generation. The use of such knowledge by the pharmaceutical industry without compensation for the intellectual rights held by communities has become a hotly debated international issue. *Access and benefit sharing* (ABS) is a new term referring to the requirement that communities must benefit from the use of their knowledge of biological resources for commercial gain, and is provided for in a protocol under the Convention of Biological Diversity.

Determining tree age

Without science it would not be possible to determine the age of large individuals of most indigenous tree species, as few indigenous tree types have clear growth rings. Where growth rings can be counted, such as in yellowwood species, a core drill can be used to drill a long wood sample out of the tree, right up to the core of the tree. In most instances carbon dating is the best method, based on the half-life of the radio-carbon isotope. In a paper published in 2013, Dr Adrian Patrut and a team of researchers reported on the carbon dating of the Glencoe baobab near Hoedspruit which has partly collapsed, putting its age at around 1 835 years. This makes the Glencoe baobab the oldest reliably dated baobab in the world, and the oldest tree in South Africa. Drs Fried von Breitenbach and Coert Geldenhuys have recorded size classes for baobab and yellowwood species respectively, thereby enabling field workers to make rough estimates of tree age. Researchers also record the numbers of individuals of tree species occurring in certain areas according to size classes, and the resultant tree population curves may provide conservation managers of forests or woodlands with useful information such as a lack of regeneration of certain species, which could lead to adaptions in management practices.

The partially collapsed Platland baobab tree. Baobabs can grow to over 1 800 years old as determined by carbon dating, but often suffer from collapses in the late stages of their life cycles – non-catastrophic in this case (Photo: René O'Connell)

Dendrochronology

This is another useful scientific field based on tree rings, as continuous growth of vascular cambium near the inner bark takes place at a different seasonal tempo, which shows up as discernible rings if a cross-section is cut through a tree. Fast growth of cambium tissue during the summer seasons forms broad light bands, while slow growth during winter seasons shows up as narrow dark bands. Rings of old tree trunks can tell us much about the changes in the climate over centuries as wetter and drier seasons followed in sequence with wider and narrower growth bands. Fire scars show up where forest fires raged, even centuries ago. Scientists can even gain information from these rings about sun-spot activity over the ages. Such phenomena are mostly detectable from trees in the temperate areas, but the few local softwood species such as yellowwoods (*Podocarpus* species) and cedars (*Widdringtonia* species) can also be used for this purpose. Many fossilised remnants of ancient trees have been found locally, from which much information can be gained of the plant life and weather patterns reigning millions of years ago.

A tomograph survey of a giant yellowwood in the Knysna Forests. Radar scans such as this can determine whether tree trunks have cavities or rot on the inside

Plant taxonomy

South Africa is a mega-diverse country, ranking as the country with the third most plant species in the world. Since the explorations of early botanists like Carl Peter Thunberg in the 18th and 19th centuries, the taxonomic classification of the rich plant life found here has never ceased. Plant families are constantly studied and species are re-categorised and renamed by taxonomists, to the exasperation of tree lovers. But new tree species are seldom discovered. A scientific paper by Dr Jack Pettigrew and a team of international scientists on the identification of a new diploid species of baobab on the basis of DNA and pollen studies published recently, has resulted in this species being named the kilima baobab (*Adansonia kilima*). At the time of going to press, local baobab expert Dr Sarah Venter was investigating this finding through field studies to verify whether sufficient grounds exist for a new species apart from the African baobab (*Adansonia digitata*).

The Department of Botany and Plant Biotechnology of the University of Johannesburg is heading a project to create a genetic barcode database of all plant and animal species in the country, including trees. This technology holds promise for law enforcement, where positive identification of protected tree species and their products may be vital for successful enforcement. It is envisaged that this technology could find its way into a hand-held device that would be able to identify plant species at an instant when a leaf sample is fed into a sensor.

Could tree experts become redundant as technology progresses? Highly unlikely, for tree conservation and management will always require knowledgeable and experienced experts able to interpret results and translate this into practical action.

These are just some examples of the tree research fields, and describing them could justify a book on its own.

A nineteenth century botanist collecting tree leaf samples – early botanists must have marvelled at the country's abundance of trees and other plants

South Africa's Forestry Industry

Relative to the country's surface area, South Africa is poorly endowed with high forest, with its natural forests covering about half a million hectares. This fact has led, over many years, to the development of an efficient commercial forestry industry in South Africa, which today contributes substantially to both the Gross National Product (GNP) and the country's exports.

Birth of the forestry industry

Pine plantations on the slopes of the Drakensberg escarpment, Mpumalanga. Forestry has changed dramatically over the past decades and in this country the industry today is a world leader in compliance with local and international certification standards for sustainable management

The development of the forest industry often runs parallel with the recorded history of the country. With timber being a prime necessity of man's existence, when settling permanently in particular, it was obvious that the Dutch colonists at the Cape would turn to the nearest sources for their timber needs – mainly the sheltered kloofs on the eastern side of Table Mountain. To facilitate matters, particular areas were assigned to concessionaries – the names of some persisting to this day in place names such as Kirsten*bosch*, Burgers*bosch*, Klaassen*bosch*. Hout Bay, as the name indicates (*hout* = wood), must have been a valuable source of timber.

With no exotic species having been introduced yet for commercial purposes (eucalypts, pines, poplars, etc.), the trees utilised at that stage were the indigenous

Early exploitation of indigenous forests

Commercial exploitation of natural forests commenced with the arrival of the European settlers in 1652. Large woodcutter communities settled first in the Southern Cape forests and later in other regions as the demand for timber grew. Timber from these forests helped to build the economy and infrastructure, supplying hundreds of thousands of yellowwood railway sleepers as well as timber for ox-wagons, ships, telegraph poles and building materials. The limited capacity of the indigenous forests was soon recognised, resulting in increasing regulation through laws and proclamations. By the late nineteenth century the state started to integrate independent woodcutters into communities in areas where labour was needed by commercial plantations. A law promulgated in 1913 required the remaining woodcutters to register and the list was closed to any new additions. In 1939 the natural forests were closed to independent woodcutters and the remaining woodcutter families were resettled.

ABOVE: The Evelyn-Pirie narrow-gauge train in an Eastern Cape forest. This was one of only two forest railways which transported logs harvested in the natural forests during the early part of the twentieth century

BELOW: Old-time woodcutters felling a yellowwood in the Knysna forest at the turn of the nineteenth century. Many of these forest giants were felled for railway sleepers

ones: yellowwoods, stinkwoods, red alder, assegai, and others, were felled wherever accessible. The actual yield of these forests will never be known, but it must have been significant.

Once the forests in the Cape Peninsula could no longer supply the demands of a growing settlement, the mountain ranges along the eastern coast were explored. The Langeberg, the Outeniqua, the Tsitsikamma, and eventually the Amatola forests, all yielded the tree treasures they had harboured for many centuries. It is reported that Governor Joachim von Plettenberg was much perturbed about their state on an inspection tour of the southern Cape forests in 1778. The 'slash-and-burn' practice of the native subsistence farmers added to this uncontrolled depletion of the forests, which would finally affect those on the northern Drakensberg range as well.

After a few unsuccessful endeavours, control of the forests was eventually seriously taken in hand during the 1870s. This was to be the turning point in the history of South Africa's forests. From that date the focus would turn towards efficient management of the indigenous forests, together with the concerted promotion of afforestation countrywide.

In 1875 the celebrated politician John X Merriman was said to proclaim: 'Yet no one who has visited Cape Town, where the numerous plantations are a standing monument to the wisdom of the founders of the colony, can deny that in suitable situations the Cape is as well adapted to the growth of forest trees as any country in the world'. Legislation followed, promoting the establishment of plantations and street tree avenues.

In 1876 the first Government plantation consisting of eucalypt trees was established near Worcester for the supply of firewood and poles to the railways. The Cape Forest Act of 1888, 'a milestone in the history of forestry', was promulgated, and remained in force until 1913 when the first national Forest Act was passed, to be followed by the Forest Acts of 1941, 1968, 1984 and 1998. The appointment in 1882 of the first Superintendent of Forests and Plantations, Count M de Vasselot de Regné, together with a team of forestry scientists (Fourcade, Heywood, Hutchins, and others), laid the foundations for a well-managed forestry industry in South Africa, with the training of foresters and judicious management of existing (indigenous) forests as priorities. Together with the necessary knowledge, two other factors crucial towards establishing a healthy and productive plantation industry immediately received attention. The first of these was to determine which exotic species would be best suited for planting in South Africa – this was done through the testing of seeds and planting methods. (Forestry and related research, which grew from humble origins in South Africa, was later, in the 20th century, to be highly acclaimed internationally.)

Secondly, nurseries had to be established to facilitate the distribution of seedlings. The sophisticated nurseries established countrywide furthermore attest to the persistence of forestry scientists in providing the industry with the best possible material. The various arboreta, too, serve as show blocks of these research efforts.

Systematic afforestation initially made but modest progress. Yet in 1897 when, with the outbreak of rinderpest, 50 000 poles were needed for the erection of fences, they were delivered within 14 days, from wattle plantations established for the supply of firewood to rural people in the Eastern Cape. The discovery of gold and diamonds in the country during the last quarter of the 19th century, and the subsequent expansion of industries, placed large pressures on the little timber available. Plantations of eucalypts, pines and wattles were established on the Witwatersrand in particular, to supply the needs of the mines and the people. In 1902 the total afforested area amounted to 26 626 ha, of which 18 215 ha belonged to the private sector.

Serious commercial afforestation eventually started after 1902, with the result that, in 1914, on the outbreak of World War I, some 140 000 ha of exotic plantations existed countrywide, 22 500 ha of which were State forests. Nevertheless, a timber shortage experienced at that stage demonstrated the extent to which the country was still dependent on imports. Afforestation was consequently accelerated, upon which the erection of sawmills, mainly State-initiated, was to follow, as well as of timber preservation plants.

The industry today

World War II would precipitate large-scale involvement by the private sector in afforestation and its related activities. Large forestry companies came into being, which set free the necessary large capital that could be invested in what is today a flourishing industry in South Africa. Around 1,3 million ha are covered by plantations today – mainly pines, eucalypts and wattles. Sawmills and pulp factories are virtually exclusively in private hands. The industry also opened its doors to small farmers, particularly in KwaZulu-Natal. These small-scale timber growers already number more than 20 000,

The role played by the early Dutch governors

Mention should be made of the efforts of three early Dutch Governors: Jan van Riebeeck, Simon van der Stel and his son Willem Adriaan van der Stel, all realised the necessity for the establishment of plantations – preferably exotic trees that would grow faster than the indigenous species. Van Riebeeck imported seed from Europe and Indonesia and established European oak (*Quercus robur*), stone pine (*Pinus pinea*) and cluster pine (*Pinus pinaster*), as well as olive, mulberry and camphor trees in the Company's Garden and further afield. Of these the European oak fared best. Simon van der Stel followed suit with his well-known oak tree planting endeavours that included the planting of 16 000 oak trees along the slopes of Table Mountain in 1689 – the first true plantation to be established in South Africa. By 1692 a plantation of 1,7 ha consisting of oak and pine trees was already in existence near Stellenbosch. In 1700 Governor WA van der Stel commenced with the establishment of the Newlands plantation – regarded by later forestry experts as the starting point of systematic afforestation in South Africa.

Apart from primary wood production by plantations, associated industries like sawmills play an important role in job creation and adding value to the timber industry (Photo: C Chapman/SA Forestry))

making a substantial contribution towards poverty alleviation as well.

Ongoing research and modern management and industrial techniques are responsible for our healthy, vigorous man-made forests not only yielding their related products, but also providing the traveller with breath-taking panoramas – a boon to the tourism industry as well. South Africa is nowadays not only self-sufficient in respect of the forestry industry's products, but also exports these products to almost every corner of the world, even to traditionally timber-producing countries. South Africa's paper and pulp companies have become successful world players, with factories in many countries. Back home the forestry and forest products sectors provide employment to some 210 000 people, each probably supporting a household of a further five people or more. The industry is also fully committed to conservation in its various aspects. In this respect South Africa has the distinction of having the highest percentage of Forest Stewardship Council (FSC) certified tree plantations in the world.

From a country 'without trees', as described by Max O'Rell in 1894, '... having bare mountains and being without trees generally, just as the indigenous inhabitants who wore little clothing', South Africa has progressed in a relatively short span of time to a country where conservationists already find it necessary to raise objections against afforestation – and the only country where a permit is required specifically for the establishment of a plantation!

Afforestation is considered a water use activity by the National Water Act, therefore requiring a water use licence. As a result of stringent controls and the withdrawal of plantations in sensitive areas like wetlands, the net increase in the commercial plantation area has slowed down to the extent that just over 10 000 ha were added during the last decade.

Trees

I think that I shall never see
A poem as lovely as a tree

A tree whose hungry mouth is pressed
Against the earth's sweet flowering breast;

A tree that looks at God all day
And lifts her leafy arms to pray;

A tree that may in summer wear
A nest of robins in her hair;

Upon whose bosom snow has lain
Who intimately lives with rain;

Poems are made by fools like me
But only God can make a tree.

Joyce Kilmer
1886–1919

Tree Families

CYATHEACEAE
Tree Fern Family

Approximately 600 species of the tree fern family occur worldwide, mostly in the northern temperate climatic zones. Two tree-like ferns occur in South Africa in the forests and high-rainfall grassland areas. Both species have unbranched stems covered with brown scales and are crowned with arching feather-like leaves. Both species are protected.

Cyathea capensis (**forest tree fern**) occurs from the Western Cape through the eastern parts of southern Africa to Tanzania. It has a graceful slender stem of up to 4 m. The leaves are up to 3 m long with a tangle of green hair-like structures that later on turn brown at the base. These ferns are abundant in the Knysna-Tsitsikamma forests, with extraordinarily large concentrations in some areas, such as the Valley of Ferns near Diepwalle, a popular picnic site on the Knysna-Uniondale road.

Cyathea dregei (**grassveld tree fern**) is more widespread, with the exception of the southern and western regions, where it is completely absent. The stem is sturdy, 450 mm in diameter and up to 5 m tall. The leaves lack the hair-like structures of the forest tree fern at their bases.

The Mondi Tree Fern Reserve, a Natural Heritage Site near Sabie in Mpumalanga, probably contains the greatest concentration of grassveld tree ferns in the country. Some 1 200 plants, 1 to 5 m high, occur in an area of 3,3 ha.

Forest tree fern in its natural habitat, the Knysna forests, Western Cape

The grassveld tree fern has a wide distribution

ZAMIACEAE

The Cycad Family

Zamiaceae, the cycad family, consists of eight genera with 140 species, occurring in the Americas, the West Indies, Australia and Africa. It is a cone-bearing family; the general characteristics are an (usually) unbranched trunk where existing, i.e. in tree species, and large compound leaves. Cycads are scientifically one of the most interesting existing plant groups. They represent the relics of an ancient flora that dominated the earth's vegetation during the Mesozoic Era some 200 million years ago, when dinosaurs roamed the planet. The dinosaurs disappeared completely at the end of the Era, while cycad species managed to survive in spite of competition from highly successful flowering plants.

These dauntingly striking plants are objects of reverence to some peoples, of envy, to the unsuccessful gardener, and of illegal appropriation by many who are aware of their value. A single specimen of this palm-like cone-bearing 'tree' in a garden may serve as a status symbol, proudly dominating its environment with its large leaves, enhanced by the colourful cones resembling pineapples. Some cones are covered with a dense brownish wool. Mostly, however, they are hairless and range in colour from bright orange-yellow to orange-brown and even scarlet. The fleshy outer layer of the seeds is also very colourful, ranging from scarlet to orange to red to amber to yellow. The naked seeds consist of a fleshy outer layer, often edible, encasing a mostly poisonous kernel. The plants are dioecious, i.e. with male and female cones on different plants. The female cones are usually larger than the male ones.

Only the genus *Encephalartos* occurs in southern Africa, from Malawi and Zimbabwe southwards. South Africa boasts some 33 *Encephalartos* species in total, of which 23 are classified as trees. These so-called African cycads are easily confused with the true cycad of the genus, *Cycas thouarsii*, the Malagasy cycad, an exotic and popular plant grown in gardens locally.

Encephalartos species are all remarkable. Some have adapted to grow under dry conditions; the leaves of these are covered with a bluish wax to retain water efficiently. In others, such as *E. horridus* (a shrub), the leaves are not only covered with this wax but they are also shaped and arranged so that they shade each other (twisted out of the plain of the main axis).

The tireless botanist Thunberg was the first person to describe an *Encephalartos* in South Africa. In November 1772 he observed Khoi people preparing bread from the tree by removing the pith of a large trunk, tying it in a goatskin and burying it for a month to ferment. This was then ground into a flour and formed into cakes, cooked or baked in hot ash. (The genus name *Encephalartos* is the Greek for 'bread within'.)

The species described by Thunberg was *Encephalartos longifolius*, the Suurberg cycad. It is a tree up to 3 m high with a sturdy trunk, bearing some of the largest cones in the genus – the female ones may weigh up to 35 kg – with red seeds 5 cm long. As the name indicates, this cycad is abundant in the Suurberg, but also occurs on the eastern part of the Groot-Winterhoek Mountains, both mountain ranges in the Eastern Cape. It was the Suurberg cycad that poisoned General Smuts and his commando when they camped in the Suurberg and ate the seeds of cycads in fruit during the Anglo-Boer War. In his book *Commando* Deneys Reitz gives a detailed account of this event. The commando was in flight before the British and General Smuts was so ill that two men had to hold him upright on his horse. Reitz, however, erroneously named the cycad *E. altensteinii*, which does not occur on the Suurberg.

A number of South Africa's more exceptional *Encephalartos* tree species are described below.

Encephalartos transvenosus: Modjadji cycad

The species name *transvenosus* refers to the transverse veins on the leaves. A network of veins can be seen criss-crossing between the parallel veins of a leaf held up to the light.

The Modjadji cycad, perhaps the best known of the southern African species, is restricted to the northern and eastern parts of Limpopo, where several colonies occur. Succeeding generations of Rain Queens of the Lovedu tribe, the Modjadji, have protected these particular plants – hence the common name. The most important colony is found in the Modjadji Nature Reserve near Modjadjiskloof, which was proclaimed a national monument in 1936. Thousands of these trees grow in this grove of several hectares, commonly known as the 'Rain Forest'.

The tallest tree measures 13 m. It has a sturdy trunk and its age has been estimated at over 500 years. The cones, which are yellow, appear two to four together, with the male cones measuring some 40 × 15 cm and the female ones up to 80 × 30 cm, and weighing almost 40 kg.

Both the Modjadji and Wood's cycads, as well as several others, have very sturdy stems that mostly stay upright.

Encephalartos eugene-maraisii Verdoorn: Waterberg cycad

This cycad has a single upright stem up to 4 m high, while old specimens tend to be procumbent. The species was discovered by Eugène Marais in 1925. When he died in 1936, the location was not known. Thanks to the tireless efforts of his niece, Dr Inez (IC) Verdoorn, South African botanist and cycad scholar, it was tracked down in 1944.

In *Trees in South Africa*, September 1987, Dr Verdoorn tells the following story to Mr Dick Findlay:

A year or two before his death – I can't remember the exact date – Uncle Eugène (the youngest child in my mother's large family

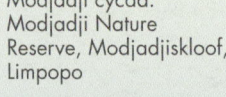

Modjadji cycad: Modjadji Nature Reserve, Modjadjiskloof, Limpopo

and she the second youngest) came to see me at the National Herbarium in connection with his Stapelias *which he wanted named. In the course of our talk I mentioned that I was working on the cycads in our country. He then asked what the name of the cycad that grew in the Waterberg was. I answered that cycads did not grow there. I added, 'They are known only from the eastern regions of our country'. He averred that there were cycads growing on the Palala Plateau and that many years previously (1925), when he was visiting there, he sent a specimen to Dr R Marloth (analytical chemist and botanist of Cape Town) because some children had become seriously ill after eating the seeds. I remarked that if Dr Marloth had kept the specimen we ought to have it as the National Herbarium had inherited Dr Marloth's herbarium. Together we searched the* Encephalartos *sheets and to my delight found the specimen. But we were astonished to find that according to the label the specimen came from Nelspruit, 'collector E. Marais'. In E. Marais' presence I changed the locality to Palala Plateau, Waterberg and Uncle Eugène promised to take me there to see the plants. But he never got so far.*

After his death, I determined that I would find the plant somehow and eventually interested an Extension Officer – Mr P Tourien, who was to be stationed at Potgietersrus – in the search. He was triumphant in 1944 and Dr Dyer took me to see it. I described the species in the SA Journal of Botany 11,1 (1945). There you can read the same story told in a less personal way.

Eugène N Marais died in 1936. He was a Pretoria-based advocate, Afrikaans writer and poet and naturalist interested both in plants and animals, who scientifically documented his observations. A number of his books were translated into English and other languages. Marais' observations on the Deadbeat ana trees are referred to under the Thorn Tree Family.

Encephalartos middelburgensis: Middelburg cycad

The Middelburg cycad is a scarce subspecies found only in the Middelburg (Mpumalanga) area, with fewer than 500 plants occurring in the wild.

One of these, a female plant on the farm Bankfontein, growing along the Cycad Hiking Trail, was declared a national monument in 1994. It consists of five stems, the tallest being 7,8 m high, still standing upright. Two stems branch to form

Multi-stemmed procumbent Middelburg cycad

Dr Duncan MacFadyen, Manager: Research and Conservation, E. Oppenheimer & Son, inspecting a giant *Encephalartos middelbergensis*, 800 years old, Mpumalanga

three crowns each, resulting in the stems being procumbent on account of the weight of the plant – a feature that is characteristic of quite a few cycads. The trunk of one such Middelburg cycad, several metres high, was leaning considerably when visited by members of the Cycad Society of SA in 1974. In 1989 it was leaning to a far greater extent, and when visited again in 1991 it was procumbent. The age of the Bankfontein cycad has been estimated at 500 years.

Encephalartos natalensis: Natal cycad

The Natal cycad occurs from the Transkei (Eastern Cape) to northern KwaZulu-Natal. The main stem is 25 to 40 cm in diameter, mostly erect but sometimes reclining. The leaves are compound and up to 3 m long, the young leaves and cones coated in a brown wool. The cones, up to five borne on one plant, are yellow, large, with orange-red to scarlet seeds. Three Natal cycads at the Monteseel Township on the R103 from Pietermaritzburg to Durban, skirting the Valley of a Thousand Hills, were declared national monuments in 1951. All are female plants; the tallest is about 6 m high, with its rootstock estimated at about 1 000 years old and the stem and branches over 250 years old.

The Rendsburg Cycad Colony, a Natural Heritage Site in the Vryheid area, KwaZulu-Natal, harbours thousands of Natal cycad trees, some of them up to 3 m high. Several other heritage sites feature Natal and other cycads, such as the Mananga Cycad Colony near Komatipoort in Mpumalanga, containing some 5 000 Piet Retief cycads (*Encephalartos senticosus*; formerly *E. lebomboensis*).

Encephalartos woodii: Wood's cycad

A single giant, multi-stemmed male cycad was discovered in 1895 by Mr J Medley Wood, curator of the Durban Botanical Garden, in the Ngoye forest in KwaZulu-Natal. This species apparently became extinct in the wild in the early 1900s. However, many plants grown from offshoots thrive today – all of them male. Two of the offshoots from the original plant can be seen in the Durban Botanical Garden, while material sent to other gardens in South Africa and overseas is still flourishing.

Wood's cycad is a large tree, up to 6 m tall, with leaves up to 2,5 m arching downwards, and showy orange cones. This apparently forest species, which dates back a probable 500 years, is now sadly considered extinct in its natural state.

Natal cycad, Baynesfield, KwaZulu-Natal

Encephalartos inopinus: Lydenburg cycad

The discovery of a new cycad species is usually a newsworthy event. In spite of their extraordinary, palm-like appearance, making them very conspicuous, new species were described as recently as 1996. One such discovery happened in 1955, on the farm Onverwacht (Dutch-Afrikaans

for 'unexpected') in the Lydenburg/Mashishing district, Mpumalanga. Dr RA Dyer, who described the plant, decided on the species name *inopinus*, which is the Latin word for 'unexpected'.

Encephalartos dyerianus: Lillie cycad

This cycad species is found only near Mica in Limpopo, named after the farm Lillie where it was first found. A colony of some 500 plants, several up to 4 m tall, occurs on rocky hills in the area. It was later classified as a new species, *dyerianus*, having been mistakenly regarded for many years as *E. eugene-maraisii*.

The rare Lillie cycad is found only near Mica in Limpopo Province

Conservation and threat

The realisation by the general public of the value of cycads has had various consequences – positive, in the sense that cycads have become sought-after garden objects, which has led to wide interest in their growing and has probably saved some species from extinction. On the other hand, theft of, and illegal dealing in, cycads have become a common occurrence. To combat this and to protect collections of cycads and rare groups of plants in nature, an anti-theft microchip-implanting device has been produced. Removing cycads from their natural sites is unnecessary too, as these plants are nowadays commonly available from nurseries. Where cycads are planted legally, gardeners assist in conserving South Africa's *Encephalartos* for posterity.

Special mention has to be made here, too, of the pivotal role played by the Lowveld National Botanical Garden in establishing a cycad gene bank.

Environmental crime inspectors at National and Provincial levels are at the forefront of the fight against illegal trade in cycads.

The colourful cones of the female ferox cycad

PODOCARPACEAE
The Yellowwood Family

Podocarpaceae, the yellowwoods, boast a fairly extended family of seven genera and 110 species occurring throughout Africa, South America, Japan, New Zealand, the West Indies, Polynesia and Burma. Related to conifers (pines, cedars and cypress trees), they do not bear flowers but produce small, primitive cones instead. Yellowwoods are evergreen and are usually grown for their attractive foliage. Unlike that of other conifers, the seed is borne on a woody or brightly coloured base or receptacle. The genus name is derived from the receptacle (*podocarpum* = foot and fruit).

The four yellowwood species occurring in South Africa's indigenous forests count among the country's most important forest trees. They are:

Podocarpus latifolius (**Real yellowwood**) yields a much sought-after wood, often used in combination with other, darker woods such as stinkwood, and nowadays fetching astronomic prices. It occurs along the coastal areas from the Western Cape through to Limpopo.

Afrocarpus falcatus (**Outeniqua yellowwood**) is the yellowwood tree with the smallest leaves, but it grows to become the largest. It occurs from the southern Cape along the mountain ranges on the eastern coast through to Limpopo.

An Outeniqua yellowwood on the farm Kempslust near Utrecht, KwaZulu-Natal, is mysteriously linked to Shaka, the great Zulu leader. Legend has it that he stayed in a cave below the tree. Unfortunately, the tree died of an unknown cause some years ago. The present owner of Kempslust, Johan Kemp, planned to plant a new tree to mark the place, as both the tree and cave are revered by the local people.

Podocarpus henkelii (**Henkel's yellowwood**) – from the Eastern Cape and KwaZulu-Natal – has long, hanging leaves. It is a popular ornamental plant and the most widely planted for this purpose of all the yellowwood species.

Podocarpus elongatus (**Breede River yellowwood**) is the rarest and smallest of the yellowwood trees. It is confined to the Western Cape and southern parts of the Northern Cape.

The yellowwoods were declared the national trees of South Africa in 1976.

Giant Outeniqua yellowwood trees having escaped the woodcutter's axe in the Knysna-Tsitsikamma forests

The strange shape of a yellowwood planted at Vergelegen, Somerset West

large quantities in the forests and yielding a most workable multi-purpose wood, yellowwood trees were felled, almost to extinction in those forests worked by woodcutters, to obtain the best quality timber for purposes of construction, wagon-building, furniture, etc. – the latter are prestigious objects nowadays, as are yellowwood flooring and ceiling boards. Beautiful yellowwood furniture is manufactured by a number of furniture factories in the George-Knysna area, and the historic Dutch Reformed Church in George boasts beautiful yellowwood woodwork.

In spite of their prehistoric appearance due to long threads of grey lichens (old man's beard) drooping from their crowns, the age of South Africa's yellowwoods does not come near to challenging world records. None of the yellowwoods dated so far has been found to be older than 1 000 years. Radiocarbon testing by Dr JC Vogel at the CSIR has determined the age of South Africa's giant podocarps to be probably between 600 and 1 000 years.

All four species are protected in terms of the National Forests Act as well as by some provincial ordinances. Yellowwood trees occurring naturally, even those standing in private gardens, may therefore not be felled without a permit.

South Africans are proud to acknowledge the role played by these trees in the more recently documented development of the country. Once conveniently obtainable in

Visitors to the forests are usually overwhelmed by the size of the Outeniqua yellowwoods and are fascinated by their age. A true forestry story goes that when a group of tourists once argued about the age of one of the forest giants, a woodcutter nearby told them that the tree was 804 years old.

A yellowwood to the rescue

A giant Outeniqua yellowwood at the mouth of the Kleinbos River in the Tsitsikamma can boast the unusual achievement of saving the lives of two young brothers – and did South Africa's forests a good turn. One of the young men was the late Dr DR de Wet, then district forest officer (DFO) in Knysna.

Dr de Wet's brother came by light aeroplane, a Rearwin, from Pretoria to fetch him at Knysna so that they could spend Christmas with their parents in 1937. He was supposed to land on Thesen's Island, but due to bad weather landed in a wheat field 400 m long on the bank of the Keurbooms River near Plettenberg Bay.

The next day, after an almost impossible take-off, the brothers found themselves in thick mist on their way to Port Elizabeth. As visibility was bad, they followed the white foam line on the coast. Suddenly there were two foam lines and they realised that they were flying up one of the deep river mouths. At this stage it was impossible to turn back in the narrow ravine. They just succeeded in gaining enough height to climb out of it, but struck one of the bulging Outeniqua yellowwood crowns that protruded above the forest canopy. The aeroplane slid down the gigantic trunk and landed on its nose, coming to rest against the trunk. Other than the scare created by a young branch of 6 cm that just missed Dr de Wet's head, neither brother suffered a scratch. A memorable experience for a DFO who later became the Secretary of the Department of Forestry!

TREE FAMILIES

Henkel's yellowwood trees, Ntsekeni forest, Eastern Cape

Astonished at the exactness of the number, they asked him how he knew that. 'That's easy', he answered, 'four years ago Dr Phillips, a researcher, told a group of students that this tree was 800 years old.'

Many noted yellowwood trees are found in the Western Cape, Eastern Cape, KwaZulu-Natal, Mpumalanga and Limpopo. They are mostly tall or generally big trees. On the farm Groothoek near Steelpoort in Mpumalanga three Outeniqua yellowwood trees occur in the savannah along a stream in the Groothoek Valley. These trees are typically stunted, with tapering trunks – a sure sign that they are growing in a dry area.

In 1947 six trees were planted in the garden of the hotel in the Royal Natal National Park in the northern Drakensberg area of KwaZulu-Natal, four of which are positively identified as *Podocarpus henkelii* (Henkel's or Natal yellowwood). These four trees were planted by King George VI of Britain, the then Queen Elizabeth, and their two daughters, the Princesses Elizabeth (Queen Elizabeth II) and Margaret, during the British Royal visit to South Africa. Trees were also planted by General JC Smuts, then Premier of the Union of South Africa, and Senator Hosking. It has been reported that the tree planted by Senator Hosking died and was replaced with another by his son, Gerald, in 1984. (The Park derived its name from this particular Royal visit.)

Two *Podocarpus latifolius* (real yellowwood) trees at Ngome plantation, KwaZulu-Natal, are reminders of another Royal event, a forest picnic, on 13 June 1939. The Duke and Duchess of Devonshire (the Duke was then Colonial Secretary of Britain), travelled from Nongoma to Vryheid. At Ngome, in a clearing in the indigenous forest, they were treated to tea and typical South African delicacies such as koeksisters and milk tart. The couple each planted a real yellowwood tree at the forestry quarters.

Outeniqua yellowwood trees are fairly often seen in gardens in Pretoria. One such tree in Lys Street, Riviera, planted in 1935 by a Mr Immelman, is now the largest known yellowwood in Gauteng. Also, many yellowwoods, some even larger than the Lys Street tree, were established along streets in Yellowwood Park, Durban.

Outeniqua yellowwood trees along a hiking trail in Blouberg Nature Reserve, Limpopo

CUPRESSACEAE

The Cypress Family

Cupressaceae, the cypress family, contains 22 genera occurring in both the Northern and the Southern Hemispheres, with only one genus native to South Africa, namely the *Widdringtonia*. A fair number of the genus *Cupressus* (cypresses) are planted in South Africa, being popular mainly for ornamental purposes. Characteristics associated with these widely known exotic cypresses generally apply to all members of the family. The young leaves tend to be needle-like, but become scale-like when mature. Male and female cones occur on the same tree, the males being small and the females globose and woody. The wood is fragrant, resinous and highly inflammable.

This latter characteristic causes the three *Widdringtonia* species growing naturally in South Africa to be described both as rare and remarkable. These trees, all containing an aromatic resin, are particularly susceptible to fire, almost exploding into flames, and consequently burning to death. This accounts for their occurring only in small numbers in South Africa – mostly in narrow ravines or on rocky outcrops where they are protected from fires.

While the **Widdringtonia nodiflora (mountain cypress)** will only grow into a small tree or, more aptly, a shrub, the other two *Widdringtonia* species are medium-sized trees. These two species, although resembling each other very closely, can actually be separated according to their geographical distribution.

The better-known **Widdringtonia cedarbergensis (Clanwilliam cedar)** has the remarkable distinction of having had a range of mountains in the Western Cape called after it. Its sole locality is the Cedarberg mountain range. Its common name points to the town that can be dubbed the 'heart' of the Cedarberg, and where both the Anglican church and the Courthouse contain fittings from cedar wood.

Its particular features render cedar wood very durable – early travellers such as Barrow and Lichtenstein reported this more than two centuries ago. These reports attracted woodcutters, who settled in the area and cut a considerable number of cedar trees for saw-timber. Fortunately the felling of *Widdringtonia cedarbergensis* ceased in 1876, when the Cedarberg area was proclaimed a forest reserve and the trees were declared protected. Many of the offspring of these woodcutters, familiar with the area, and without an income on account of the small number of cedar trees left, excelled at buchu picking in the Cedarberg. Buchu picking during the first few decades of the 20th century closely resembled a gold or diamond rush, in which every mobile man, woman and child had to run to stake their claims.

Owing to their susceptibility to fire, these cedar trees usually grow in shallow soils among rocks, where they are to a fair extent protected from fire. This accounts for their generally small measurements, the trunks being short and the tree form gnarled, providing an eerie feature to the already bizarre appearance of the mountains. The weird rock formations result from millennia of wind erosion. Over several decades the Clanwilliam cedar tree population has declined, sparking efforts by the provincial conservation authorities to propagate and plant seedlings in the Cedarberg Wilderness Area.

While the Clanwilliam cedar is endemic to the Cedarberg, three specimens were found a number of years ago on the southern slopes of the Anysberg to the west of Ladismith, Western Cape, all within 50 m of a forestry path built in the 1950s. A retired foreman, one Mr Gerber, remembered building

OPPOSITE PAGE: Clanwilliam cedars outgrowing their sandstone fire guards, Cedarberg, Western Cape

Willowmore cedars in Sapreekloof, Kouga mountains, Eastern Cape

the trail and 'beautifying' it by scattering Clanwilliam cedar seeds. The Anysberg, a small, island-like mountain range linking the fynbos mountains of the southern Cape with those of the Western Cape, shows a remarkable resemblance with the Cedarberg in both the flora and rock formations – thus the ideal growing conditions for the Clanwilliam cedar.

The common names of **Widdringtonia schwarzii** (**Willowmore** or **Baviaanskloof cedar**) reveal the locality of this species to be the narrow valley pressed in between the Kouga and Baviaanskloof mountains in the Eastern Cape. This cedar reaches a height of 30 m, in contrast to the Clanwilliam cedar, which reaches only some 20 m in valleys. In spite of earlier, mostly small-scale, utilisation of the timber, a number of giant Willowmore cedar trees are still to be seen in the narrow ravines in the Baviaanskloof on the northern side of the Kouga mountains, where they are better protected from wild fires. This greatly enhances the attractiveness of an obscure and less-travelled part of the country.

The ravines where the trees grow are usually very deep. Legend has it that trees were felled at risk to one's life and that, with no other practical solution, woodcutters had to wait for a flood to convey the planks! (Due to its geography the Baviaanskloof is often flooded.)

The biggest known Willowmore cedar occurs in one such ravine called Doringkloof. Its measurements are: height 39 m and stem diameter at breast height 1,8 m. The bark has been severely damaged by rocks carried by the strong floods. Eyewitnesses have reported the existence of a large plank presumably sawn many years ago near this tree. Neither human strength nor the force of a torrent has been able to remove it from Doringkloof all these years; not so much due to its size but as a result of the difficult terrain.

Owing to their scarcity and vulnerability, much research has been undertaken on the *Widdringtonia* species to ensure their survival. The results of a study by forestry scientist Dr HA Lückhoff of the Willowmore cedar, and a survey of its natural distribution in the Baviaanskloof, accompanied by a map showing the different localities, appeared in *Bosbou in Suid-Afrika/Forestry in South Africa*, No 3, October 1963. A follow-up survey was undertaken by researchers at the then Saasveld Forestry Research Centre in the 1980s. Recent field visits by forestry officers confirmed that small but healthy populations of these cedars persist.

Willowmore cedar trees in a narrow ravine, Kouga Mountains, Eastern Cape

Clanwilliam cedar tree in the Uitkyk Pass, Cedarberg, 1936

Exotic cypresses

Exotic trees of many kinds and from many parts of the world are seen in our parks and gardens and especially in graveyards. The Karoo town of Aberdeen boasts a number of beautiful churchyard cypresses (*Cupressus sempervirens* var. *sempervirens*). The beauty of these trees is surpassed only by those in the world-renowned graveyard in Windhoek, Namibia. Dr Fried von Breitenbach once said that cypress trees are planted in graveyards because they are the diehards of the ancient world; they symbolise eternal life and they are the comforting sentinels of the hereafter.

The churchyard cypress in Beaufort West on Stand 582 was declared a national monument in 1982, and is the only one remaining of 25 such trees that were planted in the Dutch Reformed Church graveyard in 1834.

Cypress trees are known as being hardy and really durable. Unfortunately this seems no longer to be true, due to an aphid, *Cinara cupressi*, which attacks them, resulting in dead branches and sometimes causing the whole tree to die. The solution to save members of the cypress family was the introduction of a parasite feeding on the aphid.

TREE FAMILIES

ARECACEAE

The Palm Family

Arecaceae, the palm family, consists of 140 genera and more than 1 000 species, mainly growing in tropical areas. There are exceptions, however – the (real) date palm, which prefers desert conditions with their high degree of daylight intensity, especially for successful fruit production. One of the most remarkable palm trees in the world is the wax palm, a high altitude species, and the national tree of Colombia. With stem diameter of at most 60 cm at the base, these spindly trees tower up to 70 m in the sky – the tallest palm trees in the world.

Palms are not only, as Linnaeus described them, the 'princes of the plant world'; they also count among the most important trees in the world. The date palm (*Phoenix dactylifera*), the coconut palm (*Cocos nucifera*) and the (African) oil palm (*Elaeis guineensis*) are but a few of the economically important palm trees grown worldwide. Palms yield food, oils, wax, flavours, tannin, charcoal, fibre, liquor, building, plaiting and thatching materials and medicine.

Palm trees are also known and grown worldwide for ornamental purposes. With their single and mostly slender stems growing upright, attaining an impressive height in many cases, and crowned with a dense tuft of graceful leaves, palm trees enhance gardens, parks and lined avenues with their stately beauty. Variations in the crown leaves, in particular, enable identification of the various genera and species.

Five palm genera occur naturally in South Africa, all, except the ilala and wild date palms, in very restricted areas. Although of no great economic importance, South Africa's native palms are of considerable local value and importance. The leaves of some species are used extensively for basketry and plaiting, and a potent beer is brewed in some areas from the sap of other species.

One of the tallest and most beautiful of South Africa's palms is **Borassus aethiopum** (**borassus palm** or **Selati palm** or **African fan palm**). The species name *aethiopum* probably refers to the country where it was first encountered, which led to botanists regarding this species as introduced, its distribution in South Africa and Zimbabwe being 'unnatural'. The common name Selati palm, however, testifies to the contrary. The Ga-Selati River rises west of Ofcolaco and flows eastwards, into the Olifants River south of Phalaborwa in Limpopo. 'Selati' was apparently the name of a Shangaan woman.

This difference of opinion almost led to the felling of the only two Selati palms growing in the Kruger National Park. Fortunately what would have been an irretrievable loss was prevented on acceptance of their natural occurrence, and the two trees were left in peace, adding interest to the landscape in the far north-east, i.e. the Pafuri area of the Park.

Other specimens occur naturally only in a small area in the vicinity of Tzaneen in Limpopo. It is a picturesque species, with its smooth, tall, straight and slender stem reaching a height of up to 20 m, and crowned with a tuft of giant fan-shaped bluish-green leaves 4 m long

The palm-nut vulture (*Gypohierax angolensis*) or vulturine fish eagle, feeds mainly on the fruit of the Kosi palm

(petiole included), reaching in all directions, with the dying ones hanging downwards. The sight of these trees among the surrounding Lowveld vegetation is overwhelming and they seem somewhat out of place.

Obviously very rare in South Africa, the Selati palm has also been recorded from other areas in Africa and India. It is a protected plant both in South Africa and Zimbabwe.

The spirit of the Chief

A unique feature of the Selati palm is a conspicuous swelling halfway up the bole. One such tree that grew along the Tzaneen-Leydsdorp road (R36) was believed by locals to house the spirit of Chief Magoeba (also pronounced Makgoba), the last chief of the Batlou tribe, in this bulge. On the death of the tree people were satisfied that Magoeba's spirit was released. A plaque at the spot commemorates this slice of history.

Selati or African fan palm, a rare indigenous palm of the Limpopo Province

Raphia is also a small genus, mainly of Madagascar, tropical Africa and southwards to southern Mozambique, from where one species (*Raphia australis*) seemingly spread to Kosi Bay in northern KwaZulu-Natal, its sole occurrence in South Africa. The word *raphia (raffia)* is derived from the Greek word *raphis*, which means 'needle'. (There is some uncertainty as to which characteristic this refers.) The species name *australis*, which means 'of the south' (Latin), probably refers to its southern distribution.

Raphia australis (**raffia palm** or **Kosi palm**) has a relatively short stem with a maximum height of 10 m, but its crown of massive feather-like leaves, some apparently

Kosi palms showing off their large feather-like leaves

up to 18 m long, can give the tree a height of 28 m. Not surprisingly, these leaves are reported to be among the largest of living plants.

The inflorescence is impressive, too, being 3 m long, rising straight from the centre of the tree. Male and female flowers are borne separately on the same plume-like structure. The tree flowers after 25 to 30 years, and having set fruit, dies off. Between 8 000 and 10 000 fruits develop on the inflorescence, which reaches a total weight of 300 kg. The palm-nut vulture feeds on the fruits and also nests in the palms.

Because this palm grows in swampy soils it develops masses of small breathing roots around the base. It has for many years been utilised by local people, who use the strong midribs of the big leaves to build houses and construct rafts. The usefulness of the Kosi palm as a stream-bank stabiliser has been acknowledged by forestry companies, so that these trees are planted along streams, serving this purpose.

At Mtunzini in KwaZulu-Natal a grove of Kosi palms was planted some 100 years ago by a local magistrate. An official employed for malaria control followed suit and in the course of his work planted seeds wherever he thought was suitable. Many Kosi palms are still to be seen in the Mtunzini area, and the site of the original plantings (the grove near the railway station) was declared a national monument in 1942, owing to its scientific importance.

Jubaeopsis caffra (**Pondo palm**), South Africa's rarest palm, is a small tree (up to 8 m) with a very restricted distribution in the erstwhile Pondoland, Eastern Cape, lining the northern banks of two rivers, the Mcentu and the Msikaba. It is the only species in the genus, and locally it is known as the **Mkambati palm**. It is a multi-stemmed tree, with male and female flowers occurring on the same inflorescence, the male flowers on the upper and the female on the lower parts. The fruit resembles a small coconut, and the hard kernel contains a white meat (endosperm), which is relished by the local people.

Hyphaene coriacea I/L**ala palm** or **gingerbread tree**) is a handsome palm tree with somewhat stiff fan-shaped grey-green leaves. It occurs in the northern parts of the Eastern Cape, KwaZulu-Natal, north-eastern Mpumalanga and Limpopo. This palm is mostly a shrub, forming dense stands, although it occasionally develops into a small tree up to 7 m high. Male and female flowers are borne on separate trees, and fruits are produced profusely – more than 1 000 per tree – consisting of a thin, shiny, dark brown skin when ripe, which covers a layer of edible pulp, followed by a hard fibrous covering over a kernel of vegetable ivory. This was at one stage used for making buttons and for cutting small ornaments.

The ilala palm is an exceptionally useful tree, not only for the fruits, but also for its other parts. The leaves are used to weave baskets, hats, mats and other such articles, while it has been reported that the heart of the tree stem is used as a vegetable. The sap is tapped to brew an alcoholic drink

Ilala palm trees near Shingwedzi rest camp, Kruger National Park

The fruits of the ilala palm tree are favoured by elephants

Date palms established in 1880 at Pella, Northern Cape

Phoenix reclinata (**wild date palm** or **Cape date palm**, also known as **coffee palm** or **feather palm**) has a somewhat wider distribution, growing in damp spots from the Eastern Cape, through KwaZulu-Natal, eastern Mpumalanga and Limpopo, and northwards into Africa.

Unlike those of the real date palm, *Phoenix dactylifera*, the fruits of the wild date palm are poor in quality. The tree itself is, however, extremely useful. Fibres of the stem yield brushes, the fruits are eaten by local people, the sap is extracted for brewing an alcoholic drink, the heart of the crown is eaten, and the leaves are used in weaving and for making the skirts of Xhosa boys taking part in initiation ceremonies.

resembling wine, each tree producing some 50 litres. The growing tip of the tree is cut away to obtain the sap; this unfortunately causes the tree to die.

The leaves, the fruits and the growing tip of the ilala palm are eaten by elephants, and palm swifts nest in the trees.

The wild date is the one indigenous palm tree planted widely in South African gardens, being particularly beautiful when old, with its multiple reclining stems.

On guard: Canary palm trees at the entrance gate of the Mount Nelson Hotel, Cape Town

The 'princes' in the parks

Palm trees, with their dramatic tropical appearance, are sought after as garden items and are important for the garden industry in South Africa. Various species, and exotic species in particular, are planted countrywide, mainly in accordance with their climatic preferences.

Phoenix canariensis (**Canary palm**), a feature of the older parts of many cities and towns, used to be one of the most popular, being prominent in parts of Cape Town such as Camps Bay, where it withstands the severe winds exceptionally well. An avenue of Canary palms leading from the main entrance in Orange Street enhances the stately Mount Nelson Hotel in the Gardens suburb. Parks in other towns and cities also boast specimens of these large, heavy-trunked palms, their crowns of gracefully arching feather-like leaves providing a nesting place to rock pigeons in particular. These birds abound in and around a city like Pretoria, where stretches of the Apies River are lined with Canary palm trees.

A magnificent Canary palm tree avenue at the holiday resort Die Eiland in Upington, Northern Cape, on the southern bank of the Orange River, stretches over a distance of 1 041 m. This Canary palm tree avenue, reputedly the longest of its kind in the Southern Hemisphere, was declared a national monument in 1982.

Members of the genus *Washingtonia* (**petticoat palm**), probably the palms most widely planted in South Africa, grow well in the more arid regions. Two species are usually planted, namely *Washingtonia robusta* (thin-stemmed petticoat palm), with a more slender stem, and *Washingtonia filifera* (thick-stemmed petticoat palm), with

Canary palm trees standing guard in front of Cape Town City Hall

a robust trunk. Not shed, the dead leaves resemble petticoats hanging out underneath the heads of fan-like leaves. The trees also provide nesting to urbanised rock pigeons.

In Cape Town and George, Western Cape, magnificent specimens can be seen of **Sabal palmetto** (**robust cabbage palm**), while excellent specimens of **Butia capitata** (**jelly palm**) can be seen in the Arderne Garden, Claremont; the Company's Garden, Cape Town; St George's Park, Port Elizabeth, and also at the University of Pretoria. This small, attractive palm, native to Brazil, Uruguay and Argentina, has decorative grey-green arching leaves. It is a slow-growing tree, reaching a height of approximately 7 m.

A number of exotic palm tree species, mainly of tropical origin and usually frost sensitive, only thrive in South Africa's warmer, subtropical regions. Many of them have become part of the environment, enhancing the skyline of cities and towns such as Durban, Pietermaritzburg, Phalaborwa, Tzaneen, Louis Trichardt and others.

The 'phoenix' rising from the desert

Probably the best known palm worldwide is *Phoenix dactylifera* (**real date palm**). It is native to the Middle East, where the special climatic conditions necessary for successful fruiting occur in desert regions. Apart from a high degree of daylight intensity, sufficient sustainable underground water is necessary to support the trees growing in the harsh conditions of extremely high temperatures and dry air. The genus name *Phoenix* seems appropriate, referring to the mythical bird that lived in the Arabian desert, and that, after burning itself on a funeral pyre, rose from the ashes with renewed youth. The

Date plantation at Klein Pella in the Northern Cape

vigour with which the trees seem to grow in their preferred severe conditions could well attest to the myth. Incidentally, the traders of the erstwhile countries of Tyre and Sidon, called the Phoenicians, also traded in dates. A linkage between the names of the traders and their product is suspected.

Dry and hot as South Africa is, relatively few areas would provide the conditions required for the date palm to bear fruit. One such area is the lower Orange River region, i.e. the northern part of Bushmanland in the Northern Cape. The area, being half desert, is very sparsely inhabited.

At a site called Henkries, a troop of German soldiers set up camp in 1914 during the invasion of the then German West Africa, now Namibia, by South African forces. Their rations included dates, seeds of which germinated in the soil, with the resultant trees eventually producing tasty fruits. This was the unintentional birth of South Africa's date palm industry. Today the Henkries community are proud of their almost 5 000 date palm trees that provide work for several members of their community through a small industry that has put their settlement on the map. (The Henkries date palms are, however, not the oldest in the country – see insert.)

Other sites of date palms exist, such as Pella, a community some 30 km north-west of the town of Pofadder on the N8 route, which developed from a missionary post into an interesting and charming community, well known for its date palms and annual crop of cleanly packed parasite-free dates. The first date palm trees were established at Pella around 1880.

On the farm Klein Pella, west of Pella proper, Mr Gert Niemöller started experimenting in 1960 with various fodder trees as well as date palms. He found date palms promising and specialised in this crop, importing plant material from the USA in 1978. The present-day owner of Klein Pella has 13 000 date palm trees, of which 50 per cent yield 400 tons of dates annually. With the potential to double production with the existing number of trees, Klein Pella is, and will be, undoubtedly the largest date producer in the country.

Even further west from Pofadder along the N8, after some 64 km, one approaches the mining town of Aggeneys, lying in an area with little more than 100 mm rainfall per year. Aggeneys is a veritable oasis in the dry Bushmanland, boasting a 7 km long avenue of date palms, obtained from Klein Pella, along the entrance road. Date palms also enhance the local golf course. These palms were not planted for their fruit but for decoration.

The town itself is a real 'arbor town' with thriving monkey thorn trees, fever trees, ana trees and river bushwillow. To achieve this, water is pumped over a distance of approximately 40 km from the Orange River.

In addition to the Lower Orange River area and the Ceres Karoo, the Limpopo Valley is an area where dates could be produced and where the former Department of Agriculture had experimented with date palms. The outcome was, however, unsuccessful.

The oldest date palm trees

The oldest *Phoenix dactylifera* trees in South Africa are found quite a long way from Bushmanland. On the farm Elandsvlei, about halfway between Calvinia in the north and Ceres in the south, along the R355 traversing the Ceres Karoo, date palm trees were recorded to bear fruit as far back as 1838. Neither the age of the trees, nor by what turn of fate they happened to be planted at that particular site, is known. Offspring of these trees have been included in the Infruitec Garden.

Fruit of the real date palm

TREE FAMILIES

POACEAE

The Grass Family

The rare southern mountain bamboo on the farm Moolmanshoek, eastern Free State (Photo supplied by Willie Nel)

Poaceae is undoubtedly the most important family in terms of usefulness to man. Just think about all the grains and pastures, without which man would not be able to survive, and the bamboos (giant grasses) important for food, building and crafts, in Eastern countries in particular. Many grasses are used as lawns or as ornamental plants. Kikuyu, *Pennisetum clandestinum*, the grass species probably planted most widely in South Africa, was introduced in 1912 by botanist Joseph Burtt Davy from a single rooted shoot from East Africa. However, owing to its unrestrained spreading, kikuyu is nowadays regarded as a pest in some places.

Bamboos are arborescent grasses (i.e. tree-like in growth or appearance), with approximately 1 200 species found worldwide. They are also the fastest growing plants known, with some reputedly growing 1 m per day, and some species reach a stem diameter of 25 cm and a height of 30 m. The two kinds of Panda bears, big and small, feed almost entirely on the soft shoots of bamboo.

It was in the hollow joint of a bamboo that silkworm eggs were smuggled from China to Constantinople (today's Istanbul in Turkey) during the reign of the Roman Emperor Justinian in the 6th century AD, thereby introducing the silkworm to Western countries.

Only one bamboo species occurs naturally in South Africa, namely ***Thamnocalamus tessellatus*** (**southern mountain bamboo**), endemic to the country and listed in the SA Red Data Book. It is a miniature bamboo 1 to 5 m tall, occurring on the high mountains of the Eastern Cape and KwaZulu-Natal at altitudes between 1 600 m and 2 700 m. The westernmost distribution occurs in the Moolmanshoek Natural Heritage Site in the Rosendal district, Free State. The plant is also being protected in the Evening Star Natural Heritage Site, Clocolan district, Free State. The veins on the leaf surface mark out conspicuous small squares (*tessellate*, from the Latin *tessera* = a small square block used in mosaic). The plant flowers sporadically and then dies.

The holy bamboo of Vendaland, a solitary clump of bamboo found near Thohoyando in Limpopo, is the species ***Oxytenanthera abyssinica*** (**Holy Venda bamboo, Bindura bamboo**). It is used for ceremonial purposes and was probably introduced by ancestors of the Venda from northern countries.

As bamboo does not occur widely in South Africa, the practice of using bamboo extensively is foreign to South Africans. In Eastern countries, where most of the 1 200 species occur, it is used for a great variety of purposes: as food (young shoots), for construction and scaffolding, household goods, musical instruments and furniture, handicrafts and agricultural tools, poles for fencing and fish-pens, walking sticks, banana props, water pipes, fishing rods, laminated flooring, paper, etc. These people's everyday lives depend on bamboo in much the same way as South Africans are dependent on their timber. (An estimated 1 billion people live in bamboo huts in Eastern countries.)

There was a time, though, when bamboo species were planted in South Africa to be used for whip-sticks and fishing rods. Modern living has phased out these uses, with cart and wagon replaced by motor cars and sophisticated glass-fibre fishing rods having made their appearance. In 1975 a bamboo species was planted in the Infruitec Garden to commemorate the whip-stick industry, which was an acknowledged, though informal one in its time.

Exotic bamboo species, common in South African gardens

TREE FAMILIES

LILIACEAE
The Lily Family

Liliaceae is a vast family of 235 genera and between 3 000 and 4 000 species. *Lilium* is derived from the Celtic word *li*, which means 'white'. Hundreds of species of ornamental plants belong to this family, most of them displaying showy flowers. The rootstocks are generally bulbous, cormous or rhizomotous, all transplanting well. It is said that the madonna lily (*Lilium candidum*) is the oldest of all domesticated flowers. The major group of the family is herbaceous, and it also contains vegetables such as asparagus and onions.

A large tree aloe in the Company's Garden, Cape Town

A well-known and widespread genus of this family is the *Aloe*, occurring in Africa, on Madagascar, in the Mediterranean region, in Saudi Arabia and in India. Aloes have been used medicinally since earliest times, and still are today. The name 'aloe' is derived from the Arabic word *alloch*, which means 'bitter'.

Aloes have a long history of domestication and several South African species were cultivated in the Company's Garden in Cape Town, mostly as large shrubs. Twenty eight species were reportedly being cultivated there by 1695.

It might seem strange that plants of the genus *Aloe*, and belonging to the lily family, are classified as trees. Yet, of the approximately 150 *Aloe* species found in southern Africa, 33 reach tree height, most with a single stem and a rosette of fleshy leaves at the top. Spectacular flowers, varying from yellow to orange and red, are borne in branched or unbranched spikes.

Of the 33 aloes classified as trees only three are regarded as 'true' trees: *Aloidendron barberae* (tree aloe), *A. dichotomum* (quiver tree) and *A. pillansii* (bastard or giant quiver tree). A few other species are also described.

Aloidendron barberae (tree aloe) is the largest of all the aloe species, reaching a height of up to 18 m, with

A dazzling flowering quiver tree

a stem diameter of over 2 m at its base. Despite a restricted natural distribution, the popularity of this aloe as a focal point in private gardens and parks has ensured its survival. Massive branches form a well-rounded crown and, together with the pink to orange flowers borne in short spikes on each leaf rosette, the tree catches the eye, lending charm to a garden. A beautiful specimen, planted in 1889, is found in the Company's Garden in Cape Town. Giant specimens also occur in the Barberton (Mpumalanga) area.

The tree aloe occurs along the eastern coastal and higher rainfall areas of South Africa, from Barberton in Mpumalanga to just east of East London in the Eastern Cape, as well as in Swaziland and the southern part of Mozambique. It is often planted by rural communities on their properties as single trees or as a hedge.

Both the quiver tree (*Aloidendron dichotomum*) and its lesser known relative, the giant quiver tree (*A. pillansii*), are inhabitants of the semi-desert areas of the Northern Cape and southern Namibia. Both are protected plants and neither will really thrive in areas out of its natural environment, such as high-rainfall areas, unless special precautions are taken.

Aloidendron dichotomum (quiver tree) is a massive, sturdy aloe reaching a maximum 7 m, with a yellowish tapering trunk of 1 m and more in diameter at ground level, branching and re-branching in twos from about halfway up. (The species name *dichotomum* = dividing into two, refers to this feature.) The bark is smooth and yellow to greyish on the branches. The leaves are arranged in sparse rosettes on the tips of every branch, with canary-yellow flowers borne above the leaf rosettes.

Gertrude Ordman, one-time member of the Tree Society of South Africa, described the quiver tree as '... a naked looking tree. Somehow they seem less weird and strange away from their bare setting'.

The first documentary record of this fascinating tree, distinctive on rocky hills, dates back to 1685. Governor Simon van der

The cat's-tail aloe of the Ohrigstad Valley, Mpumalanga, with a heavy crown of multiple leaf rosettes

Tree Families

Quiver trees planted on the grave of Elizabeth Ashenden at Rooibergdam, Kenhardt, Northern Cape, where she died of tick fever in 1898. Her husband, Percey, an engineer, was at that time constructing the dam. (Photo: Elma le Roux)

Stel first observed that the San hunters used the soft branches as quivers for their arrows – hence the popular name. The flowers produce nectar in abundance, attracting bees and birds, and even baboons. As the quiver tree is one of the bigger trees in the dry Northern Cape, social weavers are attracted to the trees, resulting in their occasionally housing the huge, picturesque nests of these birds.

Several areas where quiver trees occur in large numbers are known as quiver tree forests. Such 'forests' are located on the R27 near Kenhardt in the Northern Cape, between the towns of Pofadder and Pella near the Orange River, and near Keetmanshoop in Namibia – the latter declared a national monument. The largest known quiver tree forest, containing between 6 000 and 8 000 trees, occurs on the Gannabos Natural Heritage Site in the district of Nieuwoudtville, Northern Cape. This is also its southernmost point of distribution.

The distribution range of quiver trees is slowly changing, with trees dying out in its northern distribution range in Namibia, but seemingly faring better in the south. According to some scientists, this phenomenon may be caused by climate change.

Aloidendron pillansii **(giant or bastard quiver tree)** closely resembles its better known brother, although a few differences can be observed. This tree outgrows *Aloidendron dichotomum*, reaching a height of 10 m, and has fewer strongly ascending branches, with bright yellow flowers hanging downwards from the leaf rosettes. Its distribution is even more restricted than that of the quiver tree. The most threatened plant species in Namaqualand, the bastard quiver tree enjoys protection in the Cornellskop Natural Heritage Site near Kuboos in the Northern Cape. (The 'Wondergat', a 50 m deep limestone sinkhole which was, according to Nama mythology, the dwelling of their supernatural hero Heitsi Eibib, is another feature of Cornellskop.)

Kumara plicatilis **(fan aloe)** is a small tree of 3 to 5 m, which also branches dichotomously. It is confined to the sandstone mountains of the southern part of the Western Cape. The leaf clusters are arranged in a fan-like pattern and the leaves have a pleated appearance, which gave rise to the species name *plicatilis*. The inflorescence is unbranched and only one appears on each leaf cluster. This was the first aloe to be illustrated and described, in 1799 in *Curtis's Botanical Magazine*.

Aloe marlothii **(mountain aloe)**, single-stemmed with horizontal flower spikes, is usually 2 to 4 m high, but sometimes develops into trees 8 m tall. On the farm Rietvlei (Mokopane/Potgietersrus district, Limpopo) the average height of these trees is 5 to 6 m, with single specimens reaching 8 m into the sky. A giant aloe like this, with its trunk closely packed with dry leaves and

Giant quiver trees, Cornellskop Natural Heritage Site, Kuboos, Northern Cape

its flower spikes carried horizontally (giving rise to the name 'flat-flowered' aloe) is a spectacular sight. Another single-stemmed species that grows to a height of 8 m is *A. rupestris* (**bottlebrush aloe**).

Strong medicine

Aloes, and in the case of South Africa the *A. ferox* or bitter aloe, are historically important medicinal plants. A substantial industry in the Western and Eastern Cape Provinces is based on the processing of two substances derived from bitter aloe leaves: the bitter yellow juice that exudes from just below the leaf surface, and the aloe gel produced from the inner leaf pulp, which has lately become important in the field of hair and skin care products. The juice is dried, using an age-old method, to form a dark-brown solid known commercially as 'aloe lump' or 'Cape aloes' and is, *inter alia*, used in medicines such as 'Lewensessens'. Bitter aloes planted as hedges in the Eastern Cape form 'stockades' that have become an attractive feature of rural areas. In contrast to the previously mentioned true tree aloe, the bitter aloe, which is also regarded as a tree, has a single stem with a maximum height of 5 metres.

The fan aloe of the fynbos biome spreading its leaves in typical fan-like manner. (First aloe to be described, 1799)

The red flowers of the bitter aloe, Baviaanskloof, Eastern Cape

CANNABACEAE

The Hemp Family

This small family of 170 species includes cannabis (dagga) and hop. *Celtis* is by far the largest genus in the family, with about 100 species. Five *Celtis* species occur in South Africa, including the well-known and popular *Celtis africana* (white stinkwood) and the lesser known and rare *Celtis gomphophylla* (false white stinkwood).

White stinkwood trees in winter, Manie van der Schijff Botanical Garden, University of Pretoria (Photo: MJK, Wikimedia Commons)

Two exotic *Celtis* species, namely *C. sinensis* (Chinese nettle or hackberry) and *Celtis australis* (European nettle or hackberry), were extensively planted in South Africa in the past. These two species hybridise with *Celtis africana* and their planting is therefore discouraged. (Most people know them as white stinkwood.)

Celtis africana (**white stinkwood**) was previously classified under the Elm family (Ulmaceae). It occurs widely in the moister areas of Africa, from the Western Cape to Ethiopia, and develops into large trees of up to 30 m in the forests. It is one of the most popular trees for parks, large gardens and streets in South Africa. At the Fountains

Valley in Pretoria in particular, hundreds of large and small trees can be observed.

Few people will remember the giant white stinkwood tree at the office of the Swartkops golf course. This huge tree had an unusually gnarled trunk and must have been very old. It probably died because of flower beds being created at its base. White stinkwood trees tend to die of a fungus disease *(Ganoderma)* after continuous gardening at their bases.

As most people find it difficult to distinguish between white stinkwood and the nettle trees or hackberries, the main differences are given below:

Table 5: Differences between indigenous and exotic Celtis species

Celtis africana (white stinkwood)	*Celtis sinensis* (Chinese nettle or hackberry)	*Celtis australis* (European nettle or hackberry)
Branches end somewhat pendulous	Branches stiff, upright, spreading	Branches stiff, upright
Leaves soft and hairy, especially when young; upper half finely toothed	Leaves shiny; almost hairless when older; upper half finely toothed	Leaves coarse-haired, dark, dull green; upper half with larger serrations
Berries small and yellow when ripe; approximately 4 mm in diameter	Berries orange-brown when ripe; approximately 7 mm in diameter	Berries black when ripe; approximately 10 mm in diameter

The tree that Mandela planted

In September 2008 the late Mr Nelson Mandela (former president of South Africa and a global iconic leader affectionately known as 'Madiba') planted a white stinkwood (*Celtis africana*) in Thokoza Park in South Africa's largest township of Soweto. This planting took place during Arbor Week as part of the award-winning Greening of Soweto Project launched by the Johannesburg City Parks and Zoo in that year. The tree planting also marked Madiba's 90th birthday. This beautiful tree already stands more than 13 m tall, and forms part of a memorial corner in the park which draws throngs of local and overseas visitors.

TREE FAMILIES

MORACEAE

The Fig and Mulberry Family

Moraceae, the fig and mulberry family, is a very large (more than 1 000 species) and highly interesting family of trees and shrubs of tropical and subtropical regions of the world. The genus *Ficus* (fig trees) is the largest of the six genera in the family, containing some 800 species, with 25 species occurring in South Africa. All figs have a milky latex and terminal bud sheaths protecting the growing point. These sheaths are often brightly coloured. (Readers should note that it is difficult to differentiate between *Ficus burkei* and resembling species. Taxonomic changes, necessary from time to time, tend to aggravate this dilemma.)

Large roots protruding above the ground, typical of many fig species. Moreton Bay fig in the Arderne Garden, Claremont, Cape Town

Fig trees are fascinating because of their extraordinary growth habits. These trees often have very prominent root systems, which may vary in appearance between species, from flared buttressed roots to networks of roots strangling trees or embracing rocks. In appearance some species can be described as 'walking on stilts', while others are 'stranglers' or even 'rock-breakers'. These same species can, however, grow as normal, 'well-behaved' trees under normal circumstances, e.g. when the seed germinates in open land.

Fascinating, too, is the (so-called) fruit of the fig, although those of our indigenous tree species are small and insipid when compared to that luscious specimen of the cultivated *Ficus carica* (the edible fig), probably the oldest cultivated fruit in the world. The fig, i.e. the fruit, is actually a receptacle within which the male and female flowers are found. Pollination is done by wasps entering through the small opening on the under-side of the fig. Apparently a different wasp is responsible for the pollination of each species. The figs are borne on the branches of some species, in others in colourful clusters on broom-like structures on the trunk or branches, and in still others in the leaf axils.

Fig tree leaves can be big or small, almost all are beautiful, and most are shiny. The fruit and leaves of several *Ficus* species were traditionally known and used for their medicinal healing qualities and for their high nutritional value.

A great number of exotic *Ficus* species are cultivated in South Africa. A gigantic ***Ficus macrophylla*** (**Moreton Bay fig**), with part of its roots protruding above the ground, grows in the Arderne Garden in Claremont,

Cape Town. Similar giant specimens of *F. macrophylla* grow in Port Elizabeth's St Georges Park and at Burgers Park and Melrose House in Pretoria. One Willem Wolmarans, a member of President Kruger's cabinet, settled on the farm Donkerhoek, east of Pretoria, completing his home in 1889. Many exotic trees occur on the farm, some probably dating back to the first owner. A Moreton Bay fig, planted in front of the house some time afterwards, developed into a remarkably large tree, adding to the interest of the old house.

Other interesting members of the fig family are the mulberry, known for its fruit, and the jackfruit, with enormous rough-skinned fruit, of which there is a big tree in the Durban Botanical Garden, with several elsewhere in the country. The edible fruit can weigh up to 40 kg and is too heavy to hang on the ends of branches, so is borne on the trunk and on stout branches. Some members of the fig tree family supply timber, like iroko, the timber of *Chlorophora excelsa*, which is imported from West Africa.

The *Ficus* species accounts for many of South Africa's remarkable trees. **Ficus salicifolia (Wonderboom fig)** (= 'wonder tree') is normally a medium-sized spreading tree of up to 9 m, occurring from Gauteng northwards into Zimbabwe. The widely known Wonderboom in Pretoria (City of Tshwane), is actually a complex of 74 trees with a crown cover of 2 233 m². If the fact that it consists of a group of trees is ignored, this fig tree can be regarded as one of South Africa's champion trees with an index figure of 380 (see *The Top Thirty Indigenous Trees of South Africa*).

The method of spreading of the Wonderboom is peculiar and has taken place over a period of about 1 000 years, as was determined by carbon dating. The family group consists of an inner circle of trees, with a second concentric circle having been formed where the drooping branches reached the ground, resulting in new trees springing up. Three of these have given rise to new plants, forming a third circle. One of the wonders of this tree is that it was protected by the indigenous people. Chief Mzilikazi of the Matabele tribe had his kraal close by. It is said that chief Nyabela Mahlanga of the Ndzindza Ndebele was buried under the tree, and there was a belief among some people that the tree derives its growth power from the buried chief. Nyabela was imprisoned by the government of the Zuid-Afrikaansche Republiek in 1883 following an uprising of his people near Roossenekal in Mpumalanga, and released in 1899, whereafter he and some followers settled near Pretoria. He died in 1902.

In spite of its species name, *ingens* (Latin for 'large'), the **Ficus ingens (red-leaved rock fig)** is but a small to medium-sized tree, with the larger specimens tending to be straggling. In spring, when the new bronze-

Pretoria's Wonderboom fig tree in unspoilt surroundings about a century ago

Aerial view of the Wonderboom fig and its green environment (Photo: Christo van der Wath)

Robert Moffat's 'inhabited' red-leaved rock fig tree once offering hospitality by serving as a 'condominium' of 17 huts where Matabele people found protection against dangerous animals

The dense crown of a large red-leaved rock fig, North West

red leaves appear, this deciduous tree is truly an eye-catching sight.

The Moffat 'inhabited' tree, on the farm Bultfontein in the Boshoek area near Rustenburg, North West Province, is regarded as the most famous red-leaved rock fig in South Africa. Robert Moffat, from the London Mission Society, and father-in-law of David Livingstone, was stationed in Kuruman, Northern Cape, from where he undertook a journey in 1829 to Chief Mzilikazi. When passing through the Rustenburg area he saw this tree with 17 huts built in its crown, all standing on poles that reached through the branches. Notches were carved in the poles to allow access to the huts. The reason for erecting this extraordinary 'block of flats' seems to have been fear of lions. The dimensions of this remarkable phenomenon are not of record proportions. The tree was chosen as a refuge against lions only because it was the biggest and most suitable in the vicinity. Another protective measure that Moffat observed during the same trip was that huts – in fact complete villages – were built on poles to protect the inhabitants against lion attacks.

The mode of propagation of the 'inhabited' tree is remarkable. Today the original tree is surrounded by six young red-leaved fig trees that have developed where the branches touched the ground. (The farm Bultfontein was acquired by a German missionary, named Fuls, in 1877. The fifth generation of the Fuls family are still farming on Bultfontein and are protecting the tree.)

A red-leaved fig tree often mistaken for the abovementioned 'inhabited' tree, stood on the farm Boekenhoutfontein in the Rustenburg district, once owned by ZAR President Paul Kruger. When this tree was measured in 1969, it boasted a trunk diameter at breast height of 2,7 m and crown diameter of 29,6 m. Since then the tree has broken into three parts. It is still alive, but only as a tangle of branches. Some of the branches have struck root, and it is hoped that many trees will emerge from the disintegrated giant. This will however only be possible if fires are kept away from the locality.

From the plains some 10 km west of the Pretoria Wonderboom, in the Akasia municipal area, a red-leaved fig tree emerged, with dimensions that stirred the soul, especially bearing in mind that this tree species is known as a small to medium-sized tree. With a height of 14 m, the wonder of this tree lay in its large crown diameter and mode of propagation. The trunk had a diameter of 8,32 m and consisted of 12 branches emerging straight from the ground. The main branches stretched out in all directions for about 17 m. The branch ends fortunately struck root, so that at least 18 new generation red-leaved fig trees are now growing in a circle around what used to be the mother tree – one of them already measuring 7 m in height. (The mother tree died in 1999.) It was a unique experience to stand under this canopy of branches that would cover a residential plot of about 876 square metres!

A worthy successor to this fallen giant was discovered some time ago by Professor Piet Nel on his farm Rooi-ivoor in the Lydenburg/Mashishing district. (The farm now belongs to the Mamokgala Kopi Trust.)

There are many splendid specimens of *Ficus burkei* (**common wild fig**, also known as the **strangler fig**). It is always special to observe the phenomenon of an unsuspecting host tree being strangled by the roots of its guest tree! This is the result of the seeds of *F. burkei* germinating in the fork of branches of the host tree after being dropped there by birds or other animals. Long aerial roots are sent down, twining around the host's stem until they reach the ground, where they root in the soil. The aerial sections then become the stem of the new tree – with fatal results to the host as a result of their thickening and strengthening.

A most remarkable specimen of this kind is to be seen on the farm Modderfontein, in the Rustenburg district (see photograph on front cover). The seed germinated more than a century ago above the lintel of the farmhouse built by the first owners. After the house was burnt down by British soldiers in 1902, seeds germinated in the ruins, and two trunks in the course of time grew over the doorway, outlining it clearly, to join again

The massive girth of a red-leaved fig tree on the farm Rooi-ivoor in the Lydenburg/Mashishing district

Common wild fig trees on the stone walls at Vygekraal farm, Pretoria district

at the top. Some bricks are still captured in the tangle of roots. This particular tree has a bole diameter of 4,5 m and a crown diameter of 30 m. The Modderfontein fig tree is not only a striking proof of reconstruction after a devastating war, but it also serves as a monument to the healing capacity of nature.

Legends of the Bavenda tribe of the Soutpansberg refer to a big tree that grew halfway between the chief's mountain stronghold near the Hanglip peak and the present-day town of Louis Trichardt/Makhado. This tree apparently served as the chief's presence-chamber where he would keep court. Among his visitors he counted General Piet Joubert, head of the Defence Force of the ZAR; Joao Albasini, famous Lowveld pioneer, and others who were desirous of making contact with the Venda people. Many large fig trees, *F. burkei* in particular, are found in the Louis Trichardt area. The 'indaba' tree is probably the one growing on the farm Bergvliet in the district.

Four large common wild fig trees standing in a half-circle on a portion of the farm Zilkaatsnek indicate where the pioneer Ras family had constructed a temporary cattle kraal in 1842. (In those days a kraal built from strong poles planted in the soil was an absolute necessity, to protect domestic animals from lion and other predators.) Some of the poles were cut from a wild fig tree, and they afterwards started to grow. The present owners, the Scribante family, offspring of the Ras pioneers, today enjoy the luxury of a shady farmyard! (The trees were witnesses of war activities in the Anglo-Boer War, when in 1900 troops of General Koos de la Rey made camp under a nearby moepel tree – *Mimusops zeyheri* – during the battle of Zilkaatsnek.)

Eastwards of Zilkaatsnek, still north of the Magaliesberg, more evidence of pioneer habitation is found on the farm Vygekraal, in the form of several stone walls – presumably cattle kraals. Several common wild figs have established themselves on these walls, one of which developed into a shady giant with roots flowing, on both sides, over a wall two metres high. To add to the spectacle the owners of the farm have mounted the base and top of a giant matumi tree (*Breonadia salicina*, mingerhout.) next to the entrance of the kraal. (Matumi does not occur naturally in the Pretoria area, and this giant tree was salvaged from northern KwaZulu-Natal after the destructive Demoina tropical cyclone in 1984 by Mr TAP de Beer, manufacturer of wood jewels.)

A mkhulu (big) tree is the apt description for a very large common wild fig at Mkhulukei Guest Farm near the Kei River mouth, Eastern Cape. It is a major attraction at the farm. (It has still to be measured by dendrologists.)

After the Wonderboom, the next largest known *Ficus* tree in South Africa is a **Ficus sycomorus** (**common cluster fig**, also known as the **sycamore fig**) on the farm Langkloof near Munnik in the Polokwane district, Limpopo. The statistics of this tree are: trunk diameter: 3,94 m; height: 25 m; crown diameter 45,7 m; size index 336. Exactly the same size index has been recorded for yet another sycamore fig, which surpasses the abovementioned in height, but has lesser dimensions in other respects. This tree grows along the Olifants River between Hoedspruit and Phalaborwa on the farm Excellence, near Mica. Another magnificent specimen known as the Ilembe Tree grows near Kranskop in KwaZulu-Natal. This tree has multiple trunks around a hollow interior, measuring 23 m in circumference around the base.

The Bible often mentions the sycamore fig tree. The best-known reference is that of Zacchaeus who clambered up a sycamore tree at Jericho to get a better view of Jesus.

The imposing cluster fig at Ilembe, KwaZulu-Natal (Photo: Enrico Liebenberg)

There are many remarkable sycamore fig trees in Africa, of which the Segeneiti tree in Eritrea is probably the most famous. It grows in the Sycamore Valley and is not only depicted on one of the currency notes of that country but is also a tourist attraction because of its dimensions.

Growing conditions for trees at the confluence of the Limpopo and Shashe Rivers on the South Africa/Botswana/Zimbabwe border are ideal, owing to the annual flooding of the area, which leaves a rich deposit of deep alluvial soil. Here, on the property Shalimpo in Botswana, a common cluster fig has attained dimensions that almost dwarf the Munnik tree. A grave problem in the area is however the abundance of elephants that damage the giant trees. (Many more tree species grow to record size here.) To protect the trees landowners cover the lower trunks with wire mesh. Enormous specimens of sycamore fig trees occur in what was formerly the Vhembe Nature Reserve and Natural Heritage Site, now Mapungubwe National Park (declared 2004) and World Heritage Site (declared 2003) in the Musina district, Limpopo. (At Mapungubwe Hill, an important archaeological site, golden artefacts were discovered, serving as witnesses of a far developed African civilisation that thrived seven centuries ago.) Tree top walks along a raised canopy walk following the riverine forest offer magnificent views of the ana trees growing along the Limpopo River.

A tree with a rather sad history is the 'Ultimatum' tree, a common cluster fig, on the southern bank of the Tugela River in KwaZulu-Natal. This tree was declared a historical monument in 1938 because it was believed that the British issued an ultimatum to the Zulu people on the eve of the outbreak of the Anglo-Zulu War in 1878 under this tree. In 1945 it was discovered to be the wrong tree. It was however still protected as a national monument (declared in 1950), as it was of botanical interest. In 1984 the cyclone Demoina struck and floods destroyed the tree partly, which caused it to deteriorate. The course of the river was altered and the tree then stood in the river course. In 1991 a storm brewed over the rerouting of the Natal North Coast Highway, which would affect a number of historical sites, including this tree. It was decided to fell the tree and to leave a suitable stump. The rest of the tree was cut into pieces and distributed to several institutions. In 1993 the Natal Regional Committee recommended that Government Notices declaring it a historical and national monument be withdrawn.

An extraordinary *Ficus cordata*, the **Namaqua fig**, grows on the farm Abasas in northern Bushmanland, Northern Cape. Although the Namaqua fig usually grows on rocks, this tree grows in deep fertile alluvial soil, which accounts for its gigantic

Wild fig trees, 'exhibitionists of the plant world', a heart-leaved fig at Umtentweni, KwaZulu-Natal

Lonely Namaqua fig along the Orange River on the farm Abasas, Northern Cape (Photo: Jacoline Mans)

dimensions: trunk diameter at breast height 4,78 m, height 17 m, and mean crown diameter 32,5 m. It was reported that the Abasas tree was almost completely inundated during the flood of 1974. Fortunately it recovered completely from this watery ordeal.

Banyan figs are fig trees raised on stilt-roots dropped from the main horizontal branches. This is necessitated by the particular locality of these trees, which is coastal and swamp forest. This explains the common nature of the only banyan species in South Africa, **Ficus trichopoda** (**swamp fig**), occurring in KwaZulu-Natal and northwards along the East African coast. As this distribution roughly coincides with that of the hippopotamus, the same name is used in isiZulu for both the tree and the hippo. This had led to the tree previously being described as *F. hippopotami*.

The monster fig of Calcutta

Ficus benghalensis, the (Indian) banyan tree, has had the reputation since earliest times of becoming a big tree. According to legend, the whole army of Alexander the Great once set up camp underneath a banyan tree.

A giant specimen of *F. benghalensis* can be seen in the Durban Botanical Garden. This tree is however a mere dwarf in comparison with one of the same species growing in the Calcutta Botanical Garden. According to the curator of the Calcutta Garden, this monster tree, which is 232 years old, is their main attraction. Apparently a seed germinated in a palm tree even before the Botanical Garden was established in 1787. In 1925 the main trunk had to be removed because it was attacked by a fungus disease. Fortunately the disease did not spread to the rest of the tree, with its forest of prop roots. Today this tree, with its highest point a sizeable 40 m, has spread over an area of 22 165 m^2 (2,2 ha), with more than 2 800 prop roots with diameters varying from 7 cm to 80 cm, thus creating a mini forest of its own.

PROTEACEAE
The Protea Family

Proteas are, for various reasons, held in high esteem by South Africans. The Proteaceae plant family is also well known far beyond our borders. The family is composed of 60 genera and about 1 300 species, abundantly represented in South Africa and Australia, in particular, and to a lesser extent in other parts of the Southern Hemisphere. This distribution is of great importance as possible proof of a former close land connection between the two continents (Gondwanaland). No African genus or species occurs naturally in Australia, however (or elsewhere in the world), while Madagascar is home to a member of the indigenous South African genus *Faurea*.

Proteaceae, especially proteas, have superb cut flowers that keep their colour for weeks and retain their shape even longer. Proteaceae from South Africa and Australia are nowadays cultivated in many parts of the world for the flower market. The wood of the Proteaceae is beautiful, owing to the attractive wide medullary rays, resembling oak timber. The only food plant of significance among the Proteaceae is the Macadamia nut (*Macadamia integrifolia*), originally from Australia.

Fourteen genera, containing over 300 species, are found in South Africa, the majority concentrated in the south-western Cape, where they form a large part of the fynbos, i.e. the Cape Floristic Kingdom or Fynbos Biome, which is restricted to that part of the country. For the rest, Proteaceae genera and species are scattered over many parts of the country, usually in mountainous areas, where they often grow in poor soils on rocky hillsides or bare mountains, as shrubs or sometimes as trees. Trees occur only in the six genera *Protea*, *Leucadendron*, *Leucospermum*, *Brabejum*, *Faurea* and *Mimetes*. Owing to the strong association of the name 'protea', it is applied popularly to all the species occurring in the South African genera, whereas *Protea* only refers to the particular genus.

The name 'protea' is derived from that of the Greek mythological god Proteus, who could, according to legend, change his appearance at will. Carl Linnaeus, the father of botanical terminology, used this name to

Pride of the Protea family – 'my big brother is a tree' – the king protea, South Africa's national flower

describe the diversity in the appearance of these plants. (The family name Proteaceae comes from that of the genus *Protea*, which was first described.) Their brightly coloured, exceptionally beautiful flowers, totally unfamiliar in the Northern Hemisphere, first attracted the attention of early seafarers round the Cape. The first description and drawing of *Protea neriifolia* appeared in 1605 in a publication in Antwerp, Belgium, although it was mistakenly described as a thistle from Madagascar.

Protea: Sugarbushes

The genus *Protea*, with its exquisite flower inflorescences, occurs only in Africa, where it is mainly concentrated on the southern tip of the continent. Twenty seven *Protea* species are classified as trees.

Plants from the *Protea* genus generally have long, slender, tough, evergreen and often stalkless untoothed leaves, usually arranged spirally. The 'flowers', for which they are so popular, are actually inflorescences or

The krantz sugarbush on the Cocks Comb mountains near Port Elizabeth, Eastern Cape – an elusive protea seen in nature only by those who dare it on the high peaks of the Western and Eastern Cape (Photo: Donnie Erlank)

clusters of flowers, known as 'flowerheads'. Their brilliance is not due to the flowers, which are small and packed closely in large numbers in the heart of the bracts, but to the multicoloured bracts, i.e. (sometimes) bearded involucral leaves surrounding the small flowers and resembling petals. The flowers are pollinated mainly by birds, many of which, like the Cape sugarbird, are specifically adapted to extracting the nectar with their long bills; in some cases insects and even rodents perform this function.

Cultivation of proteas, both for the local and overseas markets, has become an important industry in South Africa as well as in countries such as Australia, America and Israel. Centuries ago, from about 1760, growing proteas was fashionable in England, when King George III took an interest. This craze was followed not only by wealthy English merchants and the nobility, but also spread to France, where Josephine, the wife of Napoleon Bonaparte, started cultivating proteas. She was so enthusiastic about her hobby that, together with another grower, she employed a botanist who was charged with the task of collecting South African *Protea* seed.

Eighteen *Protea* tree species occur in the winter rainfall regions and nine in the summer rainfall regions, where they grow in harsh conditions on mountain slopes.

The best known of the winter rainfall *Protea* tree species is **Protea nitida (wagon tree** or **tree protea)**. This is one of the tallest of the genus, reaching 7 m. It grows on Table Mountain, northwards to the Cedarberg and eastwards to approximately Uniondale and is a familiar sight alongside many of the mountain roads of the Cape, such as through Du Toits Kloof and the Pakhuis Pass, where it displays its blue-green foliage. The name 'wagon tree' derives from the use of the wood for making felloes (rim segments) of wagon wheels. For some time good charcoal was produced from the wood and, later on, pipe stems and bowls were manufactured at Uniondale. The bark was formerly used for tanning as well as for medicinal purposes.

Wagon trees and cone bushes colouring the sandstone mountainside of the Cedarberg, Western Cape (Photo: Zane Erasmus)

One of the most familiar *Protea* tree species in the summer-rainfall regions is **Protea caffra** (**common sugarbush**, also called the **Highveld protea** or **Natal sugarbush**). The common names indicate its main areas of occurrence. This rather unassuming small, sturdy, gnarled tree, seldom exceeding 6 m in height, with its spreading branches, short, dark and rough trunk and blue-green foliage, is very attractive when the flowers are fresh, but the old heads remain on the tree for some time, giving it an unkempt appearance. Nevertheless, this *Protea* species is responsible for a range of hills in Gauteng being called the Suikerbosrand/t and for the existence of the Suikerbosrant Nature Reserve near Heidelberg – a refuge for the city dweller and nature lover. ('Suikerbos' = sugarbush.)

With its flower heads consisting of whitish and greenish to brownish outer bracts and pinkish white to red inner bracts, *P. caffra* may be confused with **Protea gaguedi** (**African white sugarbush**), which it resembles in many aspects, although the latter has smaller leaves and longer and broader flower buds.

Protea gaguedi prefers warmer areas, often rocky soils, although, with a wide distribution, it occupies widely varying habitats. It occurs from the Soutpansberg in Limpopo through North West Province, Gauteng, Mpumalanga and Swaziland into KwaZulu-Natal and northwards into Africa. It is very common in Ethiopia. Under favourable conditions this tree, generally small and gnarled, may rise up to 7 m. It is the only *Protea* found in Namibia, on one site along the Okavango River.

Probably the most widespread of the summer-rainfall *Protea* species is **Protea roupelliae** (**silver sugarbush** or **Drakensberg protea**). Also a small, gnarled but attractive tree, it occurs on grassy hills and mountain slopes where it often forms small patches of *Protea* woodland – growing from sea-level at Port St Johns in the Eastern Cape to an altitude of over 2 000 m in the Natal Drakensberg, in the Golden Gate National Park in the Free State, and in the Blouberg Nature Reserve as well as on the northern Drakensberg. It occurs sparsely on the Magaliesberg close to Pretoria and Johannesburg. The young leaves are silvery, hence the common name. The flower heads are large and sometimes almost hidden among the leaves. At its most colourful, it is a very attractive species, which caught the attention of a Mrs Roupell, who produced a book of flower paintings, *Cape Flowers by a Lady*, in 1849. The species was named after her.

Silver sugarbush in the Wolkberg near Tzaneen, Limpopo

Leucadendron: Cone- and Yellow bushes

The genus *Leucadendron* consists of approximately 100 species, of which eleven can be regarded as small trees, all mainly concentrated in the Fynbos Biome.

The common names 'yellow bush' and 'conebush' given to members of the genus refer respectively to the colour of the leaves around the flowering heads and the little female 'cones', either because they spin when kicked or because they resemble little tops, according to folklore. Conebush foliage is particularly popular in flower arrangements.

Leucadendron species are dioecious, i.e. having the male and female flowers on separate plants. The male flowerheads are loose, spherical and not cone-like, while the female flowers are set in cone-like heads formed by overlapping bracts.

The genus owes its name to its most striking member, **Leucadendron argenteum (silver tree)** that used to grow in large numbers on the lower mountainsides of the Cape Peninsula. Remnants in their natural state can still be seen on the slopes of Lion's Head, Orange Kloof and at the Kirstenbosch National Botanical Garden. Fortunately it also naturalised on the Paarl Berg and Simonsberg near Stellenbosch, as well as in the Silwerboomkloof Natural Heritage Site on the foothills of the Helderberg, Somerset West. Early Dutch colonists called this tree *witteboom* (white tree); thus *leucadendron*, from the Greek *leukos* = white and *dendron* = tree.

The most outstanding characteristic of the silver tree (*argenteum*=silvery) is its foliage. The extraordinary silver sheen on the leaves gives forth a vivid silver glittering appearance in summer, which resembles the play of light on a mirror. This can be ascribed to the fine silky hairs covering both sides, which serve as a protective 'layer' against excessive transpiration, and are drawn flat in sunny weather while half raised in rainy weather, to allow the leaves to transpire freely – hence the dull appearance in winter. The silver leaves are sought after to enhance floral arrangements, or merely as souvenirs.

The silver tree or 'witteboom', endemic to the Cape Peninsula and inland about as far as Paarl and Stellenbosch

The tree is generally small, 5 to 7 m high, although it can reach 16 m under ideal conditions. It has a slender, graceful appearance and is popular as a garden tree, provided conditions are suitable. The bark is grey, smooth, with distinctive leaf scars, while the wood is soft and spongy, and therefore of little use generally.

In spite of its exceedingly limited distribution and having decreased in numbers as a result of increasing urbanisation in the Cape Peninsula, the silver tree can be grown elsewhere. As early as 1693 it was cultivated successfully in England. It has been described as 'probably the Cape's finest gift to South Africa's gardens as a whole'. The silver tree was the tree emblem of the former Cape Province.

Leucospermum: Pincushion trees and bushes

The genus *Leucospermum*, consisting of more than 40 species, is centred in the south-western and south-eastern parts of South Africa, with the largest concentration (30 per cent) in a narrow strip on the Bredasdorp (Western Cape) coast. While the genus name *Leucospermum* refers to the white seeds, the common name of 'pincushions' refers to the flower heads packed with narrow tube-shaped flowers with protruding styles, each ending in a club- or cone-shaped pollen presenter, thus altogether closely resembling pincushions. Some of these pincushions are as beautiful as the proteas, and often more striking in a landscape, because of the abundance of their bloom. The flower heads also produce nectar copiously, attracting mainly various sunbirds, as well as insects and beetles. The fruits somewhat resemble ticks, and this gave rise to the common Afrikaans name *luisiesboom* ('tick tree'), applied loosely to several of the species.

Six *Leucospermum* species are classified as trees, which often grow multi-stemmed from

The green tree pincushion, abundant in the Cape Point Nature Reserve

the two subspecies of *Leucospermum conocarpodendron* trees (**subsp.** *conocarpodendron* and **subsp.** *viridum*) that may reach 5 m. Both are exceptionally fire resistant, developing rounded, umbrella-shaped crowns, as a result of fires, with crooked and interlocking branches, and brilliant yellow flowerheads. This was the first species of *Leucospermum* to be described.

Leucospermum reflexum (**rocket pincushion**), which reaches 5 m in height, is most showy when in flower. The individual small flowers in the flowerhead are bent backwards and downwards, hence the species and common names.

the base. This accounts for the Afrikaans common names of *kreupelhout/kreupelboom/bos* ('gnarled tree/bush'). This applies to

Mimetes: Cape bottlebrushes

Two *Mimetes* species are classified as trees: *M. arboreus* (Kogelberg silver bottlebrush) and *M. fimbriifolius* (fringed bottlebrush). The common name 'bottlebrush' describes the inflorescence of these plants. **Mimetes arboreus** (*arboreus* = tree-like) occurs only in the Kogelberg Mountains near Betty's Bay, Western Cape, at a height of 1 000 m or more, reaching up to 6 m, with a heavy main trunk branching from about 1 m. This, together with its denser rounded crown consisting of short, recurrently forking branches, clearly distinguishes *M. arboreus* from the **silver bottlebrush** (*M. argenteus*) – formerly thought to be the same species.

Mimetes fimbriifolius (**fringed bottlebrush**) is a sturdy, rather gnarled small tree, compact (dense) and spreading, reaching 4 m, with a stem diameter of 20 cm. The leaves are densely fringed (= *fimbriifolius*), which distinguishes it from the shrub *M. cucullatus*, with which it often hybridizes. The flowers are greenish-yellow, surrounded by reddish hairy bracts, but almost hidden by the leaves. This species is endemic to the extreme south-western Cape region, occurring on the Cape

The rare fringed bottlebrush, a small tree of the Cape Point Nature Reserve

Flats, but most abundant at Cape Point, where the visitor may also watch sunbirds and sugarbirds extracting nectar from the flowers.

Brabejum

This genus consists of only one species: *Brabejum stellatifolium* (**wild almond tree**). It is unique, also in the sense that, according to written records, it was the first indigenous tree to be cultivated in South Africa. It is a densely growing shrub or tree, reaching up to 8 m in height (the tallest specimen recorded reached 9 m), with its natural distribution restricted to the Western Cape, where it flourishes, particularly along streams. This was thought to be the ideal tree to plant for hedges and for windbreaks, and so the first Dutch settlers at the Cape of Good Hope planted a hedge of wild almond trees to serve both as a boundary to their settlement and as a protection from cattle thieves. This was recorded in 1660 in the diary of their commander, Jan van Riebeeck. One hundred years after the planting of this hedge, the wild almond was named by Linnaeus. Fragments of the hedge may still be seen; the sections that occur within the National Botanical Garden at Kirstenbosch and on Wynberg Hill were both proclaimed national monuments in 1936. The original hedge was 13 km long, but suburban development in Claremont and Rondebosch resulted in its extermination in these areas. A second stretch of the hedge still exists near Klaassen Road, Bishopscourt, and was declared a national monument in 1945.

The 'almond' refers to the fruits that resemble those of the cultivated almond. Roasted kernels were used as a coffee substitute at one time. The wild almond is distinguished from the other Proteaceae in that it is the only stone-fruit bearer; the rest of the family bear small, dry nuts. The leaves are the most distinguishable feature of this tree; long, lance-shaped, irregularly toothed, with a prominent midrib, and arranged in whorls of four to six – hence the species name *stellatifolium*, which describes their star-like appearance. In the absence of flowers the tree can be identified by the large light-green leaf whorls. The flowers are sweetly scented, creamy coloured, and abundant in spikes/clusters in the axils of the upper leaves. The wild almond is indeed a beautiful tree, worthy of extensive cultivation and protection. (*Brabejum* is, interestingly, the only South African Proteaceae representative bearing a close relationship to the Australian members.)

Remnants of the 13 km long wild almond hedge planted in 1660, still flourishing

Faurea: African boekenhout (formerly beeches)

Four *Faurea* species are classified as trees: *F. saligna*, *F. galpinii* (forest boekenhout), *F. macnaughtonii* (terblanz beech) and *F. rochetiana* (= *F. speciosa*) (broad-leaved boekenhout). Their leaves are all lanceolate, differing in width in accordance with the particular species, and the flowers are bisexual, borne in terminal, solitary spikes, while the fruit is a nut with a tuft of hairs.

Faurea saligna (**Transvaal/bushveld/African/red boekenhout**) is popular for its valuable general-purpose timber, especially on game farms in Limpopo. It is usually a slender, graceful, small to medium-sized tree, but reaches 20 m in the KwaZulu-Natal bushveld. It is not restricted to wet, high-lying areas, unlike the other three species, but is rather associated with sourveld.

TREE FAMILIES

FAGACEAE

The Beech Family

Oaks (*Quercus* species), beech (*Fagus*) and chestnuts (*Castanea* species) all belong to the beech or Fagaceae family, regarded by some as the 'royal family' of broad-leaved trees. The family contains both evergreen and deciduous trees, characterised by their fruits. These may either be a nut enclosed in a cup (oaks), a burr (beech) or a chestnut (chestnuts).

A number of oaks produce edible acorns, of which it was said many centuries ago that in years of scarcity a good crop could mean wealth to a nation. Acorns formed part of the food of early mankind. In South Africa they are only used as animal feed, particularly for pigs. The genus name *Quercus* originates from *choiros*, the Greek word for pig, while 'acorn' is derived from 'oak-corn'.

No member of the beech family is native to South Africa, yet the family has played an important role in the history of the country. Slow growers in their native Western Europe, oak trees provided the required quality of timber needed for ship-building during the pre-steel era, thus playing a part in conveying many hundreds of colonists and slaves to the shores of this country. Tree lover and nature

The Vergelegen English oak tree at Somerset West, more than 300 years old

conservationist Governor WA van der Stel was responsible for the planting of the oldest still existing oak tree in South Africa (*Quercus robur*, an **English oak**) at his estate Vergelegen – now about 300 years old and verily showing its age.

It was this same WA and not his father Simon van der Stel, as popular belief goes, who initiated the establishing of English oaks as street trees in Stellenbosch – first a wagon-load full in 1701, followed by similar batches in 1709 and again in 1711. In 1797, however, most of these trees were felled and the timber was sold. The old oak trees lining the streets of Stellenbosch today were planted after that date, and they therefore boast an age of about two centuries.

As they have done during centuries past, the oak tree-lined streets are still responsible for that special atmosphere characteristic of the 'Eikestad' (Oak City), as Stellenbosch is lovingly called. Small wonder, therefore, that the English oak trees along a number of streets in Stellenbosch were declared national monuments in 1968.

Oak trees in Swellengrebel Street, Swellendam, Western Cape, were declared a national monument in 1955. Some of these trees are still the original ones planted some 250 years ago.

Another Western Cape national monument oak tree, declared in 1936, is the reputed 'Slave tree'. An English oak standing in front of the old library in York Street, George, is claimed to be one of the biggest specimens in the Southern Hemisphere. The tree was planted in 1811 by Landdrost van Kervel when laying out the town. Apparently slaves used to be tied to the chain still embedded in the tree trunk, with the old lock attached to it. These claims are rebutted from some quarters, though, thus increasing the mystery surrounding the tree. (Part of the crown has collapsed due to rot.)

Oak trees are widespread in temperate countries, more so than any other broad-leaved tree. They are evergreen or deciduous, some being shrubs, but most becoming big

A tree doctor at work on one of the precious old oak trees in George. This tree, known as the 'Slave tree', lost part of its crown

The historic English oak trees of Dorp Street, Stellenbosch

trees. In their countries of origin the *Quercus* species may live for 500 years or more, but the harsher South African climate will not allow such extreme ages. On the one hand the trees will grow faster in higher temperatures, while on the other they are exceedingly susceptible to leaf and wood fungi attacks.

A region more suited to growing conditions for the oak tree is the eastern highveld of Mpumalanga. Large clumps of English oak in the Ermelo and neighbouring districts are witnesses to the unflagging enthusiasm of Dr Aart Jurriaanse, a Dutch physician who gave medical services to the Boer forces during the Anglo-Boer War. After the war he settled in Ermelo, and upon realising the possibilities of the oak as a fodder tree, he launched a full-scale campaign to establish *Quercus robur* on his farm Kralingen and elsewhere in the area. His son and namesake, a forestry scientist, was responsible for the planting of 16 species of *Quercus* as street trees in the town of Sasolburg, Free State. Sasolburg thereby became the third 'Oak City' in South Africa, after Stellenbosch and Potchefstroom (North West). The oak tree was declared Tree of the Year by the Forestry Branch of the Department of Environment Affairs in 1990. In 1991 Sasolburg received the prestigious Arbor City Award from the Forestry Branch and the Institute for Parks and Recreation. In this same year the three 'Oak Cities' signed an agreement of mutual co-operation and loyalty.

An English oak avenue of 6,84 km in Potchefstroom, North West Province, reputedly the longest in the Southern Hemisphere, was declared a national monument in 1977. The trees were planted in 1910 and those along what was Tom Street, now Steve Biko Street, in particular, developed into a beautiful tunnel-like avenue. The trees were previously pruned to fit in below an overhead power line. After the removal of the power line the trees developed beautiful, dense, branchy crowns. An interesting story concerns this avenue that, incidentally, does not follow a straight line. Apparently one of the Town Council members was an employee at the local Agricultural College and he travelled there daily by bicycle. Following the route of

Steve Biko (Tom) Street, lined with English oak trees, Potchefstroom (Tlokwe municipality), composing, together with Stellenbosch and Sasolburg, South Africa's 'Oak City' trio

his daily bicycle ride, the avenue starts where he used to live and more or less stops where he worked. The Honourable Council Member preferred to travel in shade in summer and therefore initiated this unique avenue.

Oakdene, currently known as Pretorius House, probably the oldest existing house in Potchefstroom, dating back to 1853, was declared a national monument in 1987. It is generally accepted that the two oak trees standing in the farmyard were planted in 1868 by the first President of the Zuid-Afrikaansche Republiek (ZAR), Marthinus Wessel Pretorius, the founder of Pretoria.

Two English oaks, planted in 1860 on what was then the farm of General Piet Joubert of the ZAR, situated in what is now the Pretoria suburb Villieria, were at a stage known as 'Twee Eike' (Two Oaks), well known to residents on account of a tea garden that was run on the premises. Incessant rains in 1994 caused one to be uprooted, which led to the name change: 'Die Eik' (The Oak). The survivor has not been officially measured yet, but should probably rank among the largest English oaks in the country, being quite impressive to see. Near Die Eik, on part of the original property, a giant water oak (*Quercus nigra*) can be seen – apparently also planted by General Joubert.

Apart from these, a number of other trees belonging to the genus *Quercus* in South Africa are worthy of mention, such as an exceptionally big oak tree that can be seen on the western slopes of the Riebeek Kasteel mountains, Western Cape.

TREE FAMILIES

The northern Free State is a part of the country where the climate somewhat resembles that of native countries of the oak. On the farm Walton in the district of Harrismith two rows of English oak trees had enhanced the elegant sandstone homestead. During the Anglo-Boer War this house was not burnt in the scorched earth campaign, but was used as officers' quarters. Many of the oak trees were felled for firewood by the British officers. The tree closest to the homestead however escaped the axe and developed into one of the biggest oak trees in the country with a trunk diameter of 1,6 m, height of 24 m and crown diameter of 34 m.

This giant survivor, planted together with the 'casualties' in about 1882 by Mr Gert Jacobs, was cared for by the Jacobs generation, who had to reinforce a number of its branches to prevent them from breaking. Tree and homestead still present an exquisite twosome.

The 'Tree of Assemblage' ('Boom van Samekoms'), an English oak with strong historical associations, could be seen on the farm Blydskap, some 3 km from Kestell in the Free State, until 1991, when it was struck by lightning. (A new tree was propagated to replace the historical forebear.) The tree was apparently planted in 1838 by Voortrekker leader Piet Retief. From 1887 church services were conducted in its shade, and during the Anglo-Boer War General Christiaan de Wet occasionally made use of the tree as his 'headquarters'. In 1905 a meeting was held under the tree, when the town of Kestell was founded, and in October 1999 a peace torch, made from the wood of the tree, was lit there, to be carried to Bloemfontein for the

A giant water oak in Villieria, Pretoria, presumed to be planted in the late 1800s by General Piet Joubert of the ZAR

171

commemoration of the start of the Anglo-Boer War. The oldest inhabitant of Kestell was a Mrs Anna Susanna van Graan, who was baptised under the Tree of Assemblage in 1901. The water used for the baptism came from the fountain on the farm.

Both the town of Cradock in the Eastern Cape, as well as its district, are home to a number of **holly oaks** (*Quercus ilex*) – that tantalising tree from which Virgil's Aeneas picked the golden bough that would allow him entrance to the underworld and finally to the Elysian fields, where he was to meet the spirit of his father. Number 101, Church Street, Cradock, boasted a holly oak 19 m high, with a trunk diameter of 1,79 m and crown width of 24,9 m. This tree, presumably planted in 1850 by one Charles Scanlen, sadly did not survive a fire started – unintentionally – at its base.

The holly oak is an evergreen tree with dark green leaves, making it remarkably beautiful. Fortunately its beauty did not go unnoticed and today several younger specimens grace the town and farms in the district.

The **cork oak** (*Quercus suber*) is occasionally encountered in South African parks and gardens. Bezuidenhout Park in Johannesburg boasts the largest grove of cork oaks in the city, while a 'grandfather cork oak presents his mighty boughs to all entering Old Edwardians clubhouse', according to Mike Alfred (How green is my city, in *Saturday Star*, March 4, 2000).

The cork oak is native to Mediterranean countries and yields cork, produced from the bark. South Africa's wine industry imports millions of cork bottle stoppers every year. At one stage farmers in the Western Cape, a region of similar climatic conditions to the Mediterranean, were encouraged to plant cork oak trees in avenues and windbreaks on farms for the production of cork locally. Many cork oak trees were indeed planted but the project was eventually discontinued.

In March 2000 South Africa's largest known cork oak tree, growing in the garden at Groote Schuur, the Presidential residence in Cape Town, unexpectedly toppled over. The tree had attained giant proportions of more than 20 m in height, a 2,4 m stem diameter and an enormous crown diameter. Its early history is however not known. This giant, that had withstood all the fierce winds of the Cape for definitely more than a century, maybe two or even more, collapsed on a windless day with an ear-deafening crash. Gardeners who were busy cleaning a fountain in its shade had to flee for their lives. The only casualty was a man who collided with a pillar.

Magnificent **purple beech trees** (*Fagus sylvatica* var. *purpurea*) enhance the small Mpumalanga town of Dullstroom. One of these trees boasts a height of 20 m, bole diameter of 1,08 m and crown spread of 20 m. Several **green beeches** (*F. sylvatica*) with slightly bigger dimensions are also thriving there, as well as the typical European lime or linden trees. The trees, probably more than 100 years old, were presumably brought to Dullstroom by an immigrant from Europe who missed the trees of his northern homeland.

The **Spanish chestnut** (*Castanea sativa*) is a member of the beech family that is sometimes encountered in the cooler parts of the country, such as in Dullstroom and on the farm Ashmole Dales near Haenertsburg, Limpopo. There the Sacco family, immigrants from Italy, planted a great number of Spanish chestnuts. At one stage chestnut flour was marketed from there, but the demand was low. Pockets of chestnuts for human consumption were delivered to the fresh produce market of Johannesburg. The bulk of the production is however turned into cattle feed. (Ashmole Dales first belonged to a Mr Cooper of England, of animal medicine fame. Products such as Cooper's Dip were extensively used in South Africa to combat ticks. Mr Cooper himself however never set a foot on this property.)

The trunk of an old cork oak, Arderne Garden, Claremont (Photo: Marie Vrei/Friends of the Arderne Garden)

The biggest known chestnut tree in South Africa once grew near the town of Randfontein, Gauteng. The owner of the tree described it as '... a moody tree with many faces'. In their lush green summer outfit the branches tended to sag a little. This was followed by a profusion of bee- and other insect-ridden creamy flowers, which added another burden to the branches. When in fruit, the heavily laden branches bent towards the ground and some even touched it, only to rise again after the fruits had been shed.

In his *Historia Naturalis,* Gaius Plinius Secundus (Pliny the Elder), born AD 23, wrote extensively about oak trees and Roman laws relating to them. One of the laws was that the owner of a tree could gather the acorns of his tree even if they had fallen on his neighbour's land. He pointed out that acorns formed the chief wealth of many nations and in times of scarcity the edible acorns would sometimes be ground into flour from which bread was baked. Apparently acorns are still being roasted for human consumption in Italy today. (Pliny was always in pursuit of knowledge and this brought an end to his life. When Mount Vesuvius erupted in AD 79, Pliny was commander of the fleet at Misenum in the Bay of Naples. He ordered a light vessel to take him closer to the spectacle and took refuge on the southern shore of the bay. He was overcome by sulphur fumes and died on the beach.)

A green beech tree (left), probably the largest of its kind in South Africa, Dullstroom, Mpumalanga

PORTULACACEAE
The Portulaca/Purslane Family

The Portulacaceae family contains annuals, perennials and only two tree species, both native to South Africa. The summer annual commonly known as portulaca (also moss rose or sun plant: *Portulaca grandiflora*) is well known in many countries because of its brilliantly coloured flowers. The flat-growing weed purslane with fleshy leaves and stems is regarded as a gourmet dish among the French and Mexicans.

Porkbush, a valuable fodder tree of the valley bushveld of the Eastern Cape (Photo: Geoff Nichols)

South Africa's two portulaca trees are both the only species in their genus. *Portulacaria afra*, the **porkbush (spekboom)**, occurs in abundance in the Eastern Cape, and also northwards through the eastern parts of KwaZulu-Natal to Limpopo. Well-conserved porkbushes dominate the Rietvlei Natural Heritage Site near Oudtshoorn, Western Cape. Another unique feature of this Site is the 'Rooikoppe' (Red Hills), with their impressive rock formations.

The porkbush is a succulent shrub or small tree of up to 5 m. In the Eastern Cape in particular it serves as fodder; hence the alternative common name of **elephant's food**. Where thatching grass was uncommon in the Fish River Valley of the Eastern Cape, the local people used to thatch their huts with the dried and beaten branches of the porkbush.

When in flower, the porkbush is an exceptionally beautiful sight, being covered in small star-shaped purplish-pink flowers. It has a long garden history, having been introduced into English and Dutch gardens more than two centuries ago. It grows easily and is one of the species planted traditionally by rural people, often as hedges. Because it is so widely cultivated, it is sometimes difficult to determine whether it occurs naturally in an area, or has been introduced. (See *Protecting our Tree Heritage* for its further qualities.)

Ceraria namaquensis (**Namaqua porkbush**) is a strange-looking small tree of up to 4,5 m, occurring only in a small area of the Northern Cape (Namaqualand) and adjacent Namibia. The tree is mostly multi-stemmed from the base, with a somewhat waxy silver-grey or yellow bark. The branches are covered with small nodes, described by botanists as very reduced side branches on which tiny succulent leaves (± 5 mm long) occur in tufts. When in flower, the Namaqualand porkbush is adorned with attractive pale-pink small flowers.

This small desert tree is also known as *Hotnotsriem* (Hottentot thongs), derived from the past custom of the bark being used as cordage or thongs by the Nama people.

The Augrabies National Park is one locality accessible to the public where the Namaqua porkbush can be observed. The seemingly leafless tree fits in with the bare landscape of this unique semi-desert park.

Namaqua porkbush, a rare small tree of the Northern Cape, 'on the rocks' in the Augrabies National Park

LAURACEAE

The Laurel or Avocado Family

Lauraceae is a mainly tropical and subtropical family of great beauty and economic value. The family yields such products as cinnamon (*Cinnamomum zeylanicum*), camphor (*Cinnamomum camphora*), fruit (*Persea americana*, avocado), timber (*Ocotea bullata*, stinkwood and *Ocotea porosa*, imbuia) and bay leaves (*Laurus nobilis*). All the trees of the Lauraceae family have aromatic glands in all parts, although not all are necessarily sweet smelling. 'Laurel' is the foliage of the bay (laurel) tree used as an emblem of victory or distinction – a custom still upheld in many sports, such as motor-car racing and the Olympic Games. The laurel tree is native to Mediterranean regions, and the family is represented in South Africa by three genera, two of which have tree members.

Ocotea: Stinkwood trees

South Africa's 'tree laureate', is, ironically, called the 'stinkwood' tree, owing to the repulsive odour emitted by its freshly cut wood. This is **Ocotea bullata** (**stinkwood** or **black stinkwood**), one of only two *Ocotea* species indigenous to South Africa. The genus *Ocotea* contains over 200 species of shrubs and trees, mainly from tropical America.

Stinkwood is a medium to large tree of about 8 m to 30 m, occurring in most of the high forests of South Africa, from the Cape Peninsula to Mpumalanga, but reaching its peak in the moister forests of the Knysna region, with which it is generally associated. One of the medium high forest trees, it tolerates shade well. It is an umbrageous (spreading) evergreen tree, producing a fairly straight, clean bole in the forest, but branching relatively low when growing in the open. On young trees the bark is smooth, light grey, often with beautiful mottled patterns of pink and mauve, but rugged brown and scaly on older trees. Special features of the tree are its dark green, glossy and aromatic leaves, and the tiny swellings or nodules in the axils of the leaf veins, hence the species name *bullata*, from *bulla* = a knob or bubble (Latin). Small, inconspicuous creamy-coloured flowers are borne in small bunches in the axils of the uppermost leaves. The fruit is oval-shaped,

Grotesque trunk of a stinkwood tree in a fairytale setting of the Knysna forests known to tourists as the Garden of Eden

set in a cup closely resembling an acorn, and is popular with fruit-eating birds, fruit bats, elephants, monkeys and baboons, buck, wild pigs and even wild cats.

Stinkwood is difficult to cultivate. The tree coppices readily, however, with the shoots drawing their nourishment from a well-established root system. The shoots are very nutritious and are heavily browsed by bushbuck.

The age of older stinkwood trees has been determined at about 1 000 years. Stinkwood is a protected tree, although damage to existing trees has been detected in KwaZulu-Natal, in particular, where bark is stripped for medicinal uses.

Coppice shoots on a stump of a stinkwood tree harvested many years ago in the Knysna forest

Timber goes before the tree

(Black) Stinkwood has been called the 'prince of the indigenous timbers', being the most sought-after and expensive of South Africa's indigenous timbers. The finely textured timber ranges from a beautiful golden brown to a brownish-black, or a blend of these colours. It is fairly heavy and has a natural lustre, and is the prime choice for the manufacture of prestigious furniture. Early settlers were quick to recognise the value of this particularly durable timber, and thousands of stinkwood trees were sacrificed for such uses as railway sleepers, in slipways, ship-building, even for a water-wheel. The combination of such a sought-after wood and limited resources – South Africa's indigenous trees grow fairly slowly – inevitably led to over-utilisation of stinkwood trees, especially in the Knysna forests. Felling was forbidden for a period, and since 1964 stinkwood, together with other forest timber, has been offered to the public in small quantities, through the application of a scientific management programme by the Branch: Forestry of the Department of Agriculture, Fisheries and Forestry. Controlled culling is done of trees damaged by wind or dying off. These forests now form part of the Garden Route National Park, managed by the South African National Parks (SANParks). Sadly, the lively and colourful timber auctions were suspended some years ago.

Ocotea kenyensis (**Transvaal** or **bastard stinkwood**) occurs in patches in the forests of the Eastern Cape, KwaZulu-Natal, Mpumalanga and Limpopo. Once considered only a form of the black stinkwood, it was later recognised as an East African species: *kenyensis* = 'from Kenya'. It closely resembles the (real) stinkwood, although reaching lesser heights, and the leaves lack the distinctive knobs and the freshly cut wood the offensive smell. It is said to be a good timber tree, yielding a yellowish timber that darkens on exposure. The tree is also protected by law.

An *Ocotea* species whose timber is more readily available in South Africa and elsewhere in the world, is *O. porosa*, the imbuia from South America. Specimens of this tree can be seen in the JDM Keet plantation near Tzaneen in Limpopo.

High-class furniture is manufactured from indigenous timbers by a fairly large number of manufacturers, some in existence for generations, in the George-Knysna-Humansdorp area. While the prices of these prestigious objects are near exorbitant, window-shopping is still free … The hand-carved stinkwood pulpit in the Dutch Reformed Church in George (Meade Street) is an object of wonderment.

Cryptocarya: Wild laurel and quince trees

The genus *Cryptocarya*, meaning 'hidden nut', consists of over 40 members, mostly tropical. It is represented in South Africa by six members, known as wild laurel or quince trees:

- *Cryptocarya angustifolia* (narrow/slender leaves): blue laurel
- *Cryptocarya latifolia* (broad leaves): broad-leaved quince, bastard stinkwood
- *Cryptocarya liebertiana*: common wild quince
- *Cryptocarya myrtifolia* (myrtle leaves): myrtle quince, wild camphor tree
- *Cryptocarya woodii*: Cape quince, bastard camphor tree
- *Cryptocarya wyliei*: red quince.

Cinnamomum camphora: The camphor tree

Camphor and cinnamon are both commonly used in South African households. Both names date back many ages: *cinnamon*, an aromatic spice from the inner bark of a South-East Asian tree, has a Semitic origin, while *camphor*, with an aromatic smell and bitter taste, has Arabic and Sanskrit origins. The camphor tree, which has become widely known in South Africa as an ornamental tree in parks and gardens, hails from South-East Asia, where it occurs naturally in China, Taiwan and Japan.

While cinnamon is yielded by the tree *Cinnamomum zeylanicum*, found only in its native South-East Asia, the leaves of the camphor tree, when crushed, emit a camphoric odour, as does the wood when sawn. Camphor is distilled from the wood. In South Africa it used to be sought after for making kists and lining wardrobes to repel insects.

This (formerly welcome) immigrant tree was established in the Cape Colony early during the 18th century by Governor WA van der Stel. The camphor trees planted on his estate Vergelegen at the foot of the Helderberg near Somerset West are an impressive sight, displaying all the typical features of the camphor tree in detail: large, gnarled surface roots at the base supporting a fairly short, burly trunk, which opens out into a dense and spreading evergreen bright-green crown. These trees, strikingly enhancing the mansion and its environs, count among South Africa's oldest introduced trees. At least three centuries old, they stand as witnesses to the conservation-minded consecutive generations of owners of the estate, among whom were celebrities such as Sir Lionel and Lady Florence Phillips, 'Punch' Barlow, and American Farms Ltd. The sight of the five camphor trees, declared a national monument in 1942, was said to have filled the British Royal family with

Camphor trees, dating back to more than 300 years, planted by Governor WA van der Stel on his farm Vergelegen, Somerset West (Photo: Mark Minter)

extreme pleasure during their South African tour in 1947. The late Nelson Mandela particularly requested to be photographed next to one of the trees during a visit of the Executive Committee of the ANC to Vergelegen in May 1991. Genetic material of these trees has been planted in the Infruitec Garden.

Other historic camphor trees are found in the Kirstenbosch National Botanical Garden. Camphor trees from China, together with *Ficus macrophylla* (Moreton Bay figs) from Australia, were planted by Cecil John Rhodes along the road from his house Groote Schuur to Hout Bay in the 1890s. His intention was to honour Queen Victoria by planting trees from all the outposts of the British Empire.

Persea americana: The avocado

The avocado pear industry in South Africa is an important one. While the 'modern' improved avocado pear tree is fairly small, trees planted from seed can become large. Such an example is found at the Westfalia Estate of Hans Merensky Holdings near Tzaneen (Limpopo), where a tree of about 50 years old and of unknown origin has a stem diameter of 1,64 m. This tree was originally grafted to the cultivar *Gottfried* and then to the cultivar *Fuerte*. It bears regular crops of approximately 500 to 1 000 kg per year.

Camphor tree lane in Kirstenbosch National Botanical Garden, Western Cape

ROSACEAE

The Rose Family

Rosaceae is a family containing 120 genera with 3 000 species, mainly from the cool climates of the Northern Hemisphere. From the viewpoint of farmers and gardeners, Rosaceae, next to the grass family Poaceae, is probably the most important plant family of all. Apple, pear, quince, plum, peach, nectarine, apricot, medlar, almond, cherry and strawberry all belong to this family. In all likelihood the best known and admired flower in the world is the rose, bringing joy to gardeners and homeowners alike.

One rose species has escaped from gardens in South Africa and now grows wild at places in the high mountains of the Drakensberg range. From these wild roses a small rose-hip industry had originated in the Eastern Cape town of Barkly East, from where rose-hips were exported at one stage. (Rose-hips are an excellent source of Vitamin C and are used in preserves.)

(The **mobola plum,** *Parinari curatellifolia*, a handsome medium-sized tree of the sandy woodlands of Limpopo and Mpumalanga, which was formerly classified as a member of the rose family, is now in a new family Chrysobalanaceae.)

The three tree genera in this family occurring in South Africa are *Leucosidea*, *Cliffortia* and *Prunus*.

Leucosidea sericea (**oldwood**) is a greyish shrub or small, many-branched tree of up to 7 m, growing in damp conditions from the Eastern Cape through KwaZulu-Natal and the Free State to the three northern provinces. Oldwood is not an exceptionally attractive tree, with its reddish-brown bark flaking off in strips and its densely clustered small greenish leaves. The leaves are jaggedly toothed and have a dark green upper and greyish-green hairy lower surface, and are occasionally used medicinally. Being fast-growing and hardy, oldwood may become troublesome under favourable conditions, forming impenetrable thickets. It is regarded by many farmers as an invader.

The common name 'oldwood' may refer to the old gnarled twisted trunks or to the wood burning slowly as if it were old and rotting. A second common name, 'troutwood', refers to the belief that the presence of these trees in mountainous areas is an indication that the streams are fit for trout-stocking.

The genus *Cliffortia* (**wild rice-bushes**) contains nearly 80 plant species, all African and mainly shrubs, concentrated in the Western Cape where they form part of the Fynbos Biome. One of these shrubs, affectionately called the 'climber's friend', is a sturdy, spiny-leaved plant growing among rocks, not only providing hand- and footholds to rock climbers but also firewood on uncomfortable rock faces – a real friend in need.

Four *Cliffortia* species are classified as trees, of which *Cliffortia arborea* (**star tree**) is the most remarkable on account

The mobola plum – a former member of the Rose Family – develops into a handsome tree with a well-rounded crown

of its appearance and limited distribution. It is a large shrub or small tree of up to 5 m, confined to the Calvinia-Fraserburg-Sutherland area in the Northern Cape. An endemic population of 150 star trees occurs along the slopes of the Aasvoëlkrans in the Nuweveld Mountains in the Sterboom Natural Heritage Site, Sutherland district. Some time in the past these trees were so abundant on the mountainsides near Calvinia that they were cut and sold for firewood. The leaves are needle-like, spiralling along short lateral branches in star-like rosettes; hence the common name.

The genus *Prunus* (**stone-fruit trees**) contains more than 100 species, which include important fruit trees such as cherry, peach and plum. (*Prunus* is the Latin word for 'plum'.)

Prunus africana (**red stinkwood** or **bitter almond** or **wild almond**) occurs in high natural forests from tropical Africa along the mist-belt areas of Limpopo and Mpumalanga through KwaZulu-Natal to the Eastern Cape, where a small number are found in the Bloukrans forest, their southernmost habitat.

Red stinkwood is an attractive tree, also for gardens, with rough blackish-brown bark, smooth, dark green glossy leaves and small white, fragrant flowers. The fruits are spherical, about 10 mm in diameter, pinkish-brown, and intensely bitter. The wood is hard and heavy, reddish-brown, but with limited use owing to its splitting and twisting. When the Woodbush forest near Haenertsburg (Limpopo) was exploited, red stinkwood trees were therefore left untouched, with the result that magnificent examples still occur in these forests.

Red stinkwood can be regarded as one of the very large trees of South Africa, as is shown in the table *The Top Thirty Indigenous Trees of South Africa*.

Red stinkwood is noteworthy on account of the medicinal value of its bark, which is used, not only where the tree occurs, as a treatment for a number of ailments, but also internationally. This bark is the major source of an extract used to treat benign prostatic hyperplasia, an increasingly common health problem of older men. The suppliers of bark are Cameroon, Democratic Republic of Congo, Kenya and Madagascar, and the main importers are France and Italy. As a result of use pressure, trade in the products of the tree is now regulated by the Convention on International Trade in Endangered Species (CITES).

As already mentioned, the apple tree belongs to the rose family. An apple tree tracing its ancestry to the famous tree under which Sir Isaac Newton is reputed to have sat when an apple fell on his head, leading to the theory of gravity, was planted in the garden of the CSIR in Pretoria on 1 July 1963. The

Red stinkwood trees develop into large forest trees, the bark, utilised for medicinal purposes, supplied by central African countries

National Physical Research Laboratory of the CSIR had presented its counterpart in England in 1959 with a cutting from the wild almond hedge planted by Jan van Riebeeck in 1660. By way of exchange the English Physical Research Laboratory made available to the South African CSIR a cutting of the Newton apple tree cultivar *Flower of Kent*. (A descendant of the CSIR apple tree was planted in the Infruitec Garden in 1973.)

Two historic pear trees (**Pyrus** species) on the sidewalk in Donkin Street in Beaufort West (Western Cape) were declared national monuments in 1980. These trees were planted in 1850 and 1860 respectively. Beaufort West, previously known as Hooy Vlakte (Hay Flats), has an interesting history of street tree planting. The story is told in the book *Hooy Vlakte* by WGH and S Vivier. Many pear trees still adorn the streets of Beaufort West.

Genadendal (Valley of Mercy), near Greyton, Western Cape, is the oldest mission station in South Africa, established in 1738 by the missionary Georg Schmidt of the Moravian Church. Genadendal was, among other things, known for its garden where Georg Schmidt planted a pear tree which is still standing today. Schmidt apparently held church sermons and kept school in the shade of the tree. The tree was blown over by storms twice, in 1838 and 1962, but has survived – a real symbol of faith and immortality. The church, with the churchyard containing the tree, is a declared national monument.

Two pear trees planted by Johannes Nicolaas Britz around 1825 on the farm Bloemfontein where the city of Bloemfontein was founded in 1846 were kept alive for more than 160 years until they died in 1990 and 1999 respectively.

The London missionary Robert Moffat was a remarkable man, not only an outstanding missionary but also a courageous pioneer-traveller with a keen sense of observation. He was a gardener by training and occupation and made use of his experience to lay out large gardens around the Kuruman Mission Station which he had founded in 1824. (Kuruman lies in the Northern Cape, on the N14.) A plaque in this old garden indicates the place where an almond tree used to grow and under which David Livingstone proposed to Mary, daughter of Moffat.

Clear proof of bark stripped from a tree for medicinal purposes

Vintage fruit

The most important member of the rose family and oldest living fruit tree in South Africa still bears fruit in the Company's Garden in Cape Town after more than 350 years. It is a sweet saffron pear planted during the office of Governor Jan van Riebeeck. A tree produced from a cutting of it was planted in the Infruitec Garden in 1975.

Sweet saffron pear tree in the Company's Garden, Cape Town, dating from the 1660s

FABACEAE: SUBFAMILY MIMOSOIDEAE

The Thorn Tree Family

One of the largest and most widely distributed families is the pod-bearing family with hundreds of genera and 12 000 species. Formerly called Leguminosae, deriving its name from the word 'legume', a seed pod, the family name has now been changed to Fabaceae. The plants of this family are mostly 'consumer friendly', with many yielding food to man and animals (peas, beans, clover, liquorice, gum). Liquorice is obtained from the roots of several *Clycyrrhiza* species, while gum arabic is obtained from thorn trees, especially in the Sudan, and is used as a food thickener, as well as in sweets, adhesives and paints. The shrubs producing South Africa's popular rooibos and honey teas also belong to this family. Most members of the family have root nodules containing bacteria that have the ability to fix nitrogen and enrich the soil.

The Fabaceae family is divided into three subfamilies:
- **Mimosoideae**: Petals reduced or absent. Flowers are many and in distinctive spherical heads or elongate spikes.
- **Caesalpinioideae**: Petals may be absent. Flowers are often showy and large, with the back petal larger and of a different shape or colour.
- **Papilionoideae**: Flowers are markedly asymmetric, with three different petal forms creating the pea flower or butterfly flower.

Mimosoideae

The recollection of that feel of fire when a thorn penetrates the heel of an unwary barefoot child might tend to prejudice the average person against South Africa's thorn trees. Yet these same thorns, which are actually modified stipules (attachments or extensions to the leaf), are the particular feature that distinguishes all Africa's thorn tree species (*Vachellia* and *Senegalia* species) from the mainly thornless or 'unarmed' Australian species known as wattles.

One of the major tree species of the arid regions is the **camel thorn** (*Vachellia erioloba*). Beautiful stands of these trees occur in the north-western part of the Free State and in the North West and Northern Cape Provinces. Mention was made of these trees by the English missionary Robert Moffat in his book *Missionary Labours*. With a dark green, spreading crown bearing bright yellow globose flower heads that yield a thick, curved grey pod, the trees provide shelter and an excellent fodder for stock. They are, moreover, a popular habitat of social weaver birds, mainly of the Northern Cape, whose huge nests are built in the crowns of the trees, adding to the beauty and interest of the camel thorn.

The name 'camel thorn' is actually a mistranslation from the Afrikaans 'kameeldoring', which means 'giraffe thorn'. Standing out so prominently in the otherwise mainly flat environment, these trees were portrayed in profusion by the eminent early 20th century South African painter JH Pierneef – a laudable channel for their protection.

The tree may reach up to 16 m in height, and the dark brown pith wood is exceptionally hard, durable and heavy, with a mass of 1,2 tons per cubic metre. Once used as mining props in the early mining days of Kimberley, the wood is nowadays mainly sought after as firewood. It has been listed as a protected tree species as a result of over-use of this tree species, which plays

A thorny issue

The genus name *Acacia* is derived from the Greek word *akanthos*, meaning 'thorn'. The name has become symbolic of, and even synonymous with, the African savannah. A very thorny issue is, therefore, the *Acacia* name change. Australian botanists insist that their 1 000 thornless species keep the name *Acacia*, while a different name should be given to the 150 thorny African species. This vastly ironic request seems to be based on the surprisingly overwhelming number of *Acacia* species found in Australia. A dispute of this kind gives meaning to the expression 'It is Greek to me …' To date this highly unpopular name change has not yet been accepted generally by local botanists and the public alike (as is also evident from papers delivered at prominent local environmental symposia like the annual Savanna Science Network Meetings).

For the purpose of this book the new genus names of *Vachellia* and *Senegalia* are used. Acacias occur in Australia, while the *Vachellia* and *Senegalia* species mainly occur in Africa, Madagascar, throughout the Asia-Pacific region and in the Americas – a total of 1 350 species, of which some 40 in South Africa.

Massive social weaver nest in a camel thorn tree in the arid Northern Cape (Photo: Shutterstock)

Tree Families

A camel thorn tree that served as a clock tower at the Stadt school for over a century, Mahikeng, North West

a keystone ecological role in its arid and semi-arid habitats, sustaining much diversity in fauna and also the flora growing in its shade.

Camel thorn trees are host to the *Gonometa* moth. The cocoons serving as a casing to the pupae are a source of wild silk. Beautiful and useful silk is spun from these cocoons by the Textile Division of the CSIR in Port Elizabeth.

At a private enterprise in Graskop, Mpumalanga, *Gonometa* cocoons, harvested from mopane and camel thorn trees, are processed on a large scale. Apart from hands needed for gathering the cocoons, the actual processing (washing, spinning, weaving, etc.), is vastly labour intensive, thereby actively supporting the Italeng Project for jobless South African women.

Notable camel thorn trees

Mokopane (Potgietersrus) in Limpopo also boasts fine specimens of camel thorn trees lining the streets. The use of elongated telephone poles where these valuable and beautiful trees are in the way of overhead telephone lines ensured that the trees were not mutilated. At Moorddrif ('Murder Drift'), south of the town, two camel thorn trees used to mark the spot where 33 members of a party of Voortrekkers died in 1854 in a clash with the local tribe of Chief Makapan. Both these trees, declared national monuments in 1940, have died. The trunk of one has been removed and is exhibited in the Arend Dieperink Museum at Mokopane.

The 'Breakfast tree', a large well-known camel thorn tree near Douglas, Northern Cape

In 1981 a camel thorn tree known as the 'Rebellion Tree' on the farm Van Rooy's Vley, Gordonia district, Northern Cape, was declared a national monument. Under this tree less than 1 km from the farm house, General Manie Maritz declared a rebellion against the Government of the Union of South Africa on 9 October 1914. With little success, however: In Kuruman, near by, stands the 'Truce Tree' or 'Silent Witness'… General Jan Kemp, with 1 200 rebels, on their way to join the German forces in Namibia during the Rebellion, invaded Kuruman with the purpose of replenishing their rations. He was however compelled to accede to an armistice, also in the shade of a camel thorn tree!

In Schweizer-Reneke, North West, a camel thorn tree reportedly used to accommodate up to 800 or more pupils in its shade. Known as the 'School Tree', it served as a classroom and general meeting place. It died some years ago.

A lone camel thorn tree standing alongside the bridge over the Sundays River at Graaff-Reinet on the N9 to Middelburg (Eastern Cape) marks the spot where the old wagon road also crossed the river. The origin of this tree is unknown – the seed might have been sown there by one of the many ox-wagons that transported goods to and from Kimberley, which lies in camel thorn country.

Moorddrift monument, Mokopane (Potgietersrus). Both the original Moorddrif camel thorn trees died some years ago; one of which is now displayed in the local museum, and the other replaced with a monkey thorn tree

Saving a camel thorn forest at the 'Town under the Trees'

Kathu Forest is a unique woodland dominated by camel thorn trees (*Vachellia erioloba*) just north of the town of Kathu in the Northern Cape. This woodland of about 4 000 hectares, known as Kathu Forest because of the exceptional size and density of the tree cover, is one of a number of such camel thorn woodlands known in southern Africa. One of the densest concentrations of Stone Age archaeological sites in the world is also found here, with thousands of ancient tools having been excavated, as well as the bones of an extinct elephant species. These sites are situated in parts of Kathu Forest, and also in adjoining areas.

The uniqueness of Kathu Forest was recognised as early as 1919, when it was declared a State Forest. In 1956 this State Forest was deproclaimed to allow for the establishment of the town of Kathu near the site where the Sishen mine was about to start operations. The town developed in the southern portion of Kathu Forest, and the result was a unique landscape that earned it the nickname 'The Town under the Trees'. Several properties covering the largest part of the Kathu Forest was registered in 1995 as a Natural Heritage Site by the Department of Environmental Affairs and Tourism at the request of various landowners. This included the town of Kathu, a private nature reserve owned by Sishen (Kumba Resources) to the north of the town, and the adjoining remainder of the farm Uitkoms. Although the various landowners agreed to protect Kathu Forest on these properties, the Natural Heritage Programme is voluntary.

In 2006 the Kathu Forest Working Group was established to investigate ways to protect the forest, involving all government levels and stakeholders in the area. This working group was established in response to a request from the Wildlife and Environment Society of SA to the Minister of the former Department of Water Affairs and Forestry to protect the forest, which was at that stage being threatened by increasing development. The rapidly expanding town of Kathu borders on the south of this area. This working group decided that Kathu Forest first had to receive protected woodland status, and then steps had to be taken to establish formal nature reserves on as many land parcels as possible.

Kathu Forest was mapped and three woodland classes were identified on the basis of the size and density of the trees. Core areas with dense and high trees are mainly situated on aquifers which supply the tree roots with perennial water. Around these areas the woodlands are subjected to dry seasons and droughts, and are vulnerable to a lowering of the water table by mining and other land uses. Small groups of trees within the forest are dying inexplicably, and researchers are trying to determine the causes.

Magnificent camel thorn trees in the Kathu Forest, Northern Cape

Kathu Forest was declared a protected woodland under Section 12 of the National Forests Act on 10 July 2009. This protection means that current land uses (agriculture and conservation) may continue, but that no land uses that will significantly alter the natural environment will be allowed. It also means that indigenous trees in the demarcated area are protected and may only be cut under a licence from the Department of Agriculture, Forestry and Fisheries (DAFF), save for small quantities of household firewood. The vision is to gradually create nature reserves within and around the protected woodland with even higher conservation status, and in 2009 the Kalahari Gholf en Jag Landgoed (Estate) agreed to create the first formal reserve of about 2 000 ha under the Stewardship Programme of the Department of Environmental Affairs, as an offset (compensation) for development bordering on Kathu Forest. Currently Kathu Forest is being re-declared along wider boundaries.

The camel thorn tends to hybridise with a smaller 'brother', **Vachellia haematoxylon** (**grey camel thorn**). Described by the botanist Burchell as 'a beautiful species of *Acacia* with a hoary complexion', this latter tree is a most beautiful sight in the wild, with its ghost-like grey foliage caused by a covering of grey hairs on exceedingly minute leaflets (0,5 × 0,6 mm). Because of the tiny leaves Burchell originally named it *Acacia atomiphylla*. The present species name *haematoxylon* is the Greek for 'blood-red wood'. This shrub or small tree, reaching a maximum height of 6 m in contrast to the 16 m of *V. erioloba*, has an even more restricted distribution, occurring in the dry Kalahari sand region of South Africa and Namibia.

Both species are slow growing, developing very long taproots, and are therefore difficult, or impossible, to transplant. Gardeners are however more successful with the cultivation of camel thorn away from their natural habitat, and cultivated trees are occasionally encountered in Pretoria and elsewhere. The grey camel thorn is seldom cultivated and, as in the case of the quiver tree, it would probably be less striking outside its unique natural setting.

Another fine thorn tree species, remarkable both for its size and its flowering habit, is **Senegalia galpinii** (**monkey thorn**). In contrast to the two camel thorn species (height 16 m and 6 m respectively), the monkey thorn reaches a height of 25 m and more – the maximum height having

Giant monkey thorn tree near Rust De Winter, Limpopo

been reported as about 40 m. This can be ascribed to its distribution mainly along river courses, where water is available, in the savannah regions of North West, Mpumalanga and Limpopo in particular, and in the neighbouring countries of Botswana, Zimbabwe and Mozambique. Clumps of tall monkey thorns grow along the Crocodile River near Thabazimbi (North West) and the Olifants River near Groblersdal, Mpumalanga.

The species name *galpinii* comes from the botanist Dr EE Galpin, a well-known plant collector active in the late 19th to early 20th centuries, who first collected the species in the Naboomspruit (Mookgopong), Limpopo, area. One of the Galpin descendants later established an attractive avenue of monkey thorn trees on Mosdene, the former Galpin family farm and now a Natural Heritage Site.

The monkey thorn offers a marvellous sight in spring, when, before the new leaves appear, distinctive red-brown to purple flower buds cover the tree (uncommon among thorn tree species), to burst open into yellow or creamy yellow flower spikes, with the straight, brown pods sometimes borne in profusion completing the cycle.

Apart from large specimens along the rivers in Mpumalanga and Limpopo, two particular locations for viewing the monkey thorn at its best are the Rust de Winter area some 30 km eastwards off the N1 (Pienaarsrivier offramp) and the farm Hermanusdorings, in the district of Vaalwater, Limpopo, where a row of 40 monkey thorn trees were apparently planted a century ago. As it adapts well to cultivation and is reasonably fast growing, the monkey thorn is often planted in gardens and parks, lending dignity and pride to its environment. Exceptionally large monkey thorns are reported to grow at Shalimpo, Botswana, near the border with South Africa at the confluence of the Limpopo and Shashe Rivers. Gigantic specimens are also found on the farm Modderfontein in the North West district of Rustenburg, planted about 80 years ago.

Large planted monkey thorn trees in Pretoria can be observed at the Rietondale experimental farm of the Agricultural Research Council and on the campus of the University of Pretoria. A remarkably large monkey thorn grows on the premises of APBCO Insurance Brokers, corner Lynnwood Road and Kings Highway. Word of mouth has it that, when it was still Lynnwood farm, farmers used to camp under this tree with their ox-wagons and horse-carts when attending Holy Communion (Nagmaal). The horse-carts were used on Sundays to travel from the camping terrain under the tree to the church and back.

Monkey thorn tree branches spread widely and tend to break. To prevent this, APBCO has supported the heavier branches with steel cables. The APBCO building was designed so that the windows face the tree, offering visitors a magnificent view of the tree as they enter the building.

Tsukudu Lodge, north of Pretoria, boasts a large monkey thorn tree named 'Kigeli', with stem diameter of 2 m and crown width of 39 m. A visitor from Burundi had asked the lodge management to name the tree Kigeli after a Rwandese king of whom he was a descendant. The tree seemingly reminded him of the king: big and strong.

Senegalia galpinii was adopted as the national tree of the former Bophuthatswana, where thousands of these trees were planted during the rule of President Lucas Mangope.

The well-preserved APBCO monkey thorn, Lynnwood, Pretoria

Senegalia burkei (**black monkey thorn**) nearly matches the monkey thorn in magnificence. It does however not grow to the same size and is not as spectacular in flower because the latter appear later in spring when the tree is in full foliage.

Senegalia nigrescens (**knobthorn** or sometimes called **crocodile bark**), a smaller tree than the monkey thorn and black monkey thorn, displays the same characteristic of having reddish-brown flower buds. They open into creamy blossoms in early spring to cover the leafless trees, giving them 'an air of loveliness' according to Eve Palmer. The knob thorn is a familiar tree in the Lowveld where it sometimes occurs in almost pure stands. In the Kruger National Park it is one of the tree species most targeted by elephants, often stripping its bark or pushing trees over, leading to a decline in sub-adult and mature trees in parts of tis distribution range.

Vachellia hebeclada (**candle pod acacia**) is either a shrub or small tree up to 7 m high, but typically squats on the ground as a tangle of branches, usually from a few metres to 15 m in diameter. Of the three subspecies occurring in southern Africa, the typical subspecies *hebeclada* is widespread, with its habitat being the drier inland areas of South Africa.

The Afrikaans common name *trassiedoring* refers to the figurative hermaphroditic characteristic of this tree species, which bears both hooked and straight thorns. The English common name speaks for itself – the pods are indeed characteristically upright candle-like objects. The candle pod is thought to be one of the host plants of the desert truffles, a delicacy in some parts of the Kalahari desert.

A spreading giant

When comparing the average measurements given above, the extraordinariness of one specimen on the farm Koufontein (cold fountain) near Alma (Modimolle district) in Limpopo is undeniable. This candle pod acacia tree covers an area of more or less 2 500 m², with a crown recently measured at 61 m from one end to the other. The tree could have been much larger, had it not been severely cut back from time to time to prevent its invading the surrounding fields. At least the Koufontein candle pod thorn tree has provided the owner of the farm with many tons of firewood over the years. This remarkable tree experienced troubled times when it witnessed the burning of the farmstead by British soldiers during the Anglo-Boer War.

The Koufontein candle pod is extraordinary in many respects. The protective canopy of a small part of the tree close to the homestead served as a blacksmith's shop for many years. Here two generations of Bronkhorsts repaired their wagons and sometimes those of their neighbours. The work bench was one of the horizontal branches on which the farmer installed a vice.

A treasure such as this tree does however not come without its problems. According to the present owner, Mr Jan Bronkhorst, the fourth generation farming on Koufontein, a profusion of birds is attracted to the tree. These birds also feed on invasive plant species, with the result that seringa and mulberry trees develop in the tangle of branches to such an extent that they have to be removed from time to time.

The candle pod acacia on the farm Koufontein, Modimolle (Nylstroom). This tree is a tangle of stems and branches up to 61 metres in width

Particularly conspicuous in the grassland of the central KwaZulu-Natal districts, where they sometimes form pure stands are **Vachellia sieberiana** var. **woodii** (**flat-crowned paperbark** or **Natal camel thorn**). These trees, occurring in the higher rainfall regions of South Africa, also give character to the Drakensberg escarpment areas in KwaZulu-Natal, Mpumalanga and Limpopo. A special and unique community of paperbark trees occurs in the Daisy Kopje Natural Heritage Site in the Barberton district, Mpumalanga.

With attractive flat crowns emanating from the widely branching habit of the trees, *V. sieberiana* have been propagated extensively for planting in parks and gardens countrywide, where they usually thrive under conditions similar to their natural habitat. The common name 'paperbark thorn' describes a particular feature of the bark, which tends to be corky and sometimes peels in papery strips or flakes.

What makes *V. sieberiana* so striking is that the spread of the crown may occasionally be immense, starting from a comparatively low height from the ground. One such specimen grows on the farm Stellenrust near Karino on the N4 between Nelspruit/Mbombela and Komatipoort in Mpumalanga. It has already reached tourist-attraction status because of the many visitors who stop there every day to marvel at the 'pancake' tree. Although the tree is only 5,6 m high, the crown diameter is 23 m. The Walters family cares for the tree and protects it against fire by regularly cutting the grass around it. Besides the fact that any small fire will kill the tree completely, trees exposed to fire have less spreading crowns than their well-protected brothers.

A larger, but also extraordinarily beautiful paperbark thorn tree can be seen at the De Hoek sawmill, about 15 km from Tzaneen in Limpopo. This fine tree has a wide spreading crown of approximately 30 m diameter.

A paperbark thorn tree that used to grow in the garden of the erstwhile Administrator's residence in Pietermaritzburg was declared a national monument in 1936. It was believed that the Volksraad of the Republic of Natalia in 1842 decided to accept the conditions of capitulation to the British under this tree. It is generally believed that paperbark trees do not grow much older than 150 or 200 years and this tree unfortunately died in 1969.

Vachellia xanthophloea (**fever tree**) is always associated with low-lying moist areas. The tree received its common name

A landscape painted in a sulphurous yellow by thousands of fever trees, Pafuri area, Kruger National Park (Photo: René de Klerk)

from early travellers who associated it with malaria areas before the cause of the disease was understood. The fever tree is most striking and is one of South Africa's more exceptional trees, owing to the colour of its trunk and branches. The species name *xanthophloea* – the Greek for 'yellow' – is an understatement, and the description by Elsa Pooley of 'smooth lime-green with sulphurous powdery surface' is more apt. A magnificent fever tree forest in the northern part of the Kruger National Park is known to many people. Similar 'forests' occur in northern KwaZulu-Natal – breathtakingly spectacular at the Nyamithi and Bhanzi Pans in the Ndumu Game Reserve, for instance – at Komatipoort (Mpumalanga) and elsewhere in South Africa. The fever tree is widely cultivated nowadays for ornamental purposes, often seen as street trees far outside its preferred habitat. Fever trees 30 m high have been spotted by members of the Dendrological Society in the Tuli Block in Botswana, bordering on the Limpopo River.

One of the most imposing South African trees of this subfamily is *Faidherbia albida* (**ana tree**), formerly *Acacia albida*. The ana tree can be classified as very large, with mature trees reaching a height of up to 30 m, supporting widely spreading crowns of up to 30 m in diameter (almost covering a plot of 1 000 m^2). When young, the trees grow tall, thin and straight, but with age they develop a spreading crown. The deep nitrogen-fixing root system, together with masses of pods providing excellent animal fodder, makes the tree a good choice in agroforestry systems, as is practised in various African countries. It can also be cultivated in parks and, preferably large, gardens. The pods are unusual, being conspicuously curled and twisted; hence the nickname of 'apple-ring thorn-tree'. Ana trees could well be described as 'topsy-turvy' (Afrikaans 'agterstevoor'). Unlike the majority of trees, they are in full leaf and flower in winter, while leafless in summer.

The South African distribution of the ana tree covers the wooded grassland and riverine forests of KwaZulu-Natal, Mpumalanga and Limpopo. A characteristic of the tree is that it also occurs along rivers in deserts, such as the Namib, where it develops into unexpectedly huge trees.

The 'Eugène Marais ana trees', impressive giants at Deadbeat farm, Limpopo

Tall stories: Eugène Marais' Deadbeat trees

An interesting article by the nature-loving journalist Eugène Marais praising the ana tree appeared in the newspaper *Die Vaderland* on 3 December 1933. Marais argued that South Africans are unaware of the country's giant trees, comparing the ana tree (which he called *apiesdoring* = the monkey thorn tree) favourably with America's giant redwood trees. He claimed that the ana trees along the Magalakwen

(Mogalakwena) River on the farm Deadbeat in the district of Mokopane (Potgietersrus), Limpopo, exceeded the American giants in several respects. Marais estimated these ana trees at 60 m in height, also claiming that the alluvial sand around the trunks of some was 30 m deep, and that 7 200 men would have a square yard (± 0,836 m^2) each available if they stood in the shade of the largest tree at noon!

These exciting, although exaggerated, claims serve as proof of how difficult it is to estimate the height and size of trees. The actual height of the tallest of these 'Eugène Marais' trees at Deadbeat is 24 m, and 827 men would be able to stand in its shade as described. The trees are still there to be seen and still raise debate in the media from time to time – impressive giants, fortunately protected by caring people. It has been reported that this stand of trees has lost some of its former glory, with some trees already dead and others suffering crown die-back.

About 15 km north-west of Mokopane another outstanding group of ana trees, known as the 'Livingstone trees', used to attract interest. It is doubtful whether Dr Livingstone ever saw these trees, which were declared a national monument in 1940. Disaster struck when all the trees, with the exception of a few young ones, died around 1990 as a result of the groundwater supply being cut off through excessive extraction of water from the Mogalakwena River for agricultural purposes. The biggest of these trees in fact slightly surpassed the Eugène Marais trees.

Impressive well-kept ana trees can be seen at the Forever Resort, Tshipise, in Limpopo. Further north, at Mapungubwe, SANParks protect a patch of Limpopo riverine ana forest against destructive elephants. Visitors to this spot can enjoy an exhilarating treetop walk.

A number of shrubs, lianes or trees, of the genus *Entada*, also belong to the subfamily Mimosoideae. An exquisite but rather scarce species in South Africa is **Entada rheedii** (sea bean), with a scattered distribution in the coastal forests of northern KwaZulu-Natal, although more widely found in tropical Africa and other tropical regions.

The sea bean is a very large woody forest climber that may attain tree stature. Its flowers are small, fluffy creamy-yellow spikes up to 23 cm long, while the fruit is an enormous flat woody pod measuring up to an amazing 1 m × 15 cm. Exceptionally large seeds of 4 to 6 cm in diameter are set free when the pods break up in segments and are sometimes carried down the streams to the sea, to be washed up on the beaches of the KwaZulu-Natal and Eastern Cape coast. This evidently explains the common name of 'sea bean'. While the seeds are known to many – almost everybody who has set foot on these beaches – the plant itself has been seen by very few South Africans.

Besides thorn trees, which add much to the fascination of the bushveld and lowveld and Africa

Enormous pod of the sea bean, clearly showing the bulges of large seeds. This elusive giant climber plant is only seen by a few people, while the seeds are seen by thousands on the eastern beaches of the country, where they have been washed down southwards from the rivers in northern KwaZulu-Natal and neighbouring countries

in general, the subfamily Mimosoideae includes several other fascinating genera, such as the genus *Albizia* (false-thorn trees).

Eleven false-thorn tree species occur in South Africa, with ***Albizia adianthifolia*** (**flat-crown false-thorn**) the most conspicuous because of its wide-spreading flat crown. The flat-crown was the provincial tree of the former Natal Province, and it has been retained for KwaZulu-Natal. The species name *adianthifolia* means 'with leaves like a maidenhair fern'. The leaves are indeed fern-like, large and double compound. After being picked, the leaflets close up to face one another. The flowers are not as showy as those of other albizias, and brown pods are borne in profusion. The tree has a tall, straight stem with grey-brown bark, and grows to 20 m in height. This beautifully shaped tree is ideally suited for planting in big gardens and parks in frost-free areas.

Albizia tanganyicensis (**paperbark false-thorn**) is a very conspicuous but small, 9 m high tree which occurs from the Waterberg northwards in Limpopo. This tree is remarkable because of its papery, light orange-yellow bark, which peels in patches. The species name indicates that it was first described in Tanzania, formerly known as Tanganyika. The crown is rather open with stiff, stunted branches, in comparison with the graceful flat-crown false-thorn, but the almost white peeling bark and creamy-white fluffy flower heads, which appear in spring before the leaves come out, make the paperbark false-thorn a unique tree.

The spreading crown of a flat-crown false-thorn tree, Richmond, KwaZulu-Natal

Newtonia hildebrandtii (**Lebombo wattle**) occurs in northern KwaZulu-Natal and is a large tree up to 18 m tall, with feathery foliage and a large rounded crown, occasionally up to 30 m in diameter. The scientific name honours two persons, an English-Portuguese plant collector, Francisco Newton, and a German, JM Hildebrandt.

The timber is dark brown and hard, and it is said that baby Zulu boys after birth were washed in water heated by *Umfomothi* wood (the isiZulu name) in order to confer upon them the hardiness of the tree.

The 'Australian invasion'

Five exotic acacias, native to Australia and without thorns, that can be regarded as notorious rather than remarkable are:

Acacia mearnsii (**black wattle**) is both an invader and South Africa's most profitable plantation tree. It is probably best known as a tree hated by everyone except those who utilise the wood for building, heating and cooking and those who make profits from selling its bark and wood. Products derived from the black wattle are used in the manufacture of a wide variety of essential commodities that affect the everyday lives of people around the world. These include leather-tanning materials, wood glues, paper pulp, rayon and viscose pulp, fibre board, cellophane, cigarette filters, photographic films, cosmetics, pharmaceuticals, sausage casings, sanitary ware, spectacle frames, light switches, various health care products, and explosives. The raw materials are exported to almost every corner of the world from the plantations of KwaZulu-Natal and Mpumalanga.

Acacia melanoxylon (**blackwood**) is a tall tree with a straight bole occurring mainly in the Knysna and Tsitsikamma areas of the Western and Eastern Cape Provinces, where it yields timber of outstanding beauty for high-grade furniture. These exotic trees have been interplanted in clearings within the high natural forests in the late 19th and early 20th century, yielding a timber quality unmatched by any blackwood trees harvested outside these forests. The tree also has invading qualities. Blackwood is hardy in frost conditions and it is one of the evergreen species that could be planted in the cold highveld areas where it would be less invasive.

Acacia pendula (**weeping myall**) is one of the most beautiful wattles of Australia, which grows exceptionally well in the drier areas of South Africa. With their grey-green leaves on long pendulous branches these trees are a magnificent sight on the farms and in the towns of the North West and Northern Cape Provinces. Fortunately this species does not spread naturally.

Acacia saligna (**Port Jackson**) is an exceptionally invasive species used with great success to stabilise hundreds of kilometres of sand dunes between Cape Town and Port Elizabeth. It has subsequently spread over vast areas. In places the wood was utilised as firewood and the leaves as animal fodder. Owing to its fast spread, threatening both indigenous vegetation and water resources, a programme was launched some years ago by the Plant Protection Research Institute to combat Port Jackson by means of a fungus. This proved to be highly successful, with the majority of Port Jackson plants already being affected by the fungus.

Acacia cyclops (**rooikrans** or **red eye** or **Cape coast wattle**) has also spread aggressively in more or less the same areas as *A. saligna*, and is also being purposefully combated. Rooikrans yields a high-quality firewood.

Weeping myall trees, 'treurwattel', along a farm road in the North West Province

FABACEAE SUBFAMILY CAESALPINIOIDEAE

The Flamboyant Family

The subfamily Caesalpinioideae of the family Fabaceae may well be called 'flamboyant', with its showy and gorgeously coloured flowers. Trees of this subfamily, both indigenous and exotic, are often cultivated in gardens. Exotic species include the showy *Delonix regia*, the flamboyant, *Caesalpinia* species (Pride of Barbados, Bird of Paradise bush, leopard tree), *Senna* species and bauhinias. Indigenous species are described below under a separate heading.

The best known of all the exotic flamboyant family members is void of showy flowers, but sparkles like a gem because of its other qualities. This is *Ceratonia siliqua* (**carob** or **St John's bread**), native to the Mediterranean region and widely planted in South Africa because it is evergreen and hardy. Apparently John the Baptist survived in the desert of Judaea on carob pods. In Arabia the seed of the carob was used as the measure for weighing precious stones. The word 'carat', the unit of weight for precious stones, is of Arabic origin and refers to the seed.

The carob industry is quite an important one, particularly in Spain and Portugal. The pods can be eaten, but they are usually processed and the seed separated from the rest. The seed gives carob lobe flour used in the cosmetics, rubber, leather, paper, soft drinks and food industries. The rest of the pod is used to produce carob powder, a substitute for chocolate, and is also used in the production of alcohol, stock feeds, dog biscuits, syrup and flour. South Africa imports a small quantity of carob flour annually.

The tireless agriculturist of the Northern Cape, Mr Gert Niemöller of the farm Klein Pella, also experimented with carob. He found the date palm to be more suited to the climate of the Bushmanland however, and made his carob plant material available to the former Department of Water Affairs and Forestry and to farmers working in a more suitable climate, among them Mr F Rust of the farm Eenboom, Malmesbury district (Western Cape), who established 10 ha of carob trees for the production of fodder.

Another interesting project in which carob would have featured was the Grenfell Park project, which was announced at the opening of the third annual Messina (now Musina) show in 1959. Commander HFP Grenfell wanted to ensure that Messina would thrive after its mineral resources are exhausted, and formed the Transvaal Development Company. The company was to embark on a 100 square miles afforestation scheme along the Limpopo River. The plantations would supply fibre, oils, beans, flour, kapok, tannin, rubber, cork, wax and medicines and would thus support an important industrial region with many factories. Fodder from carob would supplement the carrying capacity of the natural veld considerably. The project unfortunately did not materialise.

Flamboyant trees in flower, Makhado (Louis Trichardt), Limpopo

Indigenous Flamboyant species

Mopane trees in their late winter colours near Letaba rest camp, Kruger National Park

Umtiza listeriana (**umtiza** or **Buffalo River thorn**) is a small, spiny, evergreen tree of up to 10 m, and the only species in the genus. It has a very limited distribution, being common in the forests and kloofs along the Buffalo River at East London, Eastern Cape, but found nowhere else in the world. It is the only South African tree with an African genus name, being known as *umThiza* among local people. The species name *listeriana* honours Joseph Storr Lister, as mentioned earlier, one of the early pioneers of South Africa's forestry industry.

Umtiza has a fluted stem and the sapwood is yellow, with a small, red to purple to black, oily heartwood. It is recorded as having been used as bearings for propeller shafts in small boats, the natural oiliness providing constant lubrication.

Umtiza features fairly widely in African myth and legend. Apart from being used for medicinal purposes, pieces of bark apparently used to be hung in African huts to protect them from lightning and evil spirits. This custom seems to have fallen away.

As it is a rare tree in South Africa, umtiza has been protected since 1884 in a nature reserve of the former Department of Forestry on the Buffalo River where the Buffalo Pass crosses the river near East London. The area was later declared the Fort Grey Nature Reserve, when its management was handed over to Eastern Cape Nature Conservation. The name Umtiza Nature Reserve has been used since 1985.

Besides the umtiza and other trees of interest, the rare Narina trogon, one of South Africa's most beautiful birds, can be seen in this reserve, as well as the Samango monkey, a rare and shy animal of forests from the Eastern Cape northwards.

Colophospermum mopane (**mopane**) is also a genus with only one species. The genus name is the Greek for 'oily seed' and refers to the oil glands on the flat, wrinkled and kidney-shaped seed. The species name *mopane* is apparently derived from the Venda common name for the tree, *Mutanari*. It is a tree of the hot dry Lowveld and bushveld north of the Soutpansberg in Limpopo, and can easily be recognised by its butterfly-like, gland-dotted and turpentine-smelling

An imposing mopane tree, Kruger National Park

leaves. In dry weather and at midday the leaves fold together, with the result that the trees do not offer deep shade when it is really necessary. In spite of this unfortunate trait, the mopane is a very useful tree, both to man and his livestock:

- It provides fodder to stock and game.
- It produces an edible mopane manna with a sweetish taste. This is actually the waxy cover of the mopane psyllid on the leaves.
- The wood, with a mass of more than a ton per cubic metre, is one of the heaviest of South African timbers. The heartwood is durable and makes an excellent pole. It is also an excellent firewood.
- The irritating mopane bee *Plebina denoita* that crawls into one's ears, nose and eyes on a hot day produces small amounts of yellow edible honey, which is stored in nests in hollow trunks. A small wax tube serving as the entrance to the honey store protrudes from the trunk and gives away the secret of the bees.
- The bark provides a strong twine for hut-building and other purposes.
- The shrub mopane has straight branches, which are ideal for fencing droppers.
- The stump of the shrub mopane consists of three to four short arms radiating from the taproot. As the arms are artistically gnarled and weathered on the upper side they make attractive ornaments used in floral arrangements.
- The cocoons of the pupae of the *Gonometa* moth, which also hosts on mopane trees, provide wild silk.
- The caterpillar of the moth *Imbrasia belina* is a sought-after protein among the people of southern Africa. Mopane worms worth millions of rands are gathered each year.

Schotia is a small genus endemic to southern Africa, named after an early traveller to this country, Richard van der Schot. The best known and most commonly encountered is *Schotia brachypetala* (**weeping boer-bean**). The species name *brachypetala* means 'short petals'. The common name boer-bean (farmer's bean) indicates that the beans were used for food by early farmers. It is known that Stone Age and San people ate the boer-bean seeds, which are attached to a conspicuous yellow aril. The tree is medium to fairly big, 15 m high, with a spreading crown, half deciduous, and occurring in the dry savannah forests in South Africa, Zimbabwe, Mozambique and Swaziland.

The striking beauty of this tree species lies in the bunches of bright red or scarlet flowers, borne in spring, usually before the leaves appear. The flowers produce copious nectar that attracts birds and insects. The weeping boer-bean is one of the 'rain tree' species that are sometimes attacked by the spittle bug which sucks excessive sap dripping to the ground.

Three other boer-bean species occur in South Africa, all with exquisite red flowers except *Schotia latifolia* (**forest boer-bean**) of the Eastern Cape, which has pale-pink flowers. The name *latifolia* means 'broad-leaved', and the common name indicates that it occurs mostly on the margins of forests.

Schotia afra var. *angustifolia* (**small-leaved Karoo boer-bean**) occurs in the Little Karoo and the coastal areas of the Eastern Cape. It is a gnarled, much-branched small tree. This was the species that Richard van der Schot discovered and the species name *afra* indicates that it is from Africa.

Being beautiful trees, all the boer-bean varieties are commonly planted in gardens.

Other well-known indigenous trees of the flamboyant family with remarkable flowers are:

- *Bauhinia galpinii* (**Pride of De Kaap**), with brick-red to red flowers borne in profusion.

The protein-rich mopane worm is a local delicacy

TOP: Weeping boer bean tree displaying its crimson flowers, Sekhukhuneland

LEFT: Sjambok pod tree laden with elongated pods

- *Cassia abbreviata* (**sjambok pod**), with terminal bunches of bright yellow, scented flowers followed by up to 60 cm slender pendulous pods.
- *Peltophorum africanum* (**African wattle**) has bright yellow flowers borne in upright sprays. This is also one of the 'rain' trees attacked by the spittle bug.

Less familiar trees of the flamboyant family are:
- *Afzelia quanzensis* (**pod mahogany**): A magnificent tree of the north-eastern parts of Limpopo and KwaZulu-Natal, with a short, straight trunk up to

1 m and more in diameter and a spreading crown of 20 to 30 m. Its maximum height is approximately 25 m. The tree is deciduous, with glossy copper-coloured foliage in spring, becoming dark green with age. The scented flowers are unique, each with four green sepals from which protrudes a single flaming pinkish-red petal surrounded by greenish stamens. Even more special are the pods; 15 cm long × 5 cm broad, thick and containing six shiny black oblong beans attached to a red aril – their decorativeness is the reason for the tree's common name.

- *Cordyla africana* (**wild mango**): A rare tree in South Africa, occurring in Mpumalanga and northern KwaZulu-Natal. It grows to 20 m high, with a spreading crown, and is a tree to consider for cultivation in subtropical areas. The flowers are yellow, consisting of masses of upright stamens. The fruit is also yellow, oval and about 4 cm in diameter, with a leathery skin containing a number of flat seeds. The fruit, although it looks delicious, is tasteless. It is reported to be eaten by animals and local peoples. The genus name *Cordyla*, meaning 'club-shaped', obviously refers to the fruit.

Pod mahogany near Sagole, north-eastern Limpopo

TREE FAMILIES

FABACEAE SUBFAMILY PAPILIONOIDEAE

The Pea Family

The pea subfamily, Papilionoideae, is known for its attractive flowers in particular. (*Papilio* is a butterfly, and this refers to the form of the flowers, which resemble the wings of a butterfly.) Papilionoideae is a widespread group of about 12 000 species worldwide, containing such important plants as beans, peas, clover, sweet peas and lucerne. The flower is characteristic of the typical pea flower, with an upper petal, two side petals and two lower ones.

A number of South Africa's most attractive wild trees are members of this subfamily. The best known are the *Erythrina* or coral trees – the name indicating the colour of the flowers, which is varied hues of red. (*Erythrina*, the genus name, comes from the Greek word *erythros*, which means 'red'.)

Of the 170 *Erythrina* species, which grow mainly in tropical and subtropical areas, six occur naturally in South Africa, although with a relatively restricted distribution, owing to their growth requirements. Two species in particular, however, *E. caffra* (coast coral tree) and *E. lysistemon* (common coral tree), are prominent almost countrywide. In early spring the bright, clear orange to scarlet flowers on their leafless stalks suddenly catch the eye.

The showy flowers of the common coral tree

The trunk of a huge coast coral tree – Franschhoek, Western Cape

The natural distribution of **Erythrina lysistemon** (**common coral tree**) is given as a comma-shaped corridor from the North West Province through Limpopo, Mpumalanga, Swaziland, the eastern parts of KwaZulu-Natal, to the northern part of the Eastern Cape. A small to medium-sized tree 6–10 m high, this tree is most suitable for planting in home gardens or parks and as a street tree in areas with little or no frost, as it is easily propagated by seed or cuttings. The common coral tree was often planted by Africans on the occasion of the birth of a son, or on the grave of a chief, with the result that it is difficult to establish the natural distribution of the species.

Erythrina caffra (**coast coral tree**) has a more restricted distribution, namely a narrow corridor along the coastal area of the Eastern Cape and KwaZulu-Natal. Usually between 9 and 12 m high, it can reach up to 21 m in the forest. The Alexandria forest is said to have the tallest of these trees. Here and in other Eastern Cape forests they form a tall trunk reaching for the sun, with a small tuft of branches above the canopy, while in the open they will develop into attractive wide-crowned trees, with dense light green foliage, turning to a striking yellow autumn hue.

The flowers of *E. caffra* are orange-scarlet, with a creamy variation, and, like *E. lysistemon*, produced in early spring in large exquisite racemes of 10 cm long, before the leaves appear. The fruits of the two species resemble each other closely: they are long, thin, dark pods, constricted between the

The common coral tree is an excellent garden or street tree in frost-free areas

The exquisite flowers of *Erythrina falcata*, an exotic from Brazil, very rare in South Africa

seeds, and split open to expose small shiny coral-red seeds marked with a black spot at the point of attachment. Necklaces made from the seeds are popular, and children collect them as 'lucky beans'.

Medicinal research has shown that the seed contains toxic alkaloids and substances that prevent blood clotting, and the CSIR at one stage investigated the value of these substances in the treatment of thrombosis. Other parts of the trees are used in traditional healing to treat nervous diseases and sores.

The wood, mainly white or yellowish, very soft, light and spongy, has been used for various purposes by local people, such as for floats for fishing nets and hollowed-out trunks for troughs. Nowadays it is more commonly used for carving animals and birds. The yellow-white wood is made more interesting by colouring it with shoe polish or by scorching it with a flat piece of iron heated in a fire.

Both species grow easily from truncheons and are propagated by rural people around their kraals. The living fences of *Erythrina* in flower around water holes or kraals in some Eastern Cape districts are spectacular sights. East London, Eastern Cape, is known for the great number of well-developed coast coral trees in gardens and along the streets.

Apart from their beneficial association with man, coral trees laden with nectar attract swarms of birds and insects, which indulge in these reservoirs of sweetness.

Two other South African *Erythrina* species are regarded as trees, namely the **Erythrina latissima** (**broad-leaved coral tree**), known for its very large leaves, and **Erythrina humeana** (**dwarf coral tree**), a small multi-stemmed tree and an attractive and sought-after garden plant.

To complete the South African *Erythrina* picture, mention should be made of the shrub erythrinas, namely the ploughbreaker, ***E. zeyheri***, a big-leaved shrub with an enlarged root system, and the tambuki thorn, ***E. acanthocarpa***. The broad-leaved coral tree, dwarf coral tree and ploughbreaker all have scarlet flowers. The tambuki thorn is even more exquisite, with each flower coloured in red and green – a spectacular sight when flowering in a garden or in nature.

Other members of the Papilionoideae subfamily indigenous to South Africa, with attractive flowers, are:

Bolusanthus speciosus (**tree wistaria**): A genus with a single species named after Dr Harry Bolus, a businessman and botanist who founded the Bolus Herbarium of the Botany Department of the University of Cape Town. The Latin species name means 'beautiful' and refers to the drooping sprays of violet-blue flowers borne in spring.

Virgilia oroboides (**blossom tree**): This genus is restricted to an area along the coast from Cape Town to about Port Elizabeth. The genus name honours the Latin poet Virgil and the species name *oroboides* means resembling the flowers of *Orobus,* a genus of plants with pea-flowers. (The isiXhosa name *umzitsikama* aptly points to the particular habitat.) The tree occurs on forest fringes and is a pioneer species with a short lifespan. The sweet-scented flowers are its great attraction. They vary in colour from white to a deep rose, borne in dense bunches on the branch terminals. Many insects and birds are associated with the blossom tree but the most important insect to which this tree is host is *Phalaena venus,* the ghost moth, whose caterpillars bore into the wood.

Philenoptera violacea (=*Lonchocarpus capassa*) (**apple-leaf tree**): Only one species, occurring in the northern parts of Limpopo, eastern Mpumalanga and northern KwaZulu-Natal. The genus name *Lonchocarpus* refers to the lance-shaped pods and the species name *capassa* is based on an African name for the tree. The apple-leaf is a medium-sized tree 15 m high, bearing large sprays of small, fragrant, violet pea-like flowers in October, when it honours the name of the family to which it belongs.

Millettia grandis (**umzimbeet**): The genus name honours Charles Millett and the species name *grandis* means 'large'. The tree occurs in the Eastern Cape and KwaZulu-Natal, is usually medium-sized and has a heavy, hard and durable dark-brown wood. The flowers are borne at the ends of the branches and are colourful, purple and pea-like, developing from rusty-brown hairy buds.

Philenoptera sutherlandii (=*Millettia sutherlandii*) (**forest apple-leaf**) is a tall forest tree up to 30 m in height, occurring in the forests of the Eastern Cape and the Dhlinza and Ngoy(j)e forests in KwaZulu-Natal. The flowers of this species are pink, mauve or purple.

Xanthocercis zambesiaca (**nyala tree**) is a very large evergreen tree, up to 20 m high, with a crown diameter of 30 m and trunk diameter several metres. It occurs north of the Soutpansberg and in the northern parts of the Kruger National Park and Botswana, often in association with termite hills. The flowers are not as showy as those of other Papilionoideae members and the fruit is a berry, quite unusual for a legume. The tree is valued for its form, size and shadiness. Magnificent specimens can be seen at the Tshipise Forever Resort in Limpopo.

Jackalberry (*Diospyros mespiliformis*), of the family Ebenaceae, is another remarkable evergreen tree that occurs in more or less the same area as the nyala tree. It is also often associated with termite mounds and usually of medium size, but impressive trees of 25 m high with wide spreading crowns are not uncommon.

Pterocarpus angolensis (**wild teak** or **kiaat**) is a small to medium-sized tree in South Africa, which grows taller in Mozambique. The genus name means 'winged fruit', while *angolensis* probably describes where it was first discovered. It is an attractive tree, usually with a straight trunk and wide flattish crown. The flowers are yellow and quite showy. The flower develops into a disc-shaped pod with a bristly centre resembling large owl eyes. Wild teak is most prized for its excellent durable wood which is attractive, light brown to dark reddish-brown, very stable, of medium

Nyala trees on the bank of the Limpopo River

A giant jackalberry on the Sabie River bank in the Kruger National Park

weight and is easily worked – a most sought-after furniture timber.

In Namibia the tree is called *dolfhout*. This name had its origin with the so-called Thirstland Trek ('Dorslandtrek') that took place from 1874 to 1884, when a group of farmers (Boers from the western regions of the ZAR, the Zuid-Afrikaansche Republiek, later the Transvaal) trekked through the

The decorative twisted branches of a kiaat tree on rocky soil in the Mpumalanga Lowveld

waterless Kalahari to southern Angola and back to Namibia, where they settled in the Otavi-Grootfontein area in 1885 in the short-lived Republic of Upingtonia. One of the leaders of these Thirstland trekkers was Dolf Holtzhausen who, joined by his sons, was the carpenter of the trek.

Pterocarpus rotundifolius (**round-leaved teak** or **dopperkiaat**): This small, attractive, mostly multi-stemmed tree occurs from northern KwaZulu-Natal northwards to Limpopo. The compound leaves are shiny and roundish, as the species name indicates. Besides the beautiful shiny leaves, the other attraction of this tree is the sweet-scented flowers. They are brilliant yellow with crinkled petals. A visit to the Lowveld regions to see the dopperkiaat in flower is an unforgettable experience.

Tipuana tipu (**Tipu**): An exotic tree from Bolivia and northern Argentine, of which large specimens can be seen in Pretoria and elsewhere. A well-known tipu with crown diameter of 40 m grows on the grounds of the Hendrik Verwoerd High School in Deerness, Pretoria.

Giant tipu tree on the grounds of the Hendrik Verwoerd High School, Deerness, Pretoria

Floating trees

Conveying wood by water is general practice in many parts of the world. The most unlikely place to apply this way of transport is Namibia. Yet this was the mode of transporting logs of dead kiaat trees on the Okavango River, from Kuring-kuru to the sawpits more than 100 km downstream. Logs were tied together to form a raft, onto the centre of which a thick layer of clay was plastered to serve as a fireplace, and the crew then commenced their journey of a few days.

PTAEROXYLACEAE
The Sneezewood Family

Ptaeroxylaceae is a very small family consisting of only two genera, *Ptaeroxylon* from South Africa and *Cedrelopsis* from Madagascar.

Ptaeroxylon obliquum (**sneezewood**) is a genus of only one species from South Africa and neighbouring countries. It occurs in a variety of habitats from the Eastern Cape northwards, is of variable size, from a small shrub growing in low altitude woodland and scrub forest to a tree of 30+ m in montane forests.

The genus name *Ptaeroxylon*, as well as the family name, are derived from the Greek words for 'sneezewood', referring to the pungent sawdust from the wood, caused by a peppery volatile oily ingredient as well as an aromatic resin, both of which cause the wood to be most inflammable. This was the ideal wood for making fires by friction.

The species name *obliquum* refers to the lopsided leaflets. The trees lose their leaves occasionally, mostly after a very dry summer, when they assume a yellow rusty-red or bronze colour. Male and female flowers are borne on separate trees. The flowers are white to pale yellow and are borne in profusion.

The most outstanding feature of the sneezewood is its heartwood, which is red when freshly cut, but changes to a golden brown with time. It is fine-grained and has a satiny lustre, with a mass of 1 012 kg/m^3. A legend for its durability, sneezewood timber played an important role in the development of the country. It was used for marine works, building purposes, fence posts, railway sleepers and as an excellent firewood. Although its use for fencing might pose a risk, it has been observed that a number of sneezewood fencing posts are still standing intact after some 100 years.

Sneezewood can either be large trees in favourable climates or small shrubs where conditions are less favourable

Known for the durability of its timber, the sneezewood tree played an important role in the economic development of the country

In the course of excavations that were undertaken in the Port Elizabeth harbour in the 1970s, a number of heavy wooden baulks were found forming the roof of a storm-water drain. The timber aroused interest because of its high mass and lack of decay. Samples sent to the erstwhile South African Forestry Research Institute were identified as sneezewood.

When he delved into the history of the storm-water drain, the harbour engineer found that sneezewood and ironwood piles were used in 1856 to build a breakwater, with the sneezewood placed closer to the shore. The breakwater quickly silted up and in 1867 the piles were extracted and re-used in the construction of another jetty, where they stayed until 1880. Shortly afterwards the storm-water drain was roofed by baulks sawn from the sneezewood piles where they were excavated. After about 120 years of exposure to all kinds of eroding elements the sneezewood was still sound enough for making furniture.

In 1987 the durability of sneezewood was further demonstrated when the forester at the Fort Cunynghame plantation in the Eastern Cape unearthed a culvert built of stone and covered with sneezewood poles. The culvert was situated on the Stutterheim-Cathcart road and fell into disuse in 1946 when a new road was built. How long the sneezewood poles had been buried under gravel is not known, but the poles were still in good condition.

A wide range of medicinal uses for various parts of the sneezewood tree has been reported, as well as for snuff, as an insect repellent and as a charm.

The city of Mthatha (formerly Umtata), Eastern Cape, apparently derived its name from the isiZulu and isiXhosa names for sneezewood, namely *umThathi*.

MELIACEAE

The Mahogany Family

Meliaceae is a large tropical timber family that includes the true mahogany (*Swietenia* species), sapele mahogany (*Entandrophragma* species) and red mahogany (*Khaya* species); all are hailed throughout the world for their excellent timber.

Six genera of the mahogany family, containing eleven tree species, are indigenous to South Africa. The smallest and most exquisite of these is ***Nymania capensis*** (**Chinese lantern**), a uniquely ornamental species when in flower or fruiting, and very conspicuous in spring. The Chinese lantern has a fairly large distribution in the hot, semi-arid regions of the Little Karoo and north-westwards to the southern parts of Namibia. It is a shrub or small rigid tree 2–4 m high, bearing attractive bell-shaped pink flowers that are virtually eclipsed by the beautiful creamy-red to bright red-pink inflated (balloon-like) four-angled fruit, 3–5 cm in diameter, into which they develop.

Having caught the eye of early botanists, the species was successfully grown in greenhouses by English gardeners some 200 years ago. It grows easily from seed and is drought resistant, but does not survive in higher rainfall areas, with the result that this decorative plant is not very often seen in South African gardens.

Ekebergia capensis (**Cape ash**) is a medium to large (20 m high) evergreen or semi-evergreen tree occurring from the Eastern Cape through to Limpopo in a variety of habitats, from scrub to high altitude evergreen and riverine forests, and from sea-level to about 1 500 m above sea-level. With its small sweetly scented white flowers borne in profusion, and followed by a fleshy pale-yellow or red berry relished by birds, this is a popular garden and street tree, extensively planted in Port Elizabeth, for instance.

Two distinct variants occur: the Western Cape variant resembles the wild plum (*Harpephyllum caffrum*) from the mango family. It has a more rigid appearance than the northern variant, which is more pendulous and displays red autumn colours, in contrast to the yellow of the former. To distinguish between the Western Cape variant of the

Cape ash trees, reaching large dimensions in the indigenous forests in subtropical areas, are often seen in gardens and parks in the warmer regions of South Africa

Natal mahogany trees: popular street, park and garden trees in frost-free areas

Ekebergia and the *Harpephyllum*, detach a leaf of each and compare them. The *Ekebergia* has prominent leaf scars on the branches and, with its yellow autumn colours, differs from the *Harpephyllum* with its red autumn colours and watery substance secreted from the base of the leaf.

Legend has it that Pacaltsdorp, started as a missionary post near George, was founded around a Cape ash tree. The age of this still existing 'Tree of Meeting' is said to be 300 years.

Two *Trichilia* species occur naturally in South Africa, namely *Trichilia emetica* (**Natal mahogany**) and *Trichilia dregeana* (**forest mahogany**). For easier identification, the differences are listed in Table 6.

Table 6: Differences between *Trichilia emetica* and *T. dregeana*

	Trichilia emetica	*Trichilia dregeana*
Habitat	Open woodland	Montane and coastal forests
Size/Height	Medium sized: up to 20 m	Large: up to 30 m
Leaves	Compound, more or less rounded, hairy under-surface	Shiny compound, more or less pointed, under-surface hairless
Fruit	Rounded capsule, 2,5–3 cm in diameter, attached to stalk by means of a neck or stipe	Velvety rounded capsule, 3 cm in diameter, attached to stalk without neck or stipe

The fruits and striking seeds of the Natal mahogany tree (Photo: Ben-Erik van Wyk)

The similarities between *Trichilia emetica* and *T. dregeana* are:
- The fruit of both species split into three valves. The black seeds are almost completely covered with a red aril. The seeds are eaten by people and birds.
- The wood is most suitable for carving and woodworking.
- Bark, seeds, etc., of both species are used medicinally.

The giant *T. dregeana* growing near Mitchell Park in Durban has a trunk diameter of 2 m, height of 18 m and crown diameter of 35 m.

Melia azedarach (**seringa** or **syringa**) is an exotic member of the family Meliaceae that finds itself in the same peculiar love/hate situation in South Africa as eucalypts and wattles, being too prolific and growing too easily! The seringa, native to India, is nowadays

Forest mahogany growing in its natural habitat, Kranzkloof Nature Reserve, KwaZulu-Natal (Photo: Wikimedia Commons)

The forest mahogany is a fine shade tree and often used as a street and park tree in warm, high-rainfall areas like Durban (Photo: Garth Kloppenborg)

Forest mahogany trunk in the Old Fort gardens, Durban, KwaZulu-Natal (Photo: Wikimedia Commons)

regarded as a pest in many parts of the world. It is an extremely hardy species, growing in almost every type of soil. It bears masses of sweet-smelling lilac flowers in spring – a treat to the eyes and noses of the healthy but a torment to hay fever sufferers. The flowers are followed by masses of yellow berries, reputedly toxic.

A blessing in the arid parts of the country, seringa is a real curse in the wetter parts, where it spreads naturally. Fortunately the wood is valuable and easily workable, and both the leaves and berries are eaten by animals, the latter, however, preferably in small quantities only. The variety **umbraculiformis** ('resembling an umbrella') has a dome-shaped crown and is even more picturesque than the seringa proper.

Although exotic, a number of seringa trees were involved in historic events in South Africa. On 11 February 1859 a group of 310 dissatisfied members of the Dutch Reformed Church gathered under a seringa tree in Rustenburg, North West, and established the Reformed Church with the Reverend Dirk Postma as their minister. One of those present was SJP Kruger, who later became President of the ZAR. The original tree had to be cut down in the 1950s, and when the stump rotted away it was replaced with a granite replica in 1972. It is a national monument.

The 'Gallows Tree', a seringa in Griquatown, Northern Cape, home town of the Griqua leaders Adam Kok and Andries Waterboer, is still standing. According to the local people it was planted around 1906 and legend has it that trespassers were hanged from this tree.

TREE FAMILIES

The exotic red mahogany, a fast-growing tree attaining large dimensions in South Africa – JDM Keet Forest Station, Tzaneen, Limpopo

Khaya anthoteca (**red mahogany**) is indigenous to a number of African countries, South Africa excluded. In Mozambique, Malawi and Zambia it is an important timber tree.

In spite of its being an exotic, it is planted as an ornamental tree in the warmer regions of South Africa, as well as on a smaller scale in plantations, specially for furniture timber. This striking, fast-growing evergreen tree can develop into very large specimens. Impressive examples can be seen at the New Agatha and JDM Keet (Zomerkomst) plantations near Tzaneen, Limpopo, now managed by Komatiland Forests, at Tshipise Forever Resort and at the Merensky Hotel, Phalaborwa. The largest known tree in this species is a buttressed giant more than 60 m tall, with diameter at breast height (buttresses included) of over 5 m, growing in the Chirinda forest, eastern Zimbabwe.

A further number of noteworthy trees at JDM Keet includes, *inter alia*:
- *Hevea braziliensis* (rubber tree)
- *Ocotea porosa* (imbuia)
- *Enterolobium contortisiliquum* (black ear)
- *Eleaocarpus grandis* (blue fig, giant blueberry ash)
- *Brachystegia spiciformis* (msasa)
- *Azadirachta indica* (neem)
- *Entandophragma* species (mahogany).

EUPHORBIACEAE
The Milkbush Family

This huge, widely distributed and most interesting heterogeneous family of 4 000 species worldwide includes plants from small flat-growing garden herbs to peculiar succulents to ordinary broad-leaved trees. The family is well represented in South Africa.

Although many people are ignorant about the wide variety of euphorbias – mostly referred to as 'cacti' – the euphorbias in one form or another are known to almost everybody. Humans have become dependent on members of this diverse family for a variety of purposes: rubber, for tyres and other articles (*Hevea braziliensis* – rubber tree), medicine (e.g. *Ricinus communis* – castor-oil plant), starch for smoothing paper and for food (*Manihot esculenta* – bitter cassava or tapioca plant), garden plants (*Euphorbia pulcherrima* – poinsettia), wood for furniture (*Spirostachys africana* – tamboti), etc. A milky or watery latex is exuded by a large number of euphorbias. The latex is mostly poisonous and has played a considerable role in the preparation of arrow poison, the treatment of ailments and in witchcraft since the early history of mankind.

Hyena poison tree on the Gifberg, Vanrhynsdorp, Western Cape

Hyaenanche globosa (**hyena poison**) is a shrub or small evergreen tree approximately 4 m high, restricted to the Vanrhynsdorp and Clanwilliam districts of the Western Cape Province, where it occurs in fynbos veld. Apart from its restricted occurrence, the hyena poison is also the only species in this genus. The genus name *Hyaenanche* means 'hyena poison' – the pounded seeds were used as arrow poison by the early San people, and also in bait to poison hyenas. It was observed by the botanist Lambert, who named the tree accordingly. It was also one of the plants first observed during the Van der Stel expedition to Namaqualand in 1685.

Like many of the Euphorbiaceae, the hyena poison is dioecious, i.e. with male and female organs on different plants, and the flowers are wind-pollinated. On the Gifberg ('Poison Mountain') near Vanrhynsdorp, which derived its name from this interesting plant, specimens of these trees have been found with a height up to 3,75 m and crown diameter of 8,5 m.

The tree sometimes causes deaths among stock, especially when the latter are brought in from elsewhere. It happens when they drink water from sandstone hollows where it has accumulated together with hyena poison leaves, or if animals accidentally eat a dry leaf together with grass.

Cleistanthus schlechteri (**false tamboti**) is also the only one in its genus. It is a small to medium-sized tree up to 20 m in height, of the northern coastal area of KwaZulu-Natal, where it plays an important role in Zulu culture. The wood is dark brown, hard and durable, and is used for building and carving, while the bark is used medicinally.

Androstachys johnsonii (**Lebombo ironwood** or **wild quince**), once again the only one in its genus, is a small, medium to tall tree usually occurring in dense stands in the Soutpansberg and Lebombo mountain ranges in Limpopo, where it forms dense, almost khaki-coloured patches. It is also dioecious, with the flowers being wind-pollinated.

The dark brown wood is very durable, hard and heavy, and is used in hut building and fencing. According to Coates Palgrave, Lebombo ironwood poles used for building huts in the Shingwedzi and Punda Maria camps in the Kruger National Park were still sound after 40 years. Apparently the African names *Msimbiti* or *Msambir* mean 'ironwood'.

Schinziophyton rautanenii (**manketti** or **feather-weight tree**) grows in Kalahari sand in Namibia, Angola, Botswana and Zimbabwe, the northernmost part of the Northern Cape and in a very small area in the western part of Limpopo. The tree has a spreading crown with a slightly thickset trunk and branches with golden-grey smooth bark resembling a leafless baobab tree. The wood is creamy-white, soft and very light, with a mass of about 200 kg/m^3, as against the 910 kg/m^3 of the Lebombo ironwood.

The plum-shaped fruit (± 4 × 2,5 cm) consists of an edible pulpy outer layer, eaten both by humans and elephants. This layer encloses a very hard woody kernel, containing the best part of the fruit, a nut, which serves as an important food. The nut is protected by a thin but very hard inedible shell. The nuts are usually pounded and boiled to separate the edible and inedible parts. Kernels are often found in abundance in elephant dung where the manketti occurs; the nuts remain edible after cleaning and preparing.

Spirostachys africana (**tamboti**) is also a genus containing only one species and only from Africa. In South Africa it occurs in the

Manketti trees, like baobabs, are most impressive when leafless

bushveld and lowveld regions as well as in KwaZulu-Natal. Many legends surround the tamboti – mainly about its beautiful and durable aromatic wood, its poisonous properties and its 'jumping' seeds.

Spirostachys, the genus name, is the Greek for 'spiral flower-spikes'. The tiny flowers are arranged spirally in short brown catkin-like spires, with the male flowers at the top and the female ones below. The fruit is a three-lobed capsule that splits open with a popping sound to release the seed. The fruit often becomes infested with the larvae of a small grey moth, *Emporia melanobasis*. As the fruit becomes dry, the larvae flex inside, causing the fruit to 'jump' into the air – hence the common name of 'jumping-bean tree'. The fruits are then avidly collected by children as a curiosity.

Tamboti hardwood is dark brown and beautifully figured – one of the most beautiful of all South African woods. It is oily, has a fine texture, is heavy ($\pm$ 850 kg/m^3), durable, and has a pleasant spicy odour, which has led to the tree also being called 'African sandalwood'. (Sandalwood is both the scented wood of a sandal-tree from India, as well as the perfume derived from it.) Tamboti wood was used by indigenous peoples as a perfume or as a scented necklace. The wood is however unsuitable for fires for cooking, as the smoke will poison the food. The sap of the tree is poisonous and contact might result in blistering of sensitive skins, as well as severe pain if it enters the eyes. In spite of the poisonous qualities, however, the sap, roots and bark were used traditionally for medicinal purposes for a wide variety of complaints.

Tamboti is a protected tree under the provincial legislation of Limpopo and Mpumalanga. The Mosdene Natural Heritage Site in the Mokopane (Potgietersrus) district contains prime examples of tamboti communities.

The genus *Euphorbia* (tree euphorbias and milkbushes)

This is the largest genus in the Euphorbiaceae family, with approximately 2 000 species worldwide, ranging from herbs to shrubs to trees. Some 250 species are indigenous to South Africa, a number of which are trees of exceptional form and to some extent resembling the cacti of the Americas.

These euphorbia trees (about 25 species) are largely succulent spiny trees, occurring more commonly in the wetter eastern parts of the country than in the more arid west. Euphorbias are largely conspicuous in a landscape and usually have distinct trunks crowned with a cluster of succulent and often angled branches constricted into segments. The leaves are rudimentary and they tend to shrivel and fall off soon after their appearance. Flowers and fruit are borne together with the spines along the angles of the branches.

Euphorbias all exude a toxic latex when damaged. It is sometimes used medicinally – which at times in the past proved to be fatal, this again linking the latex with magic. For instance, in the Eastern Cape two euphorbias are planted near huts where twins have been born, to ward off harmful influences.

The branches of the candelabra tree extend to branch anew, giving rise to its common name

The Lebombo euphorbia, almost unknown, only occurring in the north-eastern areas of the Limpopo and Mpumulanga Provinces

Legend has it that the genus *Euphorbia* was named in 25 BC by Juba II, king of Mauritania, who was married to the daughter of Anthony and Cleopatra, in honour of his physician. Euphorbos, a Greek, whose name, meaning 'well-fed', was applicable both to plant and physician!

The tree euphorbia is also known as 'naboom' (Afrikaans), which is presumably a corruption of the Khoi word *gnap*, meaning 'strong' – emphasising the vigorous tree growth. The Zulu and Xhosa people do not differentiate between the species, all of which are known to them as *umHlonhlo*.

Euphorbia tirucalli (**rubber euphorbia**) is a spineless tree reaching a maximum height of 9 m, with slender pencil-like cylindrical branches forming a dense crown that closely resembles a broom. This tree occurs from the Eastern Cape northwards through Central Africa, where it is often used as a live fence around the houses of rural people.

With the exception of *Euphorbia ingens* (**candelabra tree**), all euphorbias shed their lower branches. In the case of *E. ingens* the lower branches grow, extend and branch again in a candelabra fashion, to form huge trees 9 m tall and 8 m in crown diameter – hence the species name, which means 'large'.

Synadenium cupulare (**dead-man's tree** or **crying tree**) is a shrub or small tree 1,5–4 m high, with succulent stems and leaves. It occurs from KwaZulu-Natal to Mpumalanga and Limpopo. The leaves have a dark green upper surface and a mottled red under-surface, and are crowded towards the branch apexes.

The tree is surrounded by many superstitions. The Zulu people, for instance, once believed that it lured people and animals towards itself, to kill them; hence the peculiar common name. Birds flying over the tree would drop dead, and the ground surrounding the trees was said to be white with bones.

In spite of these fears, the dead-man's tree is planted occasionally in Limpopo as a live fence, while elsewhere it is planted on graves to protect them from animals. Parts of the tree are used for medicines, and, being quite decorative with its red to purplish-red leaves, it is planted as an ornamental tree in gardens in the warmer regions of the country. A variety, *rubra*, has been cultivated for gardens.

Dying candelabra euphorbias in Limpopo Province – the cause of this phenomenon is being researched by FABI, University of Pretoria

CACTACEAE
The Cactus or Prickly Pear Family

Although no indigenous cactus trees occur in South Africa, members of the cactus family are well known in the country because many species were introduced. (South Africa's tree euphorbias are, however, sometimes confused with cacti.) The cactus family as a whole is native to the Americas exclusively, except for one small epiphyte, *Rhipsalis baccifera*, which occurs in South Africa and a few other countries. (Epiphyte = a plant growing, but not parasitic, on another.) The family contains a large number of succulent plants, usually leafless, with the stems modified into cylinders, pads or joints, where water is stored. A thick skin and numerous spines not only prevent excessive transpiration but damage from animals as well.

In contrast to the largely unattractive, sometimes even near deterring, appearance of the plants, most cacti, the jungle cacti that grow as epiphytes on trees and rocks in particular, have most exquisite flowers and are often seen cultivated. The striking flowers, oddly shaped in many cases, and the usefulness of a number of species have resulted in cacti being introduced to almost every corner of the world. Arid countries, like South Africa, actually welcomed these plants with open arms. A rockery planted with cacti once used to be an essential part of many South African gardens.

Today South Africa has more than her fair share of cacti. The less aggressive but more beautiful species can be admired in many gardens, the owners of which sometimes also sell these plants. *It must be stressed, however, that all cacti are potential invaders and it*

The sweet prickly pear, often planted in the past as a source of animal fodder, is now a declared invader

is not advisable to buy or sell these plants. The more aggressive species have established themselves firmly throughout the country; in the Eastern Cape in particular.

Introduced species as a rule thrive in their guest countries under favourable growth conditions, as their natural enemies do not accompany them from their home shores. Should these plant species become a pest, however, their natural enemies are usually our best allies in combating their spreading. Therefore attention is turned towards the country of origin, with scientists collecting these natural enemies and releasing them among the pest species.

This method of biological weed control was introduced to South Africa in 1913, when it was realised that the cactus *Opuntia vulgaris* (**sour prickly pear**), which was spreading vigorously along the Eastern Cape coast, had to be combated. A cochineal insect, *Dactylopius ceylonicus*, was imported and almost exterminated the cactus plants, still successfully controlling them to this day. This was probably the first example of deliberate biological control of a weed species in the world.

The well-known *Opuntia ficus-indica* (**sweet prickly pear**) was introduced to the Western Cape during Dutch East India Company rule. Its spread to the warmer Eastern Cape, where more favourable growth conditions prevailed, proved to be disastrous. By 1750 it had reached pest status. Conventional control measures had no dramatic results, and by the 1930s approximately 1 million hectares of land had become infested, from Port Elizabeth to Graaff-Reinet. The moth *Cactoblastis cactorum* and the cochineal insect *Dactylopius opuntiae* were imported and released in the infested areas. By 1945 a remarkable 75% of this terrible weed was destroyed, and today these insects are still maintaining the balance, virtually unnoticed. The only area where these insects are not very effective is close to the sea. This explains why so many sweet prickly pear plants still occur in the vicinity of Uitenhage. The infestations that had stretched as far as Graaff-Reinet, however, were efficiently wiped out by the insects.

Opuntia aurantiaca (**jointed cactus**), which probably started off in South Africa as a plant collector's item, is being kept at bay by the *Cactoblastis* moth together with yet another cochineal species.

The successes of those early eradication campaigns by the Plant Protection Research Institute of the former Department of Agriculture are almost forgotten, while the tide has turned and the cochineal insects are now regarded as pests by the average South African – both those who grow prickly pears for fodder and fruit and those who enjoy the fruit.

One of the species of cochineal is the source of a red dye that was used in Mexico when the Spaniards arrived there in 1518. Baron von Ludwig, of the Ludwig's-burg Garden in Cape Town, imported a cochineal species around 1831. He published an article on this valuable insect in the *South African Quarterly Journal* No V, stating that the annual value of the dye exported from South America was more than 500 000 pounds sterling, 'a vast amount to arise from so small an insect'. Von Ludwig, the businessman, obviously had a cochineal industry for South Africa in mind. This did however not materialise. Mexico and other South American countries are the main producers of cochineal dye – a growing industry because of the worldwide trend towards greater use of natural products.

More information on cacti and the danger they pose is obtainable from the Agricultural Research Council, Plant Protection Research Institute, Pretoria.

Cochineal on a prickly pear (Photo: Ben-Erik van Wyk)

ANACARDIACEAE

The Mango Family

Anacardiaceae is a large family with 60 genera and more than 500 species worldwide. It is noteworthy, as it includes trees yielding delicious fruit such as mango, marula, pistachio and cashew nuts, and trees with extremely poisonous qualities, such as *Smodingium argutum*, the rainbow leaf, indigenous to South Africa, *Searsia radicans*, the American poison berry, and *S. succedanea*, the wax tree, often planted in South Africa for its red autumn colours; all cause an allergic condition in some people. Lacquer is a benign product obtained from trees of the mango family. It is a gummy secretion exuded by the lac beetle *Technadria lacsa*, which feeds off such trees. The Peruvian pepper tree, *Schinus molle*, one of the best known trees in South Africa, introduced from South America, dearly welcomed by the weary, sun-drenched traveller through the arid parts of the country, and *S. terebinthifolius*, the Brazilian pepper tree, both belong to the mango family.

***Sclerocarya birrea* subsp. *caffra* (marula)** is probably the tree of Africa with which the average South African associates most readily. Marula is as South African as can be, although it occurs further northwards into Africa than its South African home ground in the bushveld areas of KwaZulu-Natal, Mpumalanga, Limpopo and also North West. The genus name is from the Greek for hard (*sklevos*) nut (*karyon*).

The marula is a medium-sized tree of up to 30 m in height. Male and female flowers are borne on separate trees. When in flower, the tree is a hive of activity, with honey-bees, flies and ants, all attracting their specific predators, frequenting the flowers. Early pioneers at one stage associated the marula tree with malaria because the tree produced fruits when malaria was at its worst. A legend grew that larvae bred in fallen fruit. This belief is not true, although mosquitoes do breed in marula trees where water collects in holes in the stems.

The most important part of the marula, however, is its fruits, which are borne in abundance during February and March. The fruit is almost spherical, up to 3,5 cm in diameter, with a pleasant-tasting thin fleshy layer covering the large stones. The stones are hard, with two to three cells each containing a small seed, which is not only edible but actually very tasty. It is however a hard task to extract the kernels. The fruits are shed when still green and ripen on the ground, where they give off a typical pleasant, strong smell. They can be eaten fresh, a real delicacy to the initiated, enjoyed as an intoxicating brew, cooked as a jelly, or savoured in an exquisite liquor available commercially. (Dubbed 'The Spirit of Africa', it was highly acclaimed both in South Africa and overseas. Voted second most favoured brand in a questionnaire, it received a golden award at an international wine and spirits competition in London; proclaimed to be 'a regular gold medallist on this prestigious platform'.) The jelly may

A marula tree on the northern perimeter of the Springbok Flats – Limpopo (Photo: Henry Breytenbach)

further be used to prepare tasty sweets, jams and beauty products.

Favourable reports have been received about the entrepreneurial opportunities offered by marula fruits when in abundance. Indigenous people in the Letaba area of the Mpumalanga Lowveld used to regard the marula as very important in their economic and social life. It was reported in 1937 that these people subsisted largely on marula nuts during winter. They had a marula culture and developed a small implement known as a *modukulo* for extracting the nut from the pip after it had been cracked open between two stones. The women spent their days cracking marula pips during the season. They also devised a net bag in which they carried the marula fruits on their heads. In those years the falling of the fruit heralded a period of festivity. With the beer being plentiful, men were prohibited from carrying weapons when the marula was in fruit, for fear of injuries.

Marula can indeed be considered the economic kingpin of the woodland trees. They support the survival of half a million rural households in many ways, from additional nutrition (rich in Vitamin C) and income, to formal jobs in projects such as the Mthala Development Centre in Mpumalanga, where 2 400 women are employed. Marula wood is also used by the informal wood-carving industry, together with wood from other exotic species.

With marula fruits showing economic potential, the Plant Production Department of the University of Pretoria's Agriculture Faculty has, through careful selection, succeeded in propagating trees bearing fruits 7 cm in diameter.

Marula fruits are easily available and seemingly sought after by stock and wild animals, including elephants. The story goes that baboons and monkeys become intoxicated on eating the fermenting fruits. This is accepted by many people as one of the

Women busy preparing a sought after marula drink, relished by locals

interesting examples of interplay between South Africa's botanical and animal worlds. No proof exists, however, to verify this.

The leaves of the marula are browsed by animals and the bark is stripped by elephants. The bark is used medically, while a dye is also obtained from it. Marula wood is pinkish-white to brown, soft, and ideal for carving of sculptures, the final products usually coloured or burnt to enhance the effect. During World War II a critical timber shortage arose and marula trees were felled in thousands for small industry, especially for the manufacture of lavatory seats. Protection was eventually warranted under the Forest Act in 1951, when the species was declared protected.

A historic marula tree in Maputo, Mozambique, under which the Voortrekker leader Louis Trichardt supposedly died in 1838, was visited by scientists from South Africa in 1985 to advise the owners of the property on which it stood about its health. At that time the tree was still healthy, measuring as follows: height 13,1 m; trunk diameter 1,08 m; crown spread 25 m. The biggest known marula tree in South Africa is 19 m in height, with a trunk diameter of 1,33 m and crown spread of 25 m. This giant grows at Kranspoort, Limpopo.

The mango family also includes the almost ubiquitous **Searsia** (formerly **Rhus**) species of South Africa. The various karee and wild currant trees are mostly small trees and are undoubtedly a boon to South Africa. They are very hardy, both against drought and frost, and are therefore widely planted for shade, shelter and as ornamental trees. More than 30 karee or wild currant species in South Africa are classified as trees. The most popular ones, used as street trees and garden plants, are the white karee, the karee and the mountain karee.

Searsia lancea (karee) trees used to grow at Karoopoort, some 40 km northeast of Ceres in the Western Cape, on the old Highway to the North. It was a well-known and popular outspan for many early travellers. This site was described by Lichtenstein and Burchell at the beginning of the 19th century. Burchell camped at Karoopoort in 1811 while travelling with his ox-wagon and made a sketch of the karee trees. Some stumps are still visible in the poort today. This site was declared a national monument in 1981 and includes three historical buildings, probably built after the completion of Michell's Pass in 1848.

Another historical karee tree is found near the De Wildt siding on the Pretoria-Brits railway line, where, at a meeting attended by thousands of his followers, General JBM Hertzog in 1912 made his vision for South Africa known as far as political, cultural, educational economical and social matters were concerned.

Other noteworthy species in the family are *Harpephyllum caffrum*, the wild plum, which is often confused with *Ekebergia capensis*, and often planted in gardens, the *Lannea* species (knob-berry trees), *Ozoroa* species (resin trees), and *Heeria argentea*, the rock ash, of which an exceptionally big specimen, presumably of a record age, grows along the Klipbokkop 4 × 4 route in the Stettyns Mountains near Worcester in the Western Cape. The latter two species are characterised by their extremely neat leaves conspicuously parallel veined. *Protorhus longifolia*, the red beech, and *Laurophyllus capensis*, the iron martin, are also indigenous trees cherished by South Africans.

Loxostylis alata (tarwood), the only species in this genus, is confined to the Eastern Cape and KwaZulu-Natal. It is a small evergreen tree, very decorative, resembling the pepper tree. Male and female flowers are borne on separate trees, the male ones in profusion in white terminal sprays. The female flowers are green, but when fertilised, the segments of the calyx grow longer and turn red, surrounding the small hard fruit in the centre. When in flower and fruit these trees are a most attractive sight.

Smodingium argutum (rainbow leaf tree) is another remarkable member of the mango family. It is a graceful deciduous tree of small dimensions, but once again, overwhelmingly attractive when in flower and fruit. The rainbow leaf tree – a flattering common name, too – occurs from the Eastern Cape through KwaZulu-Natal to the far eastern parts of Mpumalanga. Male and female flowers are borne in profusion on separate trees, the female flowers being creamy-green and their fruits produced in dense attractive bunches, each completely encircled by a red papery wing containing an aromatic oil. This beauty is deceiving, however, because the sap of the feared *intovane*, as it is called both in isiZulu and isiXhosa, is highly irritating, raising blisters and frequently causing hospitalisation. People might even be affected by the pollen and should, if they are aware of this, avoid the trees, particularly when in flower. Gardeners should be aware of these qualities of the *intovane* when intending to cultivate it.

Schinus molle **(Peruvian pepper tree)** is a small to medium-sized tree from the dry parts of the Andes Mountains from Peru to Argentina. The trees are hardy and grow in localities where few other species would survive. For this reason they are a widely known feature of the more arid western regions of South Africa.

Although they can be described as quite graceful, with their drooping branches and pink peppercorn-like fruits, the trees are still disliked by many people, who tend to associate them with the remote dry and lonely outback areas of our country. (The fruits can be used as a substitute for pepper, but it apparently can be poisonous when too much is taken.)

Indeed the traveller who turns off the N1 at Matjiesfontein near Laingsburg, Western Cape, will appreciate the sight of these trees enhancing an interesting 'oasis' along a tedious stretch of road. So also in and around many towns in the Karoo, the Northern Province, where Kimberley comes to mind, and the southern Free State.

At two rather unlikely localities, both a far cry from their preferred habitat, interesting – and impressive – pepper trees are found; one, with a thickset gnarled trunk at Groot-Brakrivier, Western Cape, planted in 1884 by Willie Searle. The second one can actually only be appreciated by those on the wrong side of the law, as well as their keepers, namely on the grounds of the Baviaanspoort jail near Cullinan, Gauteng. With its trunk diameter of 2 m and well-developed wide crown, this tree might probably lure the innocent to less innocent practices, merely to be able to enjoy the luxury of reposing under its shade… Here, too, one might well wonder as how this tree came to be planted at this particular, rather improbable place – its history being as obscure as the place where it is standing.

At Pofadder in the Northern Cape Province Mr Gert Niemöller has put quite an effort into farm research on the pepper tree, concluding an extract of the leaves to be an effective repellent to gnats and ticks. The negative effect of ticks is generally well known, whereas the extreme troublesomeness of gnats along the Orange River in summer time, both to humans and animals, is a largely unrecognised factor.

The gnarled trunk of an old pepper tree at Groot-Brakrivier, Western Cape

MYRTACEAE

The Myrtle or Eucalyptus and Guava Family

Myrtaceae is a large family with approximately 2 000 species worldwide, mainly tropical and subtropical. General characteristics are evergreen, often aromatic, leaves, and conspicuous, often showy, flowers, with a powder-brush appearance resulting from large tufts of stamens. The fruit may be fleshy (guava) or dry (eucalypt).

Indigenous South African species belonging to the myrtle family are the waterwood or waterberries (*Syzygium* species), lance-leaved myrtles (*Metrosideros*), wild myrtles (*Eugenia* species) and lavender trees (*Heteropyxis* species).

The most important trees belonging to the myrtle family are undoubtedly the reputed **eucalypts** or **gum trees** (*Eucalyptus* species) originating from Australia. A small number of species do however occur naturally in Papua New Guinea, Indonesia and the Philippines. Eucalypts are planted worldwide for various reasons. The trees provide ornamental value, shade, shelter, windbreaks and timber, while the leaves are used to produce oil. The genus *Eucalyptus* contains approximately 400 species and 200 subspecies, varieties and hybrids.

Honouring their common name, the indigenous waterberry trees mostly occur along streams or near water – Blouberg, Limpopo

Characteristic of the species is the bark – one of the features by which eucalypts can be identified. The bark can be smooth to fibrous to rough, with colours from snow-white to bluish, mottled-grey to coppery-red or purplish-green to almost black. In a number of species it is shed annually, in long strands in some cases and in blotches in others. Mainly owing to the variations in the bark, eucalypts figure in many South African landscape paintings.

Eucalypts have become part of the South African landscape, owing to their extreme adaptability. They are aggressive growers and will stand out wherever they are planted. In the Karoo regions, where indigenous trees reach but a modest few metres in height, eucalypts reach a good 20 m (See *E. salubris* below).

It is the ability of this species to grow, in exceptional circumstances, more than 1 m a month, together with its adaptability, that gives the genus *Eucalyptus* a bad reputation. This despite the fact that only a handful of the more than 70 introduced gum species have been declared invasive. In South Africa, in particular, eucalypts are detested by conservation-minded enthusiasts – apparently without realising that this species has made a mammoth contribution towards the conservation of the country's indigenous woody vegetation (*inter alia* reducing reliance on indigenous timber products like poles for construction), and is still doing so. Eucalypt plantations make a significant contribution to the country's Gross Domestic Product and the wellbeing of its inhabitants, through the wide range of products derived from the trees. (*Eucalyptus* is one of the three most important tree species established in South Africa's commercial plantations.) It is ironical that the piles of pamphlets distributed regularly and containing propaganda against the hated tree are most probably printed on paper manufactured from eucalypt timber ...

The giant manna tree on the farm Familiehoek in the Ermelo district, Mpumalanga (Photo: Nicol de Wet)

Eucalypts – pioneers from a different age

Eucalypt trees have played an important role in South Africa during the past two centuries. The very first eucalypts to be introduced to South Africa in 1828 were apparently *E. globulus*, named 'blue gum', from the colourful blue leaves. No indigenous tree could equal these eucalypts for fast growth and general hardiness. They provided shade and shelter much sooner than the slower growing indigenous trees. It was obvious then that the first commercial plantation established in South Africa for the provision of firewood for steam railway engines would consist of a *Eucalyptus* species. (See *South Africa's Forestry Industry*.)

Their reputation caused eucalypt trees to be planted fairly widely in South Africa during the 19th century. Ms Rhoda Edwards, the sister of Dick King of the legendary Durban-to-Grahamstown horseback ride, planted some trees on their farm Rietvlei (now Paradoxus) in the Cathcart district, Eastern

Cape, around 1863. One of these trees was an *E. globulus* of extraordinary dimensions. (Ms Edwards died in 1936 at the age of 102 years.)

For those unfamiliar with the heroic deed of Dick King: when the Voortrekkers defeated the British in 1842 at Congella in KwaZulu-Natal, Dick King, using two horses, covered a distance of about 1 000 km between Durban and Grahamstown in ten days to summon assistance.

Three German foresters, Fuchs, Genth and Otto Brandmüller, in the service of businessmen Nellmapius, Eckstein and Sammy Marks, respectively, greatly contributed to the establishment of eucalypts in the former Transvaal Province, previously the ZAR (Zuid-Afrikaansche Republiek). Alois Nellmapius arranged for the large-scale planting of eucalypts and other species in the Irene area by Mr Fuchs – many are still standing and many have grown to trees with record dimensions. Hermann Eckstein, again, had Mr Genth head the planting of more than a million eucalypt trees between 1893 and 1899 in the area nowadays known as Saxonwold, Johannesburg (from *Sachsenwald*). In 1925/26 most of these trees were cut down to allow urban development. About 12 diehards are however still flourishing on the corner of Empire and Wabard Streets in Parktown. The nearby Sir Lionel Phillips Park boasts big eucalypt trees too – probably also planted by Genth.

Sammy Marks, legendary entrepreneur-businessman and friend of President Paul Kruger, established a large nursery around 1895, containing more than a million English oak trees and several hundred eucalypts, at his Makouvlei estate on the Vaal River. This nursery probably served as an outlet for the distribution of many eucalypt trees. Many eucalypt trees are still standing on the Marks estate Swartkoppies near Pretoria.

There is a remarkable resemblance between the Makouvlei eucalypts and two rows of eucalypt trees along Celliers Street in the Free State town of Heilbron, as well as those standing along the sports grounds of the local primary school. The latter trees were planted in 1901 by children from the Boer concentration camp to mark the accession of King Edward

Rough-barked mountain ash trees, exceeding a height of 60 m, Benvie Arboretum, New Hanover, KwaZulu-Natal (Photo: Enrico Liebenberg)

VII to the British throne after the death of Queen Victoria. They had to fetch water for the trees from a nearby watercourse by means of a water cart, which they had to pull themselves. Further stands of eucalypt trees in Heilbron and vicinity originated from the nursery of Bourke and Evans at Vierfontein, Free State, who also provided the eucalypt trees still an integral part of the Vierfontein landscape today. Thomas (Tom) Bourke, owner of a large estate round Vierfontein, was the last of the 'eucalypt pioneers' from that period of South Africa's history.

A clump of eucalypt trees of historical importance can be seen on the right hand side of the N12 south near Klerksdorp, North West. Here Generals Louis Botha, Transvaal (ZAR) army chief, and Koos de la Rey, the 'Lion of the Western Transvaal', met with President MT Steyn of the Orange Free State and General Christiaan de Wet, Boer hero from the OFS, to discuss peace talks with the British forces. This meeting led to the declaration of the Peace of Vereeniging on May 31, 1902, which brought an end to the Anglo-Boer War of 1899 to 1902.

Eucalypts rank among the tallest trees in the world. *Eucalyptus regnans* (**mountain ash**) commonly attains a height of 50–70 m and a trunk diameter of 2–2,7 m in Australia, while specimens of 114 m tall have reliably been reported. Unfortunately these particular trees were felled before it was realised that they were actually of world record size. (It is generally accepted that the tallest tree in the world is a Californian redwood, *Sequoia sempervirens*, of 115,7 m. Experimental planting in South Africa of the California redwood was started in the early 1900s, and many of these trees still flourish in arboreta on forest stations country-wide, some exceeding 60 m in height, with stem diameters near 2 m.)

OPPOSITE PAGE: Lemon-scented gum trees Prima hostel, Paul Roos Gymnasium, Stellenbosch. Initiation of the greenhorns was an important institution at Prima some years ago. Part of their ordeal was that once a year, at a secret date, when they came from school they would find their linen, blankets and other belongings tied together and hoisted high up in these trees. An image of the twin peaks in the background ('Die Pieke') serves as the emblem of this famous school

In South Africa the tallest *Eucalyptus regnans* trees are found in the Benvie Arboretum, New Hanover, KwaZulu-Natal. A trio of impressive specimens of these trees measured near 70 m before a storm damaged one crown, which toppled over and damaged the other two as well. Now just over 61 m high, these trees survived, their massive tapering trunks offering a striking sight.

A *Eucalyptus saligna* (**saligna gum**) tree of 81,5 m is now the tallest tree in South Africa, almost matching the height of a former champion (84,4 m), unfortunately blown down in 2007 during a storm. This tree stands in a grove of tall saligna gum trees planted by the pioneer forester AK Eastwood between 1905 and 1906 at the Woodbush plantation in the Magoebaskloof, Limpopo. According to available information, this is not only the tallest tree in Africa, but also the tallest planted eucalypt in the world. It was measured in 2013 by a group of international tree climbers (see *Tree Climbing in South Africa*), almost touching the crowns of two earlier successive record holders.

Close to this stand, leading to the memorial of one of South Africa's early forestry pioneers, JT O'Connor, is a noteworthy avenue of *E. saligna* trees, reaching a maximum height of just over 70 m. These big trees, with their candle-white stems, are an impressive sight indeed, paying homage to the far-sightedness of those pioneers.

Of historical importance are the so-called International Commonwealth Plots on the Middelkop Tea Estate near Tzaneen

The gum trees of the Commonwealth plantation rise up in a green wall of of up to 80 m along the Magoebaskloof road at Middelkop near Tzaneen, Limpopo

Giant flowering-gum, Ida's Valley, Stellenbosch

(Limpopo), consisting of different species of eucalypts. During a field tour by delegates to the Fourth Empire Forestry Conference held in Johannesburg in September-October 1935 to the then Middelkop plantation, the Australians were reported to exclaim: 'This is Australia! Please conserve it for us for the world'! Eighteen years later, in 1953, a young forestry scientist was compiling a working plan for Middelkop plantation. He was visited by Mr J Kotze, then Deputy Director of Forestry (today Deputy Director-General) and the well-known forestry pioneer AJ O'Connor, retired at the time and residing in the Magoebaskloof area near Middelkop. Mr O'Connor was well aware of the request of the delegates in 1935, and the forestry scientist was instructed to stipulate the conservation of the plots in his working plan. This forestry scientist was Mr Aat van der Dussen, destined to become the Deputy Director-General of the branches Forestry and Environment of the Department of Environment in 1984.

In 1964, Middelkop and Grenshoek plantations were clearfelled to establish South Africa's own tea plantations – necessitated by international sanctions. Fortunately the stipulation regarding the conservation of the plots resulted in their being left intact. Today some of the trees are 80 m tall, towering above the surrounding green sea of tea plants. These plots have been declared Champion Trees. In spite of this additional protection measure, ten of these trees were found illegally felled some time ago.

Hans Merensky Holdings is protector of a number of remarkable eucalypts that were planted on their Westfalia Estate near Modjadjiskloof in Limpopo, before, and during the time of the late Dr Merensky, well-known geologist and nature-lover. The impressive avenue of *E. saligna* trees that led to Dr Merensky's homestead, which currently houses offices, is also jealously guarded by the company. An *E. saligna* showblock established in 1954, with several individuals up to 70 m high, has become a real showpiece of this species.

A spacing-and-thinning experiment started in 1952 at Langepan on the Siyaqhubeka KwaMbonambi plantation in KwaZulu-Natal attracts worldwide attention, with foresters and forestry scientists from all over the world marvelling at the sight of a stand of eucalypt trees *(E. grandis)* taller than 60 m and with diameters of 2 m in some cases.

Following closely on the heels (or tops) of *Eucalyptus regnans* is **Eucalyptus diversicolor (karri)**, which attains heights of 85 m and diameters of 3,3 m in Australia. In South Africa magnificent examples of karri occur in showblocks on Cape Pine's Tokai, Cecilia and Kruisfontein plantations (all Western Cape), with heights close to 60 m and diameters approximately 1 m at age 60 to 70 years. Recently the largest tree in South Africa was measured by the tree climber Leon Visser in a lane of karri gum trees on the famous Boschendal wine estate, planted more than two centuries ago (size index 483). This tree lane dethroned the mountain ash trees of Benvie Arboretum for the title of the largest trees in the country.

Exceptionally large specimens of ***Eucalyptus camaldulensis* (river red gum)** are found at various locations in Stellenbosch,

Johannesburg and Pretoria, at Skeerpoort on the site of the Van Gaalen Kaasmakerij (cheese factory), and at the Pankop village near Rust de Winter (Limpopo), all counting among South Africa's largest trees. Although not all have been officially measured yet, those of which the measurements were available have been listed as Champion Trees. The largest of these is a giant tree in Stellenbosch with a stem diameter of over 3 m and a size index of 409.

Notable for its drought resistance is *Eucalyptus salubris* (**gimlet**), from the western Australian interior. Only a small number of gimlet are found in South Africa. Look for them in places such as Matjiesfontein, Western Cape, with its captivating history in the middle of the Karoo, at Nelspoort, which used to house a large sanatorium for TB patients (owing to the special quality of the Karoo air), in Hankey, Eastern Province, Bloemfontein in the Free State, as well as in Vanwyksvlei and on Matjiesfontein farm near Calvinia, both in the Northern Cape. Hardly taller than 12 m, these trees thrive under extremely dry conditions, being a welcome and handsome sight with their smooth coppery bark and shiny bright-green foliage.

Eucalyptus viminalis (**manna gum**) is mainly planted in the cold highveld regions of South Africa. The largest known specimen grows on the farm Familiehoek of the De Wet family, Ermelo district (Mpumalanga). The history of the tree is not known.

The gigantic *Eucalyptus globulus* (**blue gum**) tree at the Houwhoek Inn near Botrivier in the Western Cape is well known to many people. The early history of the inn dates back to the pioneering days of the 18th century when it served as an outspan. Lady Anne Barnard, who stayed over at the inn in 1798, counts among its celebrity visitors. The buildings of today were completed in 1834, offering dinner, bed and breakfast for 90c!

Impressive blue gum trees also line the main street of Prince Albert, the small Karoo town at the foot of the Swartberg Mountains. These trees, planted in 1881 through the initiative of Civil Commissioner George Rainier, have been pollarded several times, but still hold their heads high. A number of blue gum trees have also escaped to the entrance to the Swartberg Pass on the Karoo side.

Eucalyptus viminalis ×*huberiana* (**rough-barked ribbon gum**) was not only established at the Benvie Arboretum in KwaZulu-Natal, but also in the Sabie area in Mpumalanga, on the Elandsdrift farm, in 1878. Now the property of Mondi, this has become an area of special interest, with the trees here having achieved giant status, boasting heights of over 40 m and stem diameters of 1,3 m.

Gigantic river red gum trees at Pankop village near Rust De Winter, Limpopo

Tree Families

PINACEAE
The Pine Family

Members of the family Pinaceae are widely distributed in the Northern Hemisphere, but almost absent south of the equator. Pine trees are of immense economic importance worldwide, also in South Africa. Characteristically the trees are evergreen with narrow, usually needle-like, leaves, and seeds borne on the scales of woody cones. The male and female cones are separate but on the same tree. Pollination is by wind. There are about 100 species in the genus *Pinus*. Other genera belonging to this family are fir, spruce, true cedar, larch, Douglas fir and hemlock.

The well-known lane of stone pine trees leading towards the Neethlingshof Estate, Stellenbosch

Little could those early settlers who introduced a number of pine tree species during the 17th century to South Africa have realised how thankful the country is today for the 'humble' pine which, together with the exotic gum or eucalypt tree, saved her indigenous forests from extinction at a critical stage in their existence. South Africa, semi-arid and therefore poorly endowed with indigenous forests, would never have achieved her ideal of becoming self-sufficient in the provision of wood and its derived products, had it not been for these benign 'invaders', which now support

a vibrant industry that compares favourably with those of countries with a much longer afforestation history.

Through the years the Department(s) of Forestry and the major timber companies have experimented with a great number of pine species (probably 60) in search of a softwood that could be established in plantations for the production of timber. Magnificent specimens of these trees can be observed in arboreta and areas of interest on many forest stations.

Several species have been declared invaders, and have caused serious infestations of especially the fynbos in some of the Western Cape folded mountain ranges. However, the pine family contributes hugely to the South African economy as a timber product, and to urban greening.

Pinus radiata (**radiata** or **Monterey pine**) was one of the first pine species introduced to South Africa. This spire-like evergreen coniferous tree, although confined to three exceedingly restricted localities in its native California, USA, has been used extensively for afforestation in the Southern Hemisphere, performing excellently in the winter and constant rainfall areas of South Africa. It is a major contributor to the country's forest industry, providing timber for end products typical of softwoods, such as rafters, flooring and furniture.

Monterey pine is not really successful in summer rainfall areas as it is prone to the fungus disease *Diplodea pinea*, particularly after hail damage. The species is also occasionally prey to the pine tree emperor moth, *Imbrasia cytherea*. In the past pigs were kept in the plantations to feed on the pupae, but nowadays a sex bait is used to attract and kill the female moths.

In contrast, **Pinus pinea** (**umbrella** or **stone pine**), a native of the Mediterranean region, spreads horizontally, forming at maturity a dense, dark green umbrella-shaped crown and producing large edible seeds or nuts. Clumps of stone pine are planted in their native countries for nut production. In South Africa the nuts are not regarded as important any more, although they are collected randomly.

A professional tree climber dwarfed high up in a Monterey pine tree, Tokai Arboretum, Cape Town (Photo: Leon Visser)

In no way regimented into straight rows like church spires, this pine species serves as an ornamental tree nowadays, in spite of its having been introduced originally for timber and nut production. True to its original habitat, the stone pine thrives near the sea in the Western Cape in particular, with its Mediterranean climate, reaching up to 20 m high, with a stem diameter of some 90 cm. Although it is of no great economic importance, the sight of the stone pines that enhance the scenery in and around Cape Town and further, remains an uplifting experience.

Even exceeding those of South Africa's 'Mother City', are the impressive stone pines of another 'Mother City' – Rome; also along the ancient Roman Via Appia southern highway from where the apostle Paul had his first view of Rome. Fascinated by these trees, the Italian composer Ottorini Respighi dedicated a charming and highly popular suite to them, named 'The Pines of Rome', written in the early 1920s.

Pinus lambertiana (**sugar pine**) is the world's tallest pine tree, native to North America where it reaches a height of more than 70 m. It has a straight but multi-branched stem and is described as a forester's nightmare. The sugar pine derives its name from a sweet resin that it exudes, which

The chir pine avenue, lining Main Road, Irene

was used as food by native Americans. The cones, which consist of flattish soft scales, are long and hang conspicuously from the branch tips.

This species has been established since 1890 in several areas in South Africa, but has not shown much promise. The largest of its kind in South Africa is a lone sugar gum at Leliehoek near Ladybrand in the Free State. Its age is not known but it has developed into a magnificent tree.

Pinus pinaster (**cluster pine**), native to the Mediterranean and North Africa, is variable in vitality and form, in accordance with its geographic origin. It grows very well on the poor sandstone soils of the Western Cape, but unfortunately has invasive properties. Table Mountain was once covered with cluster pine, especially at the cliffs on the eastern side of the mountain. It took quite a special kind of labourer, namely a 'cross between a mountaineer and a lumberjack', to eradicate the trees on those steep cliffs.

Cluster pine is not planted in the summer rainfall areas, also due to its vulnerability to the *Diplodea pinea* fungus, particularly after hail damage. Early cluster pine plantations established in the then areas of Natal, the Transkei and the Transvaal were wiped out by this fungus.

Pinus roxburghii (**chir** or **Indian long-leaved pine**), originating from the foothills of the Himalaya Mountains, has been planted fairly widely in South Africa, as windbreaks, along avenues, and for general decorative purposes. It is seldom planted for timber, on account of its slow growth rate and spiral wood, a characteristic defect.

Besides timber, chir pine can also give high yields of resin.

Well-developed specimens of chir pine can be seen in many parts of Kwazulu-Natal and Gauteng, mainly established for purposes other than timber. A noticeable example is the street trees at Main Road, bordering Irene in Centurion, which is partly lined with mature chir pine. Apparently chir was also favoured by General Jan Smuts, whose Irene farm contains several chir pine stands.

Pinus coulteri (**big cone pine**) from California is a remarkable species because of its unusually large cones containing edible seeds. The cones also have protrusions, which could turn a falling cone into a really dangerous projectile. This was the experience of one of our foresters whose outdoor camping stove was completely destroyed by one such cone when he was camping under big cone trees at a research plot in the Swartberg Mountains. That he has lived to tell the tale proves that he didn't brave the possibility of himself being the next casualty, so he probably moved to safer grounds …

Pinus halepensis has the distinction of bearing two common names, depending on the company in which you find yourself: in Jewish circles it will be called a **Jerusalem pine**; in Arabic an **Aleppo pine**. Either way, it is by far the best known of all the pines planted in South Africa, being both drought and cold tolerant. Where planted widely in Gauteng, the Karoo and the Free State, it develops into an attractive small tree. Cape Town's acclaimed Arderne Garden in Claremont however hosts a Jerusalem-Aleppo pine tree that has developed into an unrecognisable giant of more than 32 m tall, with stem diameter almost 1,8 m.

Used extensively in Israel to afforest vast tracks of desert land, the species was originally introduced to South Africa for timber production. The wood was however found to be of poor quality and it was eventually abandoned as a plantation species. In the 1980s a pine aphid found its way to South Africa, causing the death of thousands of Jerusalem pine trees.

Pinus elliotti (**slash pine**) originates from the largely summer-rainfall south-eastern parts of the United States of America. It is South Africa's second most important softwood after *P. patula* (see below), growing well in all the local climatic zones, especially the summer-rainfall areas. Slash pine develops into a fairly big tree of up to 40 m high.

Pinus taeda (**loblolly pine**) is another important plantation tree in South Africa introduced from the south-eastern USA. It is a vigorous grower on good soils, and a specimen at the Buffelsnek plantation near Plettenberg Bay has developed into a giant of 60,1 m high.

Pinus montezumae (**Montezuma pine**) and *Pinus pseudostrobus* (**false Weymouth pine**): the botanical names of these two species being somewhat confusing, it has prompted foresters to call them 'montestrobus' pines. Both develop into real forest giants.

Besides many trial plantings in the various high-rainfall areas of South Africa, small plots were established some 100 years ago in open areas in the indigenous forest on the Woodbush Forest Estate near Tzaneen. One such plot of *P. pseudostrobus* is lovingly called 'The Three Matrons', with the largest a fine 49,2 m tall, breast height diameter (dbh) 1,56 m and crown width 24,35 – aptly complimenting the special nickname. The 'montestrobus' does however not count

The 'Three Matrons'; false Weymouth pine trees at Woodbush, Tzaneen (Photo: Enrico Liebenberg)

among our most important softwood plantation trees.

Pinus patula (**patula** or **weeping pine**) is the most important softwood timber tree in South Africa. It has attractive drooping needles and reaches a height of 20–40 m. Being native to the cool and moist mountain ranges of central Mexico, it is mostly planted in the mist-belt areas of the summer rainfall regions of South Africa. In Highveld areas patula is occasionally being defoliated by larvae of the moth *Euproctis terminalis*.

TREE FAMILIES

ARALIACEAE

The Cabbage Tree Family

The Cabbage Tree family is also known as the Ivy family, after its most famous member, the ivy, *Hedera helix*. Cultivars of this species have been grown in gardens all over the world since earliest times. Another important member of the family is ginseng, a popular medicine obtained from the roots of *Panax* species. Three genera of the family occur in South Africa, namely *Cussonia*, *Schefflera* and *Seemannaralia*, of which *Cussonia* is regarded as the most important and remarkable species.

The genus *Cussonia* was named after professor Pierre Cusson, 1727–1783, attached to the University of Montpellier, France. Six *Cussonia* tree species occur in South Africa, of which only one, *Cussonia natalensis* (**rock cabbage tree**), with its simple palmate leaves, resembles an ordinary tree. Most of the other species are handsome palm-like trees with the leaves clustered at the top of a long, thin stem. The leaves are decorative, big and mostly double compound, resembling giant green snowflakes.

Cabbage trees are often seen in gardens, especially *Cussonia paniculata* (**Highveld cabbage tree**), a fairly frost-hardy species with decorative blue-green leaves. *Cussonia spicata* (**common cabbage tree**) is another member of this family that is widely planted in gardens. A particularly large giant of a cabbage tree grows in the Kurisa Moya forest near Houtbosdorp in Limpopo, towering to a height of 35 m, with a diameter of 3,7 m. Specimens of *Cussonia sphaerocephala* (**forest cabbage tree**) may also develop into unrecognisable giants in natural forests, where they attain heights of 30 m, stem diameters of 2 m and crown diameters of 20.

BELOW: The trunk of a gigantic common cabbage tree in an indigenous forest at Kurisa Moya, near Houtbosdorp, Limpopo

RIGHT: Commom cabbage tree in a forested kloof, New Agatha plantation, Tzaneen

VITACEAE
The Grape Family

The species of the Grape family found in South Africa are mostly shrubs or woody climbers. Some of these vines, like *Rhoicissus tomentosa* (common forest grape), can even reach the tops of 20 m trees.

A small number of extraordinary grape vines planted in South Africa have been described in the chapter *Trees as Monuments and in Gardens, Parks and Arboreta*. Magnificent examples of the remarkable cobas trees (*Cyphostemma* species) can however be seen in gardens locally, while several smaller specimens both in South Africa and Namibia occur in prostate form or as climbers. Four tree-like species with grotesque forms growing in Namibia are described below.

Cyphostemma currori (**cobas**) is a tree that reaches a height of 5 m, with stem diameter more than 1 metre. The bark is smooth, pale yellowish or red-brown, peeling in thin papery strips. The large green trifoliate leaves are succulent, and the fruit, a red berry borne in bunches, has a high content of oxalic acid crystals, causing severe irritation of the mucous membrane in the mouth when eaten. The tree form resembles that of a miniature baobab.

Cyphostemma juttae (**blue cobas**) can reach a height of up to 2 m and is fairly often seen in gardens in Pretoria. The large, fleshy blue-green leaves are simple but deeply lobed and sometimes trifoliate when mature. The bark is smooth, yellowish grey-green, peeling in short papery flakes. The thickset trunk has prompted an onlooker to compare it to a Sumo wrestler!

Cyphostemma bainesii (**Baines cobas**) and *Cyphostemma uter* (**Kaoko cobas**) are both smaller plants, with blue-green and green leaves respectively, but with those of Kaoko five-foliated.

As described under cobas, the rest of these trees also bear berries in bunches. All the parts of these plants contain oxalic acid crystals; this seemingly accounting for the fact that they are not browsed by animals.

TOP: A cobas tree, indigenous to Namibia, enhancing a Pretoria garden
BOTTOM: Far away from its native soil, Namibia, a blue kobas tree shows its colours in a Pretoria garden

BOMBACACEAE
The Kapok Family

Bombacaeae is a tropical tree family of 21 genera and 150 species. Some have barrel-shaped trunks and large showy flowers with five petals and numerous stamens. Kapok, used for stuffing pillows, etc., is derived from the seed plume or pappus of the silk cotton trees *Bombax* and *Ceiba*. These trees are occasionally seen in the subtropical areas of South Africa. The South American or Brazil kapok tree, *Chorisia speciosa*, is widely planted in South Africa for ornamental purposes, particularly for its large pink flowers that are borne in autumn. The balsa tree, which is known for its light wood of 160 kg/m^3, is the South American tree *Ochroma pyramidale*. Visitors to the East will remember the durian, *Durrio zibenthinus*, a huge thorny fruit, very tasty to eat but so smelly that hotel managements prohibit visitors from eating it on their premises.

While only one species each of the genus *Adansonia* is found in Africa and Australia, six species occur in Madagascar, among them the spectacular *A. grandidieri*, reaching 40 m in height, with a small tuft of branches on a tall smooth thickset trunk.

The African species ***Adansonia digitata*** (**baobab**) never fails to impress. 'A monarch? A monster? A carrot growing upside down?' – these are typical responses at the first sight of this tree. Its natural distribution is restricted to the Limpopo Province, as far south as the Soutpansberg Mountains, and to the east more or less as far as Hoedspruit, just across the border of Mpumalanga. This dry, hot country provides ideal growing conditions. The trees prefer deep, well-drained soil, although they are also often seen on the sides of mountains and hills. Many baobab trees have been planted elsewhere in South Africa, in gardens, parks and as street trees.

Owing to its grotesque form, this tree is undoubtedly the one most frequently described – perhaps the earliest records are from Egypt, and date back to 1592. One Michel Adanson, after whom the tree was named, brought seeds to Paris in 1754 and gave a true description, with drawings, of the tree. Since then the baobab has figured in the writings of many travellers and explorers, including Livingstone and Thomas Baines. The baobab also featured for 84 years as the tree emblem of the former Transvaal Province.

Large Brazil kapok tree in Pretoria, conspicuous in flower during autumn and early winter

The species name *digitata* refers to the digitate leaves, shaped like the fingers of a hand. The tree is deciduous, with the leaves being shed in early autumn and the new ones only appearing in late spring or early summer, after the first rains. Large, beautiful snow-white flowers (13–18 cm diameter) hang upside down from long stems, turning brown soon after being picked. The flowers have a lifespan of 24 hours. With a rather unpleasant odour, it is small wonder that they are pollinated by bats!

The fruits are large, 10–26 cm long, egg-shaped, with a hard woody shell covered by velvety hairs. Edible white pulp surrounds black seeds inside. The pulp is rich in vitamin, calcium and thiamine (a vitamin of the B complex, also know as *aneurin*, an antidote to certain disorders of the nerves). The pulp becomes powdery when dry, and, mixed with water, makes a refreshing drink; hence the names 'lemonade tree' and 'cream of tartar tree'.

Food provided by the baobab does not stop here. The leaves, with a high vitamin and calcium content, serve as a vegetable. Caterpillars that feed on the leaves provide protein in the diet of local peoples, while animals feed on the fallen leaves and flowers. The shoot of the germinating seed may replace asparagus, and the roots of the young trees are also reported to be edible. The wood of the relatively short cylindrical 'fat' trunk contains a high proportion of water, and relieves thirst when chewed. It may happen that the circumference of the trunk decreases in drought years as the wood loses moisture.

The smooth, coppery grey bark (5–10 cm thick) is the most useful part of the tree, producing not only an excellent fibre for various uses, but also medicinal substances. In parts of Central Africa it is used for the manufacture of ropes, mats and cloth. Trees are sometimes completely ring-barked for this purpose but they have the ability to recover from this mutilation.

Baobab trees retain their vitality for many years. The trunks may become hollow, often as a result of fire, and the uses to which they have been put are many: as houses, prisons, post offices and bars, storage barns, toilets and water reservoirs. Small wonder that these extraordinary trees, with their relatively short trunks tapering to comparatively small spreading branches, resembling witches' fingers, are surrounded by a wealth of African legend and superstition. Stories are told that they have been planted upside down, or were turned upside down by an angry hunter of a Nigerian tribe named Odede.

The baobab, when young, has a smooth, slender and tapering trunk, but when mature gives the impression of being old and decrepit, even prehistoric. It then has greyish brown bark, often folded and seamed (the typical lava-flow bark), especially in areas

Origin of the name 'baobab'

Much as the tree itself, the name 'baobab' had been an enigma for centuries. A popular assertion that it was derived from an unknown African dialect, meaning 'upside down tree', was upset in 1982 in a monograph by GE Wickens. Quoting from the *Journal of Dendrology* 3 (1& 2), 1983, Wickens mentions that, 'according to the writings of Prospero Alpino, a 16th century Venetian physician, the fruit was then known in the herb and spice markets of Cairo under the name of *bu hobab*, which is probably derived from the Arabic *bu hibab*, meaning "the fruit with many seeds". The name was obviously invented by the Cairo merchants who did not know the tree itself. The baobab fruit was brought to Egypt by caravans from Sudan and Eritrea as early as 2500 BC, probably for its medicinal properties as a febrifuge.'

The name was only revived by Adanson, who actually tried to replace the genus name *Adansonia* by *Baobab*, later Latinised to *Baobabus*, but his attempt was thwarted by the rules of botanical nomenclature. 'Nevertheless,' concludes the author, Fried von Breitenbach, 'the name baobab has been living on ever since as the most popular common name for the species'.

where the lower part of the trunk is damaged by elephants that injure the soft, fibrous trunk with their tusks and eat the fibres, in some cases mutilating it to such an extent that it has a hole right through the trunk.

Confusion about the age of baobab trees, which have a form of annual ring, has been squashed by carbon dating, which has established that most trees are much younger than was generally thought. A tree with a diameter of 7 m was found to be only 600 years old. The record trunk diameter in South Africa is more than 10 m, which gives an age of near 2 000 years. Adanson originally estimated some of the trees to be 5 000 years old, but recent carbon dating has determined the oldest local baobab at about 1 835 years.

In order to examine the age and growth rate of baobabs, Dr Fried and Mrs Jutta von Breitenbach examined 40 planted specimens between the age of 12 and 92 years growing on 11 different sites. Four different growth phases were distinguished: the sapling phase, 10 to 15 years; the cone phase, 60 to 70 years; the bottle phase, 200 to 300 years; and the old-age phase, 600 years and more (see diagram).

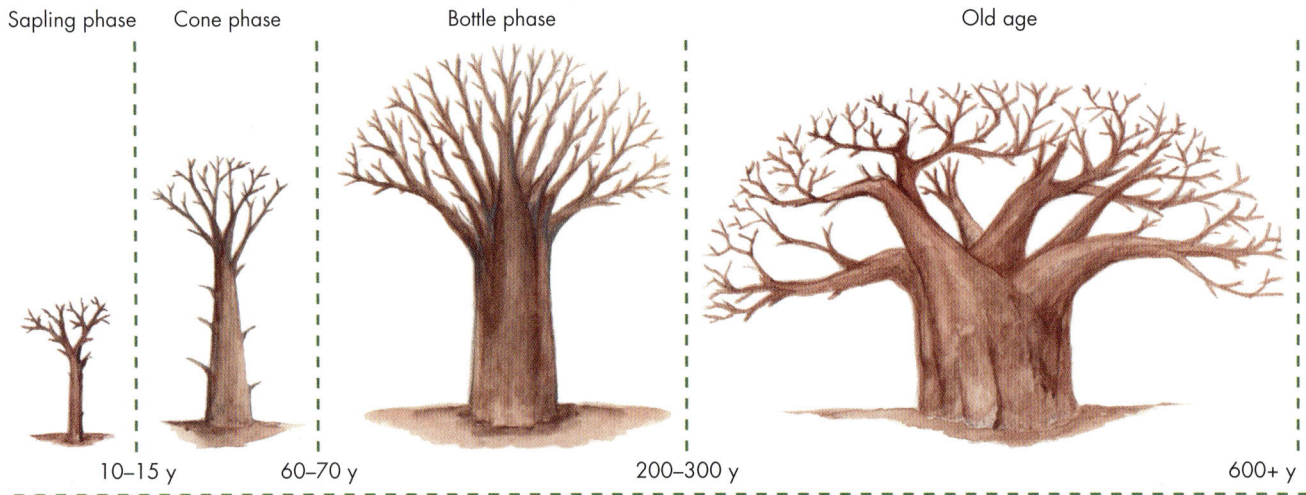

Sapling phase 10–15 y | Cone phase 60–70 y | Bottle phase 200–300 y | Old age 600+ y

Baobabs collapse into a huge fibrous mass when they die. That they catch fire spontaneously is a myth. Veld fires should get the blame for setting the heap of fibres alight. The reason why baobabs die still has to be determined. It seems as if drought plays a role because a sooty mould is sometimes noticed on stressed trees.

Fine young specimens of this protected tree can be seen on the farm Genoa between

A living monument to William Murdoch Drummond, who planted this lane of twenty trees leading to the farmhouse of Genoa, Mokopane district, in 1933

The Genoa avenue some 50 years ago

Marnitz and Tom Burke in the Makopane district, where an avenue of 20 trees was established in 1933. William Murdoch Drummond transplanted these trees from the veld 82 years ago. Today this extraordinary legacy is the pride of the present owners, Mel and Evan Sloan, who takes great care to keep the trees in good shape. Another interesting feature of Genoa is the 'Post Office' tree – a large baobab near the farmhouse that served as a post collecting point in the past.

Treating the symptoms

Dying baobabs is an emotional matter and of great concern to many people. It is a highly complex problem though, and there are no clear-cut answers. There are two known cases where ailing baobabs were treated with apparent success.

The Steyn family, who owns Naledi farm in Botswana, lost one of two diseased baobabs around 1995. They were desperate and prepared to go to great lengths to save the remaining tree. After wide consultation, they decided to treat the tree with a systemic fungicide. To their amazement and joy the tree recovered after several treatments and seems to be still healthy after more than 20 years.

The worst affected baobab at Genoa before treatment, the trunk darkened by a black fungus (Photo ± 1995)

The same treatment, with the addition of a mild insecticide, was applied to ailing baobab trees on the farm Genoa in 2004 (see photos). Since then the trees were treated five times and their general appearance improved dramatically.

Golden rules for much visited trees:
- Admire from a distance.
- Provide a boardwalk around the tree.
- If any sign of a disease is detected, obtain advice from researchers of the Forestry and Agricultural Biotechnology Institute (FABI), University of Pretoria.

On 18 August 2016 part of the famous Platland boabab collapsed (see photo on page 116). A team of specialists of FABI, including Professor Yolanda Roux (a tree pathologist), visited the Platland tree two weeks later. That investigation uncovered a fungus that was considered not to be harmful. Incidentally, this type of fungus has not been found on a boabab before. At the time of writing, the investigation of FABI was ongoing. Although the partial collapse is an upsetting event, it affords an opportunity to investigate the causes of such collapses or deterioration, which may give insight into similar conditions that afflict some boababs in southern Africa.

The tree after it was treated (Photo: Mia Sloan – 2016)

RIGHT: A tangle of branches, Glencoe baobab
BELOW: The big tree in the Honnet Nature Reserve, Forever Resorts, Tshipise

Mystique surrounds the 'Baobab forest' – an inaccessible area in the northern Kruger National Park where one or two, on average, of these giant trees occur per hectare. Similar 'forests' occur north of the Soutpansberg in the Musina area, where much of the landscape is dominated by these grotesque trees, each with its own peculiar form. Probably the best example of such a concentration of baobabs is found in the 'Forest of the Giant Baobabs' between Nwanedzi and Sagole. The town of Musina boasts a fairly large number of baobab trees, with two medium-sized specimens growing in Celliers and Smit Streets.

In 1917 experiments were carried out by the Imperial Institute of London to manufacture paper from baobab trees. A brown pulp was obtained, from which a fairly strong paper was made. It was, however, not possible to bleach the paper satisfactorily. These negative results did not prevent a certain entrepreneur named Ritter from carrying out further tests, and during World War II baobabs were exploited in the Musina area on a small scale for the manufacture of ceiling boards. Today the small factory that stood on the bank of the Sand River is only a ruin.

The erstwhile Forestry Department realised that something had to be done to protect this unique tree. In 1941 the baobab was declared a protected tree under the Forest Act. Additionally, baobab trees on a number of farms south of Musina, where the annual rainfall is 250–400 mm, were declared national monuments. On these farms the Department carried out tests with the propagation and establishing of baobab trees, and an experiment to investigate the diameter increase of these weird trees was initiated. It was found, mainly in trees with diameters of more than 2,54 m, that rainfall influences the diameter considerably. In one case a tree measured in 1931 and again in 1946, had shrunk with more than 60 cm in diameter. In 1976 the then Messina Nature Reserve, 3 898 ha in extent, was established; later managed by the Nature Conservation Division of Limpopo. In addition to many impressive baobabs and other bushveld trees, this Reserve protects rare and threatened animal species.

Other well-known baobab trees are the 'lêboom' (lying tree) along the Musina–Makhado road and the 'olifantslurpboom' (elephant trunk tree) in the Erich Mayer Park in Musina. This nickname originated from one branch that resembled an elephant's trunk, but it was unfortunately damaged by fire. The tree itself is however still healthy. The big tree in the Honnet Nature Reserve of the Forever Resort near Tshipise, known to many visitors, has an extraordinarily thick stem in comparison to its height. Other baobabs in the very big class occur on the farms Ludwigslust, Greater Kuduland and Mapungubwe, Musina district. Erich Mayer, as well as other early South African painters, made free use of baobabs as models – including 'Slurpie'.

An interesting phenomenon that can be observed among baobabs is that of multiple stems. This could be ascribed to multiple sprouting from the same rootstock. In this way a clump of nine young baobab trees has developed on the Glencoe farm. The Platland tree also demonstrates this phenomenon, while one that is a clear landmark at the Gootsa

Pan in Botswana consists of about five straight trunks that fuse at about a man's height.

While many baobab trees may become famous, some of them are actually notorious. One such is the 'Briscoe tree' in the Lebombo Mountains near the Kruger National Park's Letaba Rest Camp. The game poacher Briscoe used this magnificent baobab as a vantage point from which to shoot elephants crossing from Mozambique into the Park. Other well-known trees in the Park are the lone tree on Baobab Hill near Pafuri and the Mopane Rest Camp baobab that 'wears' many buffalo weaver nests 'in her hair' all year round.

After the Barberton gold rush in the 1880s, and some time before Leydsdorp (no longer existing) on the road to Tzaneen had acquired a pub, one Charlie Madros ran one inside the trunk of a baobab tree in the town. In the 1940s it was apparently still possible to enter the 'pub' through the back entrance. Originating from the tree pub days, the Afrikaans expression, 'Sien jou by die boom' ('Meet you at the tree') was in use for many years thereafter.

Legend has it that towards the end of the Anglo-Boer War two wagon loads of Kruger gold pounds were sent to Sabie, and then northwards towards the Olifants River in the vicinity of Hoedspruit, where the gold was hidden in a hole hacked in a baobab tree trunk. A termite queen was dug out and buried next to the tree in the hope that the ensuing anthill would cover the hole in the trunk. Reportedly, a number of serious treasure diggers had to be discouraged in order to save the Glencoe tree.

Baobab Hill with its solitary tree watching over the sea of mopane trees, a conspicuous landmark in the northern part of the Kruger National Park

The world's most corpulent trees

The tree with the record girth in the world is said to be a Montezuma cypress (*Taxodium mucronatum*) with a diameter of 11,6 m. This giant tree, with a height of 41,85 m and apparent age of 2 000 years, grows in the churchyard in the village of Santa Maria del Tule near Oaxaca, Mexico. Yet before the crown of the Glencoe baobab near Hoedspruit collapsed, the diameter of its trunk was measured at 15,9 m by the late Dr Fried von Breitenbach. Still standing and closely on the heels of the Tule tree is the 10,8 m diameter of the Sagole baobab in Limpopo.

Mexico's record-breaking Montezuma cypress

TREE FAMILIES

SAPOTACEAE

The Milkwood Family

Sapotaceae is a large family of the tropics and subtropics, with a number of species however reaching to more temperate regions. According to Palmer & Pitman the family name is derived from the Mexican tree *sapoti*, described by Linnaeus as *Achras sapote*, and the family name has been Latinised to Sapotaceae. A milky latex or juice is characteristic of this family. Chewing gum is made from the latex of some of the Central American species, while certain Malaysian species provide rubber-like substances such as 'gutta-percha' or 'ballata rubber', from which golf balls are made.

Although the approximately 20 native South African milkwood species all exude latex when damaged, none has been found as useful as the American and Malaysian species. The local species all bear fleshy fruit, some of which are very tasty both to man and animal. The **Transvaal milkplum** or **stemfruit** (*Englerophytum magalismontanum*), previously *Bequaertiodendron magalismontanum*, for instance, is a sought-after delicacy for the lover of veld fruits. Further characteristics of the milkwoods are simple, entire, alternate leathery leaves that, in the early stage, may be brownish in colour. The flowers are either axillary or borne on old wood. The seeds are shiny, with a broad scar at the point of attachment. Milkwoods are mostly slow growing and although most beautiful trees, are therefore seldom grown in gardens.

Moepel trees, well known in the Rustenburg area, reach fairly large dimensions

Giant milkwood tree at Still Bay, Western Cape

South Africa's milkwoods are concentrated along the coast, especially in KwaZulu-Natal, with a number of species occurring in the bushveld areas of Mpumalanga, Limpopo, North West and Gauteng. The common names testify either to their distribution, e.g. Natal milkplum, coastal red milkwood, Transvaal red milkwood (moepel) and the Zulu and lowveld milkberries, or to a particular characteristic, e.g. the fluted milkwood and red milkwood.

Vitellariopsis dispar (**Tugela bush milkwood**), a localised endemic of the central and upper Tugela catchment area, enjoys special protection in the Mhlopeni Natural Heritage Site in the Greytown district of KwaZulu-Natal.

The *Inhambanella henriquezii* (**milk pear**) of the dune forests of Maputaland, KwaZulu-Natal, is a magnificent sight when the new leaves appear and the entire crown is ablaze with coppery red leaves.

Doing the Sapotaceae family proud is the species ***Sideroxylon inerme*** (**white milkwood**). The genus name *Sideroxylon*, which means 'ironwood', is derived from the Greek words *sideros* = iron and *xylon* = wood, while the epiteth *imerme* means 'without thorns'. The wood has a mass of more than 1 000 kg/m^3 and is most durable. This characteristic might be ascribed to the fact that the trees consistently have to withstand the merciless impact of sea winds, as their natural habitat stretches along the coast from the Cape Peninsula eastwards as far as Kenya. (The tree is also known as 'sea oak'.) The trees are mostly low growing with many branches often leaning towards the lee side and 'huddling' close together, with flat, wind-shorn crowns. The leathery property of the shiny dark green leaves increases its wind resistance, making the tree an ideal species for survival in those harsh conditions. The flowers, unpleasant smelling, are greenish yellow, and the fruit is a black berry when ripe, relished by birds and bushpigs. Parts of the tree are used in traditional healing practices.

White milkwood is a protected species in South Africa, with several individual trees having played an important role in the history of the country and now declared national monuments. The most important white milkwood tree in South Africa, probably the first tree in the recorded history of the country, is the 'Post Office Tree' at Mossel Bay in the Western Cape. This tree grows alongside a stream where Portuguese sailors in the late 15th century came to seek fresh water. It was presumably a witness of the

The 'Treaty' white milkwood tree of the erstwhile Papendorp, now Woodstock, Cape Town

was known as Papendorp in those days.) Some sources claim that the tree served as a gallows where offenders were executed.

The 'Fingo Milkwood' near Peddie in the Eastern Cape grows at a village with the apt name of *Umgwashu* – the isiXhosa name for the white milkwood tree. It commemorates the escape of the Fingo people from war-torn Zululand. They assembled under this tree on 14 May 1835 to declare their loyalty to God and the British king.

An impressive white milkwood tree on the farm Renosterfontein in the Bredasdorp district (Western Cape) was declared a national monument in 1993. The farm has been in the possession of the Blom family since 16 January 1772, and it is believed that the farmhouse was positioned on purpose near this exceptionally big tree. It has a trunk of 1,02 m in diameter, is 9 m high and has a crown spread of 20 m. Covering 314 m^2, the dense evergreen canopy has seen the gathering of many generations of the Blom family.

The largest known milkwood tree, the 'Grandfather' of Still Bay, can be observed on the farm Langebosch in the district.

The farm Melkhoutkraal ('Milkwood Kraal') on the eastern slopes of the Knysna lagoon achieved fame as the property of George Rex, said to be the illegitimate son of George III, and one Hannah Lightfoot, who was banished from England in 1797. His reputation has ensured that his grave on the farm, as well as the milkwood trees, are among the many tourist attractions of Knysna.

important moment in South Africa's history when Bartholomeu Dias, the first man to sail round the Cape, in 1488, landed at the spot that later would become Mossel Bay. The tree only earned its name on 7 July 1501 when Joao de Nova found, in an old shoe hanging from the branches, a letter from an earlier sailor describing the adventures of Cobral's expedition and the sad loss of Dias and his ship at sea. The Post Office Tree is well over 500 years old and is still healthy. It was declared a national monument in 1938 and is one of the great tourist attractions of Mossel Bay. (It has also been declared a Champion Tree.)

Another famous white milkwood is the 'Treaty Tree' in Spring Street, Woodstock, Cape Town. This tree, which is probably older than the Castle, the first building in Cape Town, was declared a national monument in 1967. Near this tree a treaty between officials of the Batavian Government at the Cape and the commanding officer of the British troops to whom the Batavian Government surrendered, was signed on 10 January 1806. (Woodstock

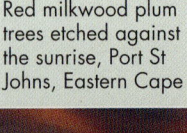

Red milkwood plum trees etched against the sunrise, Port St Johns, Eastern Cape

OLEACEAE

The Olive Family

Oleaceae is a family of about 20 genera and 300 species of trees and climbers growing in tropical and temperate areas. Some 15 species occur naturally in South Africa, the two best known to the general public being *Olea europaea* subsp. *africana* – the wild olive, and *Olea capensis* – ironwood, to both of which a fair amount of legend is attached. The wild olive used to be the tree emblem of the province of the Orange Free State.

Undoubtedly the most famous member of the family Oleaceae is ***Olea europaea*** (the **olive tree**) from the Mediterranean regions. The olive has been cultivated since 3000 BC, yielding various products, and today it is still an important agricultural product in its countries of origin. Exotic members of the olive family planted in streets and gardens in South Africa are the *Fraxinus* species (ash trees), *Syringa vulgaris* (lilac) and *Ligustrum* species (privets).

For almost a century olives have been grown commercially in South Africa, particularly in the Western Cape with its Mediterranean climate, with the Paarl district the leading area. An Italian named Costa pioneered commercial olive cultivation in South Africa. He arrived at the Cape in 1902 and, noticing the similarities between his native and adopted countries, believed he would succeed – which he did. On the farm Swartrivier in the district of Prince Albert at the foot of the Swartberg Mountains, an annual yield of 50 to 80 tons of olives is produced. This has led to the institution of an Olive Festival in April in Prince Albert. Olive trees are occasionally planted as street trees, for instance in Kimberley, Northern Cape, where the fruits are utilised by the city's people.

(With increased consumption and utilisation of olives and their huge variety of products, formal olive farming has markedly extended countrywide. Lovers of these

Wild olive trees, usually small-sized, develop into large trees under favourable climatic conditions, as is demonstrated by this one on the farm Zilkaatsnek, north of the Magaliesberg

products nowadays needn't travel far any more – olive festivals are held fairly widely in South Africa in olive-producing areas.)

Ripe olive fruits are black and unripe ones are green. When intended for oil production, the fruits are usually left on the trees to ripen, while for eating they are picked either half-ripe or ripe.

The olive is synonymous with life and plenty, and holds a unique place in the legends of mankind. Olives are said to be the oldest trees in Europe. A number of them are standing in the Garden of Gethsemane, on the Mount of Olives in Jerusalem, Israel, and are some 2 400 years of age. Material from these trees was brought to South Africa by Dr PG Marais of Infruitec, Stellenbosch. It was implanted on rootstock of the local wild olive. Ten plants were produced, of which one was planted in the Infruitec Heritage Garden on 25 August 1979. The remaining trees were donated mainly to religious communities throughout the country.

Olive trees love the sun and more or less dread humidity, therefore they are among the most drought-resistant plants. The secret of their hardiness to drought was revealed when Infruitec personnel investigated the leaves under a scanning electron microscope. The undersides of the leaves are covered with minute umbrella-shaped outgrowths that protect the stomata and prevent excessive transpiration.

Olea europaea* subsp. *africana (**wild olive**) resembles *Olea europaea* except that its fruits are smaller and are in no way largely utilised. The wild olive occurs almost throughout South Africa, growing naturally in large numbers on the southern slopes of parts of the Magaliesberg, the hills and mountainsides of the Free State, particularly in the Bloemfontein area, and on the Ghaap plateau south of Kuruman in the Northern Cape, thriving on the dolomitic soil of this low plateau. The trees are browsed by animals as far as they can reach, with the result that all these thousands of wild olive trees are pruned to the same height. An almost pure stand (about 30 ha) of wild olive trees occurs in the El Dorado Natural Heritage Site, Potchefstroom district, North West.

Another well-known, almost pure stand of wild olive trees can be seen on the farm Voëlvlei, 8 km from Piketberg on the Elands Bay road (R365). It is known as Voëlvleibos, and the sixth generation of the Rousseau family are protecting it with zeal. The majority of the trees in this 'forest' have an ancient appearance, and it can be accepted that they were there long before colonial times.

As is the case with the olive worldwide, the wild olive is held in high esteem by South Africans, who regard it as synonymous with grace, dignity and durability. The streets in many South African towns and cities are lined with wild olive trees. In spite of its small dimensions, the wood, which is hard, heavy and fine-grained, with beautiful dark embellishment, is sought after for high-class furniture and turnery work, as well as for fencing poles on account of its durability.

A gnarled and apparently very old wild olive tree in the Voëlvleibos, Piketberg, Western Cape

The wild olive is a small to medium-sized tree, between 5 and 10 m in height, but occasionally reaching up to 18 m. A large wild olive that had been a landmark at the 'Eye of the Molopo' (river) in North West until some 20 years ago had a height of 14 m, trunk diameter of 2 m and crown diameter of 21 m. It is said that Commandant JH Coetzee used this tree as a base during the Anglo Boer War. An impressive wild olive on the farm The Fountains, Pearston district (Eastern Cape), has a trunk diameter of several metres and a crown diameter of 26 m.

Many large wild olive trees are tucked away in the Magaliesberg, west of Pretoria. One specimen on the farm Zilkaatsnek measures a stem diameter more than 2 m, height 15 m and crown width 20 m.

Also, the lower Oorlogskloof or Koebee, as it is known in the Vanrhynsdorp (Western Cape) area, hides a large wild olive tree in Saaikloof. This is a remote narrow valley on the farm Klein Koebee, with access to the main ravine from the west.

On the farm Onze Rust, some 20 km south of Bloemfontein, a wild olive tree, the 'Tree of Conspiracy', was declared a national monument in 1950. President MT Steyn, President of the Republic of the Orange Free State during the Anglo Boer War years, bought the farm in 1897 and lived there with his family from 1905 until his death in 1916. He often entertained prominent visitors under this tree, which consequently became known jocularly as the 'Tree of Conspiracy'.

These trees must all have seen centuries pass …

In addition to the wood and the leaves, which serve as fodder, the bark and leaves played a valuable role in the country over the years, in particular being used to combat various illnesses. Wild olive is a protected tree in South Africa.

Olea capensis (**ironwood**) is a variable complex of evergreen shrubs and trees from a wide variety of habitats in the wetter, southern and eastern parts of the country. One of the three subspecies, *Olea capensis* subsp. *macrocarpa* (**black ironwood**) is abundant in the Knysna and Tsitsikamma forests of the southern Cape, where it is dominant and co-dominant among the medium-moist and moist forest types. It is also abundant in the mountain forests of Mpumalanga and the Limpopo Province.

Black ironwood is a medium to tall tree 17–25 m high, with a clear bole 10 m in height and 60–80 cm in diameter. It flowers profusely every second, third or even fourth year, making identification easy. Fruits are produced in extremely large quantities; 35 to 50 fruits may be borne on each panicle, and a large tree may produce 10 000 mature fruits. Some 30 000 fruits per large tree are shed prematurely every year, for various reasons, such as wind and birds feeding. The ripe fruits provide a feast to forest birds and animals. The (Cape) rock-pigeon is the main dispersal agent of ironwood seed. In the 1930s forestry scientist JFV Phillips reported that 75 seeds were removed from the crop of a single pigeon.

The sapwood of black ironwood is grey, while the heartwood is brown to dark brown and attractively embellished with black and grey streaks, with a mass of over 1 000 kg/m^3. Whereas the wood of the two subspecies *capensis* and *enervis* is rarely utilised, that of *macrocarpa* makes a fine timber which, in spite of being difficult to work, has been used for railway sleepers, piles, floor-blocks, wagon parts, including axles, and to a limited extent for furniture.

A large wild olive tree in Saaikloof on the farm Klein Koebee, Vanrhynsdorp, Western Cape (Photo: Erica Vollgraaff)

TREE FAMILIES

GENTIANACEAE
The Gentian Family

Formerly belonging to the Wild Elder family, Gentianaceae is represented in South Africa by only one species, with striking big leaves as its most prominent feature.

Anthocleista grandiflora (**forest fever tree**) occurs in South Africa in the moist forest areas, from the Swaziland border to Limpopo. In Africa it grows as far north as Kenya. It is a most striking tree with huge, simple, dark green leaves up to 1 m long and 40 cm broad clustered at the ends of the branches. This feature makes it a popular garden plant in the subtropical regions of the country.

The genus name *Anthocleista* is based on two Greek words: *anthos* = flower and *cleistos* = closed, referring to the shape of the flower. The species name means 'big-flowered', describing the flowers, which are more than 3 cm long, white and sweet-scented and borne in large branched terminal heads. The common name of forest fever tree indicates its use in treating malaria.

The forest fever tree is one of the big tree species of South Africa that sometimes attains a height of 30 m with a crown width of 20 m. In spite of the straight branchless stems, the wood is useless, being soft and non-durable.

LEFT: Forest fever trees, popular garden and park trees in subtropical areas
BELOW LEFT: Sunshine falling through the leaves of a forest fever tree
BELOW RIGHT: A forest fever tree towering over its surroundings

COMBRETACEAE

The Bushwillow Family

Combretaceae is a family consisting of 16 genera and 400 species, spread throughout most tropical countries. Five genera with tree species occur in South Africa, namely *Combretum*, *Pteleopsis*, *Terminalia*, *Quisqualis* and *Lumnitzera*. The latter is a mangrove, occurring from northern KwaZulu-Natal to Asia and Australia. (Mangroves are described under *The Beachwood Mangrove Swamp*, KwaZulu-Natal Province.)

Combretum species (bush willows) may be trees, shrubs or climbers, such as *C. microphyllum*, the flame creeper. It is a vigorous climber with crimson-red flowers and four-winged fruits, and therefore easy to recognise.

Combretum imberbe (**leadwood**) is a graceful tree of 20 m and more – the tallest of all the South African combretums. It occurs in the warm, dry areas of KwaZulu-Natal, Mpumalanga, Limpopo, and northwards to tropical Africa, with a fairly good distribution in the northern parts of Namibia. The species name *imberbe* means 'hairless', referring to the characteristic hairless grey-green leaves. The trunk is greyish and the flowers cream to yellow and sweetly scented, while the characteristically pale yellowish-green four-winged fruits give the tree a distinctive appearance.

The common name obviously refers to the wood: the heartwood is extremely hard, heavy and durable, and very suitable for fencing standards, hut poles and rustic lapa poles. Leadwood is a popular braaiwood and is nowadays also used for carving.

Leadwood is one of the most commonly found bushveld trees in South Africa. It stands for durability, because the second oldest tree of all those carbon dated at the CSIR is a leadwood of 1 050 years. It is remarkable that this tree had, at the time of dating, already been dead for 150 years.

A 'famous' dead leadwood tree at Leeupan ('Lions' Pan') in the Kruger National Park was

Given favourable conditions such as alluvial soil on river banks, leadwoods develop into large trees.

Tree Families

described in 1959 in the *Journal of the Tree Society of South Africa* as the tree probably seen by more people than any other in South Africa, because of the number of visitors swarming there to see the king of animals. After more than half a century, the Leeupan leadwood tree is still holding its naked branches artistically in the air – and it will probably do so for many years to come.

For the Herero people of Namibia the leadwood tree used to have special significance, as they believed that the tree housed the spirits of their ancestors. The melodious name for the leadwood in their language is *Omumborombonga*.

The dead leadwood tree at Leeupan, Kruger National Park – an artistic sculpture of nature. 'Please do not turn me into firewood …'

APOCYNACEAE

The Oleander Family

Apocynaceae is a family remarkable for three qualities – the beauty of their flowers, their ability to heal and their ability to kill. Various oleanders have supplied poison for arrows since the invention of the bow and arrow. The family is represented in South Africa by 17 genera and about 40 species, which may be either trees, shrubs or climbers, often with a milky sap.

An extraordinarily showy indigenous member of the oleander family is ***Adenium multiflorum*** (**impala lily**), which has a fairly limited distribution in the bushveld and lowveld areas of KwaZulu-Natal and Limpopo. It is an attraction to visitors at various rest camps in the Kruger National Park. It is a thickset succulent shrub or small tree, only occasionally reaching 3 m in height, on account of its being browsed by game and stock in spite of its apparent toxic properties. It is said to be used as a fish and arrow poison.

The impala lily flowers in winter. The large white flowers, up to 5 cm in diameter, each ending in five crinkled, delicately pointed petals bordered pink or crimson, when set against the arid winter background, never fail to catch the eye. The sight of an impala lily in full bloom is an unforgettable experience.

Adenium swazicum (**Swazi lily**) is a small shrub of about 30 cm, also occurring in the

A magnificent specimen of the impala lily in its full winter beauty – Kruger National Park

hot and dry Limpopo lowveld, but flowering in summer. The flowers vary from soft pink to rose red and maroon.

The genus *Pachypodium* (bottle trees) is represented by only two members in South Africa, one of which is an extraordinary plant carrying the extraordinary common name of 'halfmens' (= half a human). This succulent, also classified as a tree, is **Pachypodium namaquanum (elephant's trunk)** with a limited distribution in the dry rocky hills along the Orange River where the river cuts between Namaqualand and the southernmost part of Namibia. The cylindrical spiny stems tapering to the apex rarely reach 5 m in height; they are more likely to be between 1,5 and 2,5 m. The stems are usually either unbranched or branched close to the apex, and are crowned with a bunch of grey-green velvety leaves with undulating margins – remarkably closely resembling the head and particularly the specific hair-style of human beings. The tips of the stems always bend slightly towards the north. Local legend has it that these were once men from a far northern country who were changed into plants, now standing forever with their faces turned northwards.

Pachypodium saundersii **(kudu lily)** never develops into a tree, usually being less than 1 m high. It has a grotesque, swollen stem with silvery-grey bark and a few rapidly tapering branches armed with thorns, bearing lovely white flowers from April to June.

The genus name *Pachypodium*, which means 'thick foot', refers to the swollen stem. Plants of this genus occur in Africa and Madagascar only.

TOP: 'Halfmens' in its natural habitat
LEFT: A 25 year old 'halfmens' in the Crous Kaktus en Vetplant Kwekery in Pretoria
BELOW: Pachypodium trees, 25 years old, from Madagascar (also called 'halfmens' by some) in the Crous Kaktus en Vetplant Kwekery in Pretoria

BIGNONIACEAE

The Jacaranda Family

Bignoniaceae is a large family of 109 genera and 700 species, mostly vines, trees and shrubs, rarely perennials or annuals, all mainly originating from tropical America. Characteristic of the family are the generally showy trumpet-shaped or two-lipped flowers, the opposite, compound leaves, and the long pods. The family derives its name from the genus *Bignonia*, which at one stage included most of the trumpet vines, now however reclassified.

Shrubs or small indigenous trees belonging to the family include:
- *Tecomaria capensis*: Cape honeysuckle
- *Rhigozum* species: Thorny pomegranates
- *Catophractes alexandrii*: Trumpet-thorn (Gabba bush)
- *Markhamia zanzibarica*: Bell-bean tree.

The most fascinating of the indigenous Bignoniaceae is **Kigelia africana (sausage tree)**, with a single species in the genus occurring from KwaZulu-Natal to tropical Africa. In South Africa it is a small to medium-sized deciduous tree flourishing in hotter climates, being easily propagated by seed. The trumpet-shaped flowers are striking; dark maroon, with a velvety inside and yellow veins on the outside, borne in threes in 90 cm long pendulous sprays. The flowers are large, up to 15 cm in diameter.

The fruit is a club-shaped capsule resembling a sausage, dangling from the branches on long stalks. The grey 'sausages' measure between 30 and 60 cm in length and 10 cm in diameter, and weigh up to 7 kg. They contain a fibrous pulp and many seeds. According to Palmer & Pitman, it is '[h]andsome in flower, … – in fruit surprising rather than beautiful, appearing as if decorated for some practical joke with outsize sausages or loofahs'.

The plant explorer and writer David Fairchild, after whom the Fairchild Tropical Garden in Miami is named, once took seed of the sausage tree to Florida, USA, where the owner of a petrol filling station at Coconut Beach planted it. Fairchild afterwards reported that the peculiar fruit in particular attracted thousands of motorists every year and brought revenue to the owner.

Probably the best known sausage tree in South Africa is growing at the Tshokwane picnic spot in the Kruger National Park. A large thatched roof was erected underneath the tree, and it is a favourite spot for visitors

The sausage tree 'handsome in flower – in fruit surprising, as if decorated for some practical joke' (Eve Palmer)

The famous sausage tree at the Tshokwane picnic spot in the Kruger National Park (Guess why the roof?)

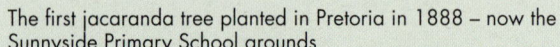
The first jacaranda tree planted in Pretoria in 1888 – now the Sunnyside Primary School grounds

to the Park to leave their vehicles and enjoy a picnic in the open. Besides the sausage tree with its strange fruits, a large jackalberry, *Diospyros mespiliformis*, is also to be admired here. The main attraction, however, are the antics of troublesome monkeys, as well as several bird species.

Jacaranda mimosifolia (**jacaranda**) is an exotic tree of great beauty with its soft fern-like leaves and profusion of purple flowers in early spring, when the tree is leafless. The species adapted exceptionally well in South Africa and spreads naturally where rainfall is sufficient, a quality which brought it into disfavour with many citizens of South Africa. The genus name *Jacaranda* is the Latinised form of the Brazilian name for the tree, which apparently means 'joyous song'. The species name refers to the mimosa-like leaves.

During October/November every year Pretoria changes into a fairy tale city. The almost unreal purple colour of the trees, and the sidewalks from falling flowers, lends a coolness to the city – even on the hottest days. Jacarandas largely contributed to Pretoria being declared Arbor City in 1984 – the first award of its kind in South Africa.

Pretoria's jacaranda tradition is more than a century old. The first two jacaranda trees were planted in 1888 in the garden of Mr JD Celliers, now the Sunnyside Primary School grounds in Celliers Street. Celliers made use of the services of a Mr Templemann, a Cape Town nurseryman, to lay out his garden. He bought the two trees from Templemann at an exorbitant price. Celliers first questioned the wisdom of the transaction but once the trees had flowered he said, 'Never were twenty pounds put to a better advantage'. It has not been reported where Templemann got the seed from but it is a fact that Baron von Ludwig, founder of the Von Ludwig's-burg Garden in Cape Town, had imported jacarandas some 50 years earlier. The two jacaranda trees in Celliers Street are still to be seen on the school grounds, where they are being cared for and protected by the school authorities and the City of Tshwane's division responsible for parks.

Several people played a leading role in planting thousands of jacaranda trees in the streets of Pretoria, and one of them even got the nickname of 'Jacaranda Jim'. Pretoria had become known as the 'Jacaranda City' and a Jacaranda Festival was held every year since 1939 except during World War II. (Apparently the town of Grafton, New South Wales, Australia, also celebrates a Jacaranda Festival every year.)

The white jacarandas in Herbert Baker Street, Groenkloof, dating from the 1960s, are a curiosity that complement the mauve/purple profusion. The white variety is said to be hardier than its purple sibling, and the white trees are in full bloom when the mauve blossoms start to fall.

Pretoria's jacarandas also brought international fame to the city. A man living in Seattle, USA, once informed the Municipality that he had named his yacht *Jacaranda*. A woman wrote from New England saying that she had been christened 'Pretoria'.

Jacaranda trees are among those listed as ornamental invader plants (Category 3), only to be used for ornamental purposes in demarcated areas.

A few other exotic trees of the jacaranda family are planted in South Africa. The **Tabebuia species (trumpet trees)** from South America are occasionally seen in the more tropical areas of the country and even in Pretoria, where they flower in profusion in spring. Three species are mainly encountered, two with yellow flowers and one with mauve flowers.

***Spathodea campanulata* (African flame)** from Central Africa decorates many cities and towns in the subtropical parts of South Africa with its tulip-shaped orange to scarlet flowers. A variety with yellow flowers is also found, but seldom seen in South Africa.

TOP: White jacaranda in Groenkloof, Pretoria
ABOVE: Jacarandas in full bloom lining a street in Pretoria

PEDALIACEAE
The Sesame Family

Pedialiaceae, the Sesame family, is a small family of annual or perennial herbs. A special feature of the family is the extraordinary forms of the fruits. (*Sesamoid* = shaped like a sesame seed, nodular.)

From the childhood wonderment at the fascinating *Tales from the Arabian Nights* when the magic words 'Open, oh Sesame!' would open new worlds, to the current emphasis on healthy foods of which sesame seeds are an important ingredient, the plant *Sesamum indicum* has long been familiar to the average household in South Africa. This herbaceous plant from India, which yields these pleasant tasting oil-rich seeds, belongs to the family Pedaliaceae.

Harpagophytum procumbens (**devil's claw**) is less favoured, although acclaimed worldwide for its medicinal properties. This low-growing plant has an interesting, intricate seed measuring some 7 × 7 cm on average, and consisting of two segments, from the sides of which 10 to 12 thorny arms bend upward like claws, ready to attach themselves to the hoof of an animal and be distributed.

One species from this family that occasionally attains tree height is ***Sesamothamnus lugardii*** (**Transvaal sesame bush**). It occurs in hot and dry areas north of the Soutpansberg Mountains in Limpopo, as well as in Zimbabwe and Botswana. The Transvaal sesame bush almost resembles a miniature baobab, with its grotesque yellowish succulent base of several metres in diameter, from which a multitude of quick-tapering erect branches sprout, studded with dark knobs, often with short sharp spines. The peculiarity of this tree (it may reach a height of 4 m) is increased by its being leafless during the major part of the year, similar to the baobab.

The Transvaal sesame bush flowers in spring from 15 cm long buds opening into beautiful white flowers that eventually turn yellow. A conspicuous spur of 6–8 mm occurs at the base of the flower tube. The fruit is a flat heart-shaped pod, with papery-winged seeds.

The odd shape of a Transvaal sesame bush near Tshipise, Limpopo

RUBIACEAE

The Gardenia Family

Rubiaceae is a widespread and varied family of 400 genera and more than 5 000 species worldwide that contains trees, shrubs and herbs with opposite or whorled leaves and usually clustered flowers but, in the case of *Gardenia* and *Rothmannia*, beautiful single flowers.

The coffee bean from the plant *Coffea arabica* is probably the best known product of the family Rubiaceae today, although the family is also famous for yielding quinine, the first drug specifically used to cure malaria. It was extracted from the South American tree *Cinchona,* the name derived from the claim that the Countess of Cinchon, wife of the Viceroy of Peru, was cured from a fever by its bark in 1638. Members of this tree family were previously, and are probably still today, used by local people to treat malaria.

The most spectacular South African tree belonging to the family Rubiaceae is **Breonadia salicina** (**Transvaal teak** or **matumi**). It is a tall evergreen tree more than 30 m high, which occurs in the Lowveld areas of Mpumalanga and Limpopo as well as northern KwaZulu-Natal.

Matumi trees along a water course in the Wolkberg, Northern Drakensberg, Limpopo

When young, the trees have narrow crowns but with age they become huge, with wide crowns. The leaves are simple and arranged usually in whorls of four. They resemble those of the oleander family, which characteristic gave rise to the common name **wild oleander**.

The outstanding feature of the matumi, besides its size, is its wood, which is hard, yellow to yellow-brown with black markings, heavy, oily and durable. It is a sought-after wood for special furniture but not readily available, because the tree is protected under the National Forests Act. Matumi trees count among South Africa's big trees, with the biggest recorded one growing on the Amorentia Estate near Modjadjiskloof in Limpopo. This giant tree has a stem diameter of 2,81 m, is 33 m high and has a crown width of 37 m, covering an area of 943 m^2. (See *The Top 30 Indigenous Trees of South Africa*.)

Very large matumi trees are being conserved in the Umhlume Natural Heritage Site, Pongola, KwaZulu-Natal, together with tree aloes, kiaat and *Euphorbia grandidens* trees (the valley-bush euphorbia).

A real giant of a tree: the Amorentia matumi (one of a triplet of giant matumi trees known as The Three Queens) near Tzaneen, one of the largest indigenous trees in South Africa

ASTERACEAE (COMPOSITAE)
The Daisy Family

Asteraceae is the largest of all the flowering families in the world, with about 900 genera and over 17 000 species worldwide, mostly herbaceous. Two well-known plants cultivated commonly throughout South Africa, the lettuce (vegetable) and the sunflower (oilseed crop), belong to this family. Characteristic features of the family are the small flowers clustered in dense heads surrounded by a ring or rings of bracts, i.e. the 'petals' of a daisy flower. The calyx is replaced by a bristly pappus that acts as a parachute to disperse the seed. This characteristic has resulted in the family being known for its beautiful compound flowers, such as dahlias, originally from Mexico, chrysanthemums from the Eastern countries, daisies and gazanias from South Africa, and asters, zinnias, cosmos, marigolds and many others from elsewhere. A large number of plants from the family are weeds, some notorious, such as blackjack, scotch thistle and burweed.

Daisies, synonymous with Namaqualand, small exuberantly flowering plants, are related to a number of remarkable South African trees

In spite of its numerical abundance, and proffering such a wealth of flowers, the daisy family is poor in trees. Six genera of trees native to South Africa appear in this family. *Brachylaena* (**wild silver oak**), with relations in tropical Africa, occurs in a variety of localities in South Africa, with the exception of the most arid regions. Various species of *Brachylaena* have a durable yellow wood tinged with brown, which is extensively used for carving purposes, especially by Kenyans, where it is regarded the best wood for this purpose after African black ebony.

Tarchonanthus camphoratus (**wild camphor bush**) is widespread in South Africa. This shrub or small tree (up to 9 m) has adapted to a wide variety of habitats and is increasingly becoming popular as a garden tree, with its thistle-form creamy-

Weird 'donkey's ears', Suurberg cushion bushes on a hill near Grahamstown, Eastern Cape (Photo: Tony Dold)

white flowers being displayed sporadically throughout the year, depending on locality and conditions. The wood is also used widely for various articles, from musical instruments to walking sticks, and the leaves have been used by Zulu women to perfume their hair. It is also known by several other names, such as **sagewood**, **wild sage** and **wild cotton**.

Oldenburgia grandis (**Suurberg cushion bush** or **donkey's ears**) is an attractive and interesting shrub or small tree (up to 5 m), occurring only in a relatively small mountainous area in the Grahamstown area of the Eastern Cape, where it grows on hard sandstone outcrops. Its characteristically gnarled form has furnished this tree with the descriptive local common name 'mountain hunchback'. The leaves, resembling those of the loquat tree, are simple, large, stiff and leathery, with a dense, hairy grey-white under-surface, and are said to be poisonous. The flowerheads are creamy-yellow, large and daisy-like, and are borne in stalked terminal clusters.

Although not trees, other members of the genus *Oldenburgia* faintly resemble the abovementioned species. Found in the Western Cape mountains only, they cling cushion-like to the rocks, resembling a swarm of bees at rest. These very peculiar plants, with their stiff grey-green leaves, are hardly discernible from the grey Table Mountain sandstone on which they grow, and they remain a wonderful phenomenon to observe.

Fallen Giants

Although trees can live for thousands of years and the oldest living organism on earth is a tree, they do not live forever. Here we pay tribute to a few of those giants that were admired by South Africans in the past. Most of these once remarkable trees died of natural causes, but in some cases human intervention played a role.

Selati or Chief Magoeba palm (Near Tzaneen)
Died of natural causes in about 1950

Nonsiang baobab (Tshipise, Limpopo)
Collapsed in 1990, a combination of uncontrolled visits and drought
Measurements: height 21 m, crown diameter 27,4 m; stem diameter 6,29 m

Molopo Eye wild olive (North-West)
Died roundabout 1990, apparently of natural causes
Measurements: height 14 m; crown diameter 21 m; stem diameter 2 m

Livingstone ana trees (Mokopane, Limpopo)
Died in about 1990, perhaps as a result of excessive extraction of groundwater
Measurements: height 34 m, crown diameter 33,5 m; stem diameter 2,37 m

FALLEN GIANTS

Rosslyn red-leaved rock fig (Rosslyn, Gauteng)
Died in 1999, possibly because of lightning damage
Measurements: height 14 m; crown diameter 34 m; stem diameter 8,32 m (measured at ground level)

Groote Schuur cork oak (Cape Town)
Collapsed in 2000 from natural causes
Measurements: Only the diameter of 2,4 m is known

Woodbush saligna gum (Woodbush plantation, Tzaneen)
Blown over by wind in 2007
Measurements: height 84,4 m; crown diameter 14 m; stem diameter 1,31 m

If a tree dies, plant another in its place.
Carl Linnaeus

Cradock holly oak (Cradock, Eastern Cape)
Died in 2005 because of a fire started by a vagrant
Measurements: height 19 m; crown diameter 24,9 m; trunk diameter 1,79 m

Bibliography

Bolsmann Eric, 1997. *Jacaranda – Splendour of Pretoria*. Be My Guest Publishers CC, Pretoria

Boon R, 2009. *Pooley's trees of South Africa: a complete guide*. Natal Flora Publications, Durban

Bradlow Frank R, 1965. *Baron von Ludwig and the Ludwig'sburg Garden*. AA Balkema, Cape Town

Carruthers J & Robin L, 2010. Taxonomic imperialism in the battles for *Acacia*: Identity and science in South Africa and Australia. *Transactions of the Royal Society of South Africa* Vol. 65 (1), February 2010, pp. 48–64

Cycad Society of South Africa. *Journals*

Dendrological Society of Southern Africa. *Journal of Dendrology*. Pretoria

Department of Environmental Affairs and Tourism, 2000. *South African Natural Heritage Programme – Annual Report 2000/2001*. Schneider Electric South Africa, Midrand

Department of Water Affairs and Forestry. *Forestry News/Bosbounuus*. Pretoria

Editors of Sunset Books and Sunset Magazine, 1988. *Western garden book*. Lane Publishing Co, California

Feiniger Andreas, 1968. *Trees*. Thames and Hudson, London

Fondation Colas, 1995. *The Road to the Largest, Tallest and Millennary Trees*. Fondation Colas, Paris, France

Hora Bayard, 1981. *The Oxford Encyclopedia of Trees of the World*. Oxford University Press, Oxford

Hyams Edward & Maquitty William, 1969. *Great Botanical Gardens of the World*. Arnaldo Mondadori, Verona

Immelman WFE, Wicht CL & Ackerman DP (eds), 1973. *Our green heritage: The South African book of trees*. Tafelberg Publishers, Cape Town

Johnson Hugh, 1984. *Encyclopaedia of Trees*. Mitchell Beazley, London

Lawes M (ed), 2004. *Indigenous forests and woodlands in South Africa: policy, people and practice*. University of KwaZulu-Natal Press. Pietermaritzburg

Liebenberg Enrico & Erna, 2015. *We are the Champions: The Champion Trees of South Africa*. HPH Publishing, Pretoria

Lückhoff HA, 1963. Die Baviaanskloof- of Willowmore seder. *Bosbou in Suid-Afrika/Forestry in South Africa No 3*, October 1963

Mucina L & Rutherford MC (eds), 2006. *The vegetation of South Africa, Lesotho and Swaziland*. South African National Biodiversity Institute, Pretoria

Olivier W, 2009. *There is honey in the forest: The history of South African forestry*. Southern African Institute of Forestry, Pretoria

O'Rell Max, 1894. *John Bull & Co*. Frederick Warne & Co, London

Palmer Eve & Pitman Norah, 1972. *Trees of Southern Africa*. AA Balkema, Cape Town

Palgrave Meg Coates, 2002. *Trees of Southern Africa* (revised edition). Struik Publishers, Cape Town

Pooley Elsa, 1994. *Trees of Natal*. Natal Flora Publication Trust, Durban

Poynton RJ, 1977. *Tree Planting in Southern Africa Vol 1. The Pines*. Government Printer, Pretoria

Poynton RJ, 1979. *Tree Planting in Southern Africa Vol 2. The Eucalypts*. Government Printer, Pretoria

Reynolds Gilbert Westacoh, 1969. *The aloes of South Africa*. AA Balkema, Cape Town

Rourke JP, 1980. *The Proteas of Southern Africa*. Purnell, Cape Town

Shone AK, ND. *Notes on the marula*. Government Printer, Pretoria

Tree Society of South Africa. *Journals*

Van der Merwe IJ, 2002. *The Knysna and Tsitsikamma forests: Their history, ecology and management*: Second (revised) edition. Department of Water Affairs and Forestry, Pretoria

Van der Walt PT (ed), 2010. *Bushveld: Ecology and management*. Briza Publications, Pretoria

Van der Zel DW & Brink AJ, 1980. Die Geskiedenis van Bosbou in Suider-Afrika Deel II: Plantasiebosbou. *SA Forestry Journal No 115,* December 1980

Van Rensburg Andrew. *Information leaflets on Trees*. Department of Forestry

Van Wyk Ben-Erik, Van Oudtshoorn Bosch, Gericke Nigel, 1997. *Medicinal plants of South Africa*. Briza Publications, Pretoria

Van Wyk Braam & Van Wyk Piet, 2013. *Field guide to trees of Southern Africa*. Struik Publishers, Cape Town

Von Breitenbach F (comp.), 1984. *National List of Introduced Trees*. Dendrological Society, Pretoria

Von Breitenbach F (comp.), 1995. *National List of Indigenous Trees (Third, revised edition)*. Dendrological Society, Pretoria

Von Breitenbach J *et al*, 2001. *Pocket list of Southern African Indigenous trees: Including selected shrubs and woody climbers:* First abridged impression, fourth edition. Briza Publications & Dendrological Society, Pretoria

Von Durckheim H, Van Wyk B & Van den Berg E, 2014. *Pocket list of Southern African indigenous trees*. Briza Publications & Dendrological Society, Pretoria

Index

A
Abasas tree 159, 160
Abies pinsapo 89
Acacia albida 191
Acacia atomiphylla 187
Acacia cyclops 114, 194
Acacia mearnsii 112, 193
Acacia melanoxylon 193
Acacia name change 183
Acacia pendula 194
Acacia saligna 194
Adansonia digitata 17, 22, 44, 47, 49, 51, 52, 58, 59, 61, 104, 117, 234
Adansonia grandidieri 234
Adansonia kilima 117
Adenium multiflorum 249
Adenium swazicum 249
Adopt a Champion Tree programme 42
afforestation 120, 121, 195
African boekenhout 167
African cycads 125
African fan palm 138
African flame 253
African oil palm 138
'African sandalwood' 213
African wattle 198
African white sugarbush 164
Afrocarpus falcatus 17, 22, 32, 40, 47, 48, 49, 52, 54, 59, 109, 131
Afrocarpus species 67
Afzelia quanzensis 198
Agathis robusta 56
Akkerdraai Oak Tree 58
Albany Thicket 15, 106, 108
Albizia adianthifolia 193
Albizia tanganyicensis 193
Aleppo pine 56, 230
Alien Big Five 26
Aloe species 73, 148
Aloe ferox 151
Aloe marlothii 150
Aloe rupestris 151
Aloidendron barberae 148
Aloidendron dichotomum 148, 149
Aloidendron pillansii 148, 149, 150
Aloidendron species 73
Amorentia Estate 23, 25, 40, 255
ana tree 23, 48, 49, 159, 191, 258
Anacardiaceae 217
Androstachys johnsonii 212
Angophora costata 69
Anthocleista grandiflora 49, 99, 246
Apocynaceae 249
apple gum 69
apple tree 180
apple-leaf tree 202
'apple-ring thorn-tree' 191
Araliaceae 232
Araucaria species 80
Araucaria heterophylla 54, 67, 76
Arbor City Award 98, 102, 103, 170, 252
arboreta 39, 69, 120, 225, 229
arborists 36
ARC Infruitec-Nietvoorbij 73
Arderne Aleppo Pine 56
Arderne Cork Oak 55

Arderne Fig Tree 55
Arderne Garden 27, 64, 67, 73, 144, 154, 231
Arderne Kauri 56
Arderne Pine 55
Arderne Turkey Oak 55
Arderne, Henry 55, 56, 67
Arderne, Ralph 40, 55, 56, 64, 67, 68
Arecaceae 138
Artocarpus heterophyllus 87
ash trees 243
assegai 120
Asteraceae 256
Augrabies National Park 174
Auraucaria heterophylla 55
Aurecon 42
Austin Roberts Bird Sanctuary 93
Australian chestnut 90
Avicennia marina 84, 109
avocado family 175
avocado tree 178
Azadirachta indica 210
azaleas 67, 89, 100

B
Babylonstoren Garden 71
Baines cobas 233
balsa tree 234
bamboo 146
banyan fig 87, 160
baobab 17, 22, 28, 49, 51, 52, 58, 59, 61, 98, 101, 104, 234–239, 258
'baobab forest' 238
Baobab Hill 239
Barringtonia species 84
bastard camphor tree 177
bastard quiver tree 148, 150
bastard stinkwood 176, 177
bauhinia 195
Bauhinia galpinii 197
Baviaanskloof cedar 136
Bay Head Natural Heritage Site 85
bay tree 175
Baynes, Joseph 40, 57, 90
Baynesfield Estate 90
Baynesfield Tulip Tree 57
Beachwood mangrove swamp 84
beech family 168
beech trees 167, 168
beefwood 56
bell-bean tree 251
Benvie Arboretum 56, 89, 225, 227
Benvie Trees 56
Bequaertiodendron magalismontanum 240
Bergplaas State Forest 34
Bergzicht Market Trees 54
Betula species 90
Bezuidenhout Park 95, 172
big cone pine 230
Big Tree Register 15, 41, 47–49
Bignoniaceae 251
Bindura bamboo 146
biological control 194, 216
biomes 15, 16, 63, 91, 102, 105–111, 151, 161, 164, 179
birch tree 90
Bird of Paradise bush 195
bitter almond 180
bitter aloe 151

bitter cassava 211
black ear 210
black ironwood 245
black mangrove 109
black monkey thorn 189
black stinkwood 79, 175
black thorn 107
black wattle 112, 193
blackwood 193
blossom tree 109, 202
Blouberg Big Trees 32, 35, 59
blue cobas 233
blue fig 210
blue gum 59, 60, 222, 227
blue laurel 177
boer-bean tree 73
Bohdi 91
Bolusanthus speciosus 91, 202
Bombacaceae 41, 234
Bombax species 234
Bonniemile Oak 56
Boom, Hendrik 64
Borassus aethiopum 138
borassus palm 138
Boscia albitrunca 44
bottlebrush aloe 151
Bo-Tuin 68
braaiwood 114, 247 *see also* firewood
Brabejum species 161
Brabejum stellatifolium 73, 167
Brachylaena discolor 257
Brachystegia spiciformis 210
Brackenhill Gum Trees 56
Brandmüller, Otto 223
Brazil kapok tree 234
Brazilian pepper tree 217
'Breakfast tree' 184
Bredenkamp, Prof Brian 76, 77
Breede River yellowwood 131
Brenthurst Garden 97
Breonadia salicina 23, 40, 48, 51, 52, 111, 158, 255
'Briscoe tree' 239
bristlecone pine 17, 41
broad-leaved boekenhout 167
broad-leaved coral tree 202
broad-leaved quince 177
Brugueria gymnorrhiza 109
Bruguiera species 84
Buddha Tree 91
Buffalo River thorn 196
Buffelsdrift baobab 28, 30, 47, 59
Buffelsnek Pine 58
Buffelsnek State Forest 27
Burgers Park 93, 155
bushman's tea 111, 116
Bushveld 15, 106, 107
bushveld boekenhout 167
bushveld mahogany 89
bushwillow family 247
Butcher Arboretum 88
Butia capitata 80, 144

C
cabbage tree family 232
Cactaceae 215
Cactoblastis cactorum 216
cactus family 215
Caesalpinia species 195
Caesalpinioideae 182, 195
Calcutta Botanical Garden 160
Californian redwood 27, 57, 58, 60, 73, 74, 225

camel thorn 17, 73, 101, 104, 114, 115, 182, 186
camphor tree 18, 27, 42, 43, 53, 60, 72, 121, 175, 177
canary palm 93, 94, 143
candelabra tree 214
candle pod acacia 189
candle-pod thorn tree 44
Cannabaceae 152
cannonball tree 87
Canterbury mulberry tree 74
Cape ash 49, 207
Cape bottlebrushes 166
Cape coast wattle 194
Cape date palm 142
Cape Floristic Kingdom 15, 16, 63, 161
Cape Forest Act 120
Cape Fynbos 15 *see also* Fynbos
Cape honeysuckle 251
Cape Point Nature Reserve 166
Cape quince 177
carbon dating 17, 116, 132, 236
carbon sequestration 108
carob 75, 90, 195
Cassia abbreviata 198
Castanea sativa 172
Castanea species 168
Castanospermum australe 90
castor-oil plant 211
casuarina 94
Casuarina cunninghamia 56
Catha edulis 111, 116
Catophractes alexandrii 251
cedar 117
Cedrelopsis species 205
Cedrus deodara 42, 55
Ceiba species 234
Celtis africana 49, 92, 94, 152, 153
Celtis australis 152, 153
Celtis gomphophylla 152
Celtis sinensis 152, 153
Centurion, The 61
Ceraria namaquensis 174
Ceratonia siliqua 75, 90, 195
Ceriops species 84
Ceroplesus species 115
Champion Tree project 38, 41
Champion Trees 19, 36, 51–60
Cheerio farm 100
cherry blossom tree 100
chestnut 168, 172, 173
Chief Magoeba palm 139, 258
Chinese hackberry 152, 153
Chinese lantern 207
Chinese nettle 152, 153
chir pine 230
Chlorophora excelsa 155
Chorisia speciosa 234
Chrysobalanaceae 179
churchyard cypress 137
Cinara cupressi 137
Cinchona species 255
Cinnamomum camphora 27, 42, 53, 60, 175, 177
Cinnamomum zeylanicum 175, 177
cinnamon tree 175
City Square Park 99
Clanwilliam cedar 134
Cleistanthus schlechteri 212
Cliffortia arborea 179

cluster fig 22
Cluster Fig Giant 52
cluster pine 121, 230
coast coral tree 200, 201
coast redwood 61
cobas 233
cochineal 216
coconut palm 138
Cocos nucifera 138
Coffea arabica 255
coffee palm 142
Colophospermum mopane 196
Colvillea racemosa 87
Combretaceae 84, 247
Combretum imberbe 17, 49, 114, 247
Combretum microphyllum 247
commercial forestry industry 118–122, 222, 229
common cabbage tree 48, 232
common cluster fig 47, 48, 52, 59, 158
common coral tree 200, 201
common forest grape 233
common sugarbush 164
common wild fig 22, 47, 48, 57, 59, 157
common wild quince 177
Commonwealth Plantation 42, 53
Company's Garden 64, 65, 66, 73, 74, 121, 144, 148, 149, 181
Compositae 256
conebush 164
Conservation of Agricultural Resources Act of 1983 39, 113
conservation, tree and forest 18, 104–113, 186
coral trees 200
Cordyla africana 49, 199
cork oak 55, 60, 172, 259
Cornellskop Natural Heritage Site 150
Corpulent Big Five 28
Corymbia ficifolia 55
cottonwood tree 58
Couroupita guianensis 87
Cradock holly oak 259
'cream of tartar tree' 235
crocodile bark 189
crying tree 214
Cryptocarya angustifolia 177
Cryptocarya latifolia 177
Cryptocarya liebertiana 177
Cryptocarya myrtifolia 177
Cryptocarya woodii 177
Cryptocarya wyliei 177
Cryptomeria japonica 89
cultural significance 18
Cupressaceae 134
Cupressus species 134
Cupressus sempervirens var. *sempervirens* 137
curiosity value 44
Cussonia natalensis 232
Cussonia paniculata 232
Cussonia sphaerocephala 49, 232
Cussonia spicata 48, 59, 232
Cyathea capensis 124
Cyathea dregei 124
Cyatheaceae 124
cycad family 125
cycad gene bank 98, 130

Index

cycads 111
cycads, illegal trade 130
Cycas thouarsii 125
Cyphostemma bainesii 233
Cyphostemma currori 233
Cyphostemma juttae 233
Cyphostemma uter 233
cypress 82, 134, 137
cypress family 134

D

Dactylopius ceylonicus 216
daisy family 256
Daisy Kopje Natural Heritage Site 190
Dalene Matthee (Big) Tree 32, 54
Dan-Ben-Hannah vine 74
date palm 75, 138, 144, 145
dawn redwood 73, 75
De Vasselot de Regné, Count M 120
De Waal Park 69
Deadbeat ana trees 191, 192
dead-man's tree 214
deforestation 110
degradation, forest 110
Delonix regia 195
dendrochronology 117
deodar cedar 42, 55, 82
Desert Biome 15
devil's claw 254
'Die Eik' 170
Diepwalle State Forest 32, 34, 124
Diospyros mespiliformis 203, 252
Diplodea pinea 229, 230
'dolfhout' 203
donkey's ears 257
dopperkiaat 204
Dracaena draco 80
dragon trees 80
Drakensberg protea 164
Duiwelskloof 99
Durban Botanical Garden 87, 129, 155, 160
durian 234
Durrio zibenthinus 234
dwarf coral tree 202
dwarf mobola 45

E

Eastern Cape Monarch 23, 32, 33, 54
Eastern Cape Pine 56
Ebenaceae 203
ecosystems 15
ecotones 109
edible fig 154
Eikenhof Arboretum 78
'Eikestad' 169
Ekebergia capensis 49, 207, 219
El Dorado Natural Heritage Site 244
Elaeis guineensis 138
Eleaocarpus grandis 210
elephant's trunk 250
elm family 152
Emporia melanobasis 213
Encephalartos altensteinii 125
Encephalartos dyerianus 130
Encephalartos eugene-maraisii Verdoorn 126, 130
Encephalartos horridus 125
Encephalartos inopinus 129
Encephalartos lebomboensis 129
Encephalartos longifolius 125
Encephalartos middelburgensis 127, 128
Encephalartos natalensis 129
Encephalartos senticosus 129
Encephalartos transvenosus 126

Encephalartos woodii 87, 129
Englerophytum magalismontanum 240
English oak 42, 45, 53, 54, 55, 56, 58, 65, 72, 94, 169
Entada rheedii 192
Entandophragma species 207, 210
Enterolobium contortisiliquum 210
Ernest Oppenheimer Garden 102
Erythrina acanthocarpa 202
Erythrina caffra 200, 201
Erythrina falcata 91
Erythrina humeana 202
Erythrina latissima 202
Erythrina lysistemon 200, 201
Erythrina zeyheri 45, 202
eucalypt 94, 113, 120, 221, 222
Eucalyptus camaldulensis 26, 53, 54, 56, 57, 59, 226
Eucalyptus citriodora 56
Eucalyptus diversicolor 40, 56, 60, 226
eucalyptus family 221
Eucalyptus ficifolia 55
Eucalyptus globulus 59, 60, 222, 227
Eucalyptus grandis 58, 59
Eucalyptus maculata 42, 53
Eucalyptus microrys 53
Eucalyptus paniculata 53
Eucalyptus regnans 56, 61, 89, 225
Eucalyptus saligna 26, 52, 53, 57, 58, 60, 61
Eucalyptus salubris 227
Eucalyptus species 53, 221
Eucalyptus viminalis 227
Eucalyptus viminalis × *huberiana* 89, 227
Eugenia species 221
euphorbia 73
Euphorbia grandidens 255
Euphorbia ingens 214
Euphorbia pulcherrima 211
Euphorbia tirucalli 214
Euphorbiaceae 211
Euproctis terminalis 231
European hackberry 152, 153
European lime 172
European nettle 152, 153
European oak 121
Evening Star Natural Heritage Site 146
exotic bamboo 147
exotic species 26, 112, 120, 137, 143, 154, 193, 194, 208, 210, 215, 221, 229, 243, 252

F

Fabaceae 182, 195, 200
Fagaceae 168
Fagus species 168
Fagus sylvatica 172
Fagus sylvatica var. *purpurea* 172
Faidherbia albida 23, 48, 49, 191
false flamboyant 87
false tamboti 212
false Weymouth pine 58, 231
false white stinkwood 152
false-thorn trees 193
fan aloe 150
Faurea galpinii 167
Faurea macnaughtonii 167
Faurea rochetiana 167
Faurea saligna 167
Faurea speciosa 161, 167
Faurea speciosa 167
feather palm 142

feather-weight tree 212
Fernwood Trees 60
ferox cycad 130
fever tree 190
fever tree forest 191
Ficus benghalensis 160
Ficus burkei 22, 47, 48, 57, 59, 157
Ficus carica 154
Ficus cordata 49, 159
Ficus hippopotami 160
Ficus ingens 49
Ficus macrophylla 27, 45, 55, 58, 60, 68, 93, 154, 178
Ficus natalensis 49
Ficus polita 49
Ficus religiosa 91
Ficus salicifolia 22, 43, 44, 47, 51, 75, 155
Ficus sansibarica 49
Ficus sycomorus 22, 40, 45, 47, 48, 52, 59, 158
Ficus thoningii 59
Ficus trichopoda 160
fig family 154
fig tree 154
'Fingo Milkwood' 242
firewood 114, 182, 194 *see also* braaiwood
flamboyant family 195
flame creeper 247
flatcrown false-thorn 193
flat-crowned paperbark 190
flat-flowered aloe 151
Flower of Kent 74
forest apple-leaf 203
Forest Big Five 32
forest boekenhout 167
forest boer-bean 197
forest cabbage tree 49, 232
forest fever tree 49, 99, 246
forest mahogany 88, 208
forest tree fern 124
forestry industry 39, 222, 229
Fraxinus species 243
Free State National Botanical Garden 83
Fremont cottonwood 102
fringed bottlebrush 166
fruit tree, oldest 181
Fynbos Biome 15, 72, 109, 161, 164

G

gabba bush 251
'Gallows Tree' 209
Gannabos Natural Heritage Site 150
Garden of Gethsemane 17, 244
Garden of Remembrance 73
gardenia family 255
Geekie, John 40, 56, 89
Genadendal 181
Genadendal pear tree 74
General Sherman tree 61
genetic barcoding 117
gentian family 246
Gentianaceae 246
Gethsemane olive tree 74, 75
ghost moth 202
giant blueberry ash 210
giant quiver tree 73, 148, 149, 150
giant redwood 61
giant-tree climbing 36
gimlet 227
Ginkgo biloba 75, 90
Glencoe baobab 28, 42, 47, 51, 116, 239
Golden Gate National Park 164

Gonometa moth 184, 197
Goudveld State Forest 32
Graaff-Reinet vine 74, 81
Grahamstown Botanical Garden 80
'Grandfather of Still Bay' 52
grape family 233
grass family 146
grass tree 89
Grassland 15
grassveld tree fern 124
Greefswald Forest 107
green beech 172
green tree pincushion 166
grey camel thorn 187
grey ironbark 53
Groote Schuur 72, 172, 178, 259
Grootvadersbos Redwood Grove 57
growth rings 17, 116
guava 113
guava family 221
Gum Tree Corner 58, 85
gum trees 94, 221
Gypohierax angolensis 138

H

Hakea gibbosa 113
'halfmens' 250
Hampton Court Palace vine 74
Hanging Tree 55
Hantam National Botanical Garden 102
Harold Porter National Botanical Garden 73
Harpagophytum procumbens 254
Harpephyllum caffrum 207, 219
Hazeldene farm 90
Hedera helix 232
Heeria argentea 219
hemp family 152
Henkel's yellowwood 131, 133
Henkries date palms 145
Herbert Baker Chapel Trees 57
Hermann Eckstein Park 95
Heritiera species 84
Heteropyxis species 221
Hevea braziliensis 210, 211
Hexrivier orange tree 78
Highveld cabbage tree 232
Highveld protea 164
Himalayan spruce 89
Hippocrates tree 74
historical significance 18
Hogsback Redwood Giant 60
Hohenort Grove 60
holly oak 172, 259
Holy Venda bamboo 146
Honnet Nature Reserve 238
'Hotnotsriem' 174
Houwhoek Inn Tree 60
Huon pine 17
Hyaenanche globosa 212
hyena poison tree 211, 212
Hyperion tree 61
Hyphaene coriacea 140
hypsometer 42

I

Ida's Valley Giant 55
ilala palm 140, 141
Ilembe Tree 45, 59, 158
illegal harvesting 111
Imbrasia belina 197
Imbrasia cytherea 229
imbuia 175, 176, 210
impala lily 249
Ina Paarman Oak 60
'indaba tree' 158
Indian banyan tree 160
Indian long-leaved pine 230

Infruitec Garden 73, 81, 145, 147, 178, 181, 244
Infruitec Gum Tree 57
Inhambanella henriquezii 241
International Commonwealth Plots 225
intovane 91, 220
invader species 39, 112, 113, 193, 194, 216, 229, 253
Irene Champion 53
Irene Estate 94
iroko 155
iron martin 219
ironwood 67, 243, 245
Isaac Newton apple tree 74
Isidenge pine 42
ivy family 232

J

jacaranda 65, 104, 113, 252
jacaranda family 251
Jacaranda mimosifolia 65, 104, 252
jackalberry 203, 252
jackfruit 87, 155
Jameson Park 88
Jan Celliers Park 92
Jan Kempdorp poplar avenue 102
Japanese cedar 89
JDM Keet Arboretum 99, 176, 210
jelly palm 80, 144
Jerusalem pine 230
Johannesburg parks 95
jointed cactus 216
Joubert Park 96
Jubaeopsis caffra 80, 140

K

Kaoko cobas 233
kapok family 234
karee 73, 219
Karoo Biome 15
Karoo Desert National Botanical Garden 73
karri (gum) 40, 56, 60, 226
Kathu Forest 186
keystone species 115
khat 111
Khaya anthoteca 210
Khaya species 207
kiaat 203
Kigelia africana 251
kilima baobab 117
Kindergarten Giant 59
King Edward VIIth Tree 32, 34, 52
King of Ga-Ratjeke baobab 28, 29, 47, 58
king protea 161
Kirstenbosch National Botanical Garden 63, 72, 73, 165, 167, 178
knob-berry trees 219
knobbly fig 49
knobthorn 189
Knysna–Tsitsikamma forests 40, 78, 79, 109
Kogelberg Biosphere Reserve 17, 73
Kogelberg silver bottlebrush 166
Koo apple tree 74
Kosi palm 98, 138, 139, 140
Koufontein candle pod thorn tree 189
krantz sugarbush 162
'kreupelboom' 166
'kreupelhout' 166
kudu lily 250

L

Kumara plicatilis 150
Kurisa Forest Giant 59
Kurisa Moya forest 232
KwaZulu-Natal National Botanical Garden 85
Kweekskool Tree 54, 76

lacquer 217
Lagarostrobos franklinii 17
lala palm 140, 141
lance-leaved myrtles 221
Lannea species 219
latex 154, 211, 213, 240
Lauraceae 175
laurel family 175
laurel tree 175
Laurophyllus capensis 219
Laurus nobilis 175
lavender trees 221
leadwood 17, 49, 114, 247
Lebombo ironwood 212
Lebombo wattle 193
'lêboom' 238
Lecythidaceae 84
Leeuwenhof 68
Leguminosae 182
'lemonade tree' 235
lemon-scented gum 51, 56
leopard tree 195
Leucadendron argenteum 63, 109, 165
Leucadendron species 161, 164
Leucosidea sericea 179
Leucospermum conocarpodendron subsp. *conocarpodendron* 166
Leucospermum conocarpodendron subsp. *viridum* 166
Leucospermum reflexum 166
Leucospermum species 161, 165
Ligustrum species 243
lilac 243
Liliaceae 148
Lilium candidum 148
Lillie cycad 130
lily family 80, 148
linden tree 172
Linnaeus, Carl 18, 138, 161, 167, 240
Liriodendron tulipifera 57, 90
Lister, Joseph Storr 40, 53, 69, 196
Livingstone (ana) trees 192, 258
Livingstone, Dr David 81, 156, 181, 192, 234
loblolly pine 58, 231
Lombardy poplar 54, 104
Lonchocarpus capassa 202
London plane 53, 74, 85
Lost City Botanical Garden 101
Louis Botha Park 99
Lowveld cabbage tree 38, 59
Lowveld National Botanical Garden 98, 130
Loxostylis alata 219
Ludwig's-burg Garden 62, 65, 66, 73, 216, 253
'luisiesboom' 165
Lumnitzera species 84, 247
Lydenburg cycad 129

M

Macadamia integrifolia 161
macadamia nut 161
madonna lily 148
Magennis Park 81
Magoebaskloof Giants 52, 61
mahogany 210
mahogany family 207
maidenhair tree 75, 90
Malagasy cycad 125

mammoth tree 73
Mananga Cycad Colony 129
manatoka tree 75
Mandela, Nelson 76, 153, 178
mango family 207, 217
mangroves 84, 85, 109, 247
Manie van der Schijff Botanical Garden 91
Manihot esculenta 211
manketti 212
manna gum 227
Mapungubwe National Park 159
Marais, Eugène 126, 127, 191
Marico Tree 57
Markhamia zanzibarica 251
Marriot's Lane 53
marula 74, 107, 217
Matthee, Dalene 32, 54, 79
matumi 22, 23, 25, 40, 48, 51, 111, 158, 255
medicinal use 116, 151, 180, 202, 206, 246, 254, 255
Melia azedarach 208
Melia azedarach var. *umbraculiformis* 209
Meliaceae 84, 207
Melrose House 93, 155
Melville Koppies Nature Reserve 96
Merensky, Dr Hans 53, 60, 99, 226
Merensky Lane 60, 99
Mesembryantheaceae 73
Metasequoia glyptostroboides 73, 75
Metrosideros species 221
Mhlopeni Natural Heritage Site 241
Middelburg cycad 127
milk pear 241
milkbush family 211
milkbushes 213
milkwood 52
milkwood family 240
Millettia grandis 203
Millettia sutherlandii 203
Mimetes arboreus 166
Mimetes argenteus 166
Mimetes cucullatus 166
Mimetes fimbriifolius 166
Mimetes species 73, 161, 166
Mimosoideae 182
Mimusops zeyheri 158
mingerhout 158
Misty Grove 58
Mitchell Park 88
Mkambati palm 140
mobola plum 179
Modjadji cycad 91, 126
Modjadji Nature Reserve 126
moepel 158
Moffat 'inhabited' tree 156
Moffat, Robert 81, 156, 181, 182
Molopo Eye wild olive 258
Mondi Tree Fern Reserve 124
monkey puzzle 80
monkey thorn 23, 25, 48, 57, 187
Monterey pine 56, 229
Monteseel Township 129
'montestrobus' pines 231
Montezuma cypress 28, 61, 239
Montezuma pine 231
Moolmanshoek Natural Heritage Site 146
mopane 196
mopane bee 197
mopane worm 197
Moraceae 41, 154
Moreton Bay fig 27, 45, 55, 58, 60, 68, 72, 93, 94, 154, 178

Mosdene Natural Heritage Site 213
moss rose 174
mottled spine-tail swift 44, 51
Mount of Olives 17, 244
mountain aloe 150
mountain ash 56, 61, 89, 225
mountain cypress 134
msasa 210
Mucuna novo-guineensis 87
mulberry 121, 155
mulberry family 154
mutanari 196
Muvuyo wa Makhadzi 51
Myoporum laetum 75
Myrtaceae 221
myrtle family 221
myrtle quince 177

N

'naboom' 214
Nama Karoo 15
Namaqua fig 49, 159
Namaqua porkbush 174
Napoleon willow 74
Natal camel thorn 190
Natal cycad 129
Natal fig 49
Natal mahogany 208
Natal sugarbush 164
Natal yellowwood 133
National Forests Act 19, 21, 38, 51, 105, 111, 132, 186, 255
National Herbarium 91
National Heritage Resources 18, 19
National Heritage Resources Act of 1999 18, 19, 104
national monument (trees) 93, 96, 126, 129, 143, 159, 169, 181, 185, 190, 192, 219, 238, 242, 245
National Protected Area Expansion Strategy 106, 107
National Register of Big Trees 39, 47
Natural Forest 15, 106, 109
natural forests, early exploitation 118, 119, 120
Natural Heritage Site 89, 124, 129, 146, 150, 150, 165, 174, 180, 186, 188, 190, 213, 241, 244, 255
natural woodlands 15
neem 210
Nellmapius, Alois Hugo 53, 94, 223
Newlands plantation 121
Newton apple tree 181
Newtonia hildebrandtii 193
Nonsiang baobab 258
Norfolk Island pine 54, 55, 67, 68, 76
Northcliff Oak 55
nyala tree 23, 48, 49, 203
Nymania capensis 207

O

O'Connor tree lane 52
'Oak City' 77, 169, 170
oak trees 93, 104, 168 *see also* beech family
Ochroma pyramidale 234
Ocotea bullata 67, 175
Ocotea kenyensis 176
Ocotea porosa 175, 176, 210
oil palm 138
Old George–Knysna road 78
Oldenburgia grandis 257
oldwood 179
Olea capensis 243, 245
Olea capensis subsp. *macrocarpa* 67, 245

Olea europaea 243
Olea europaea subsp. *africana* 243, 244
Oleaceae 243
oleander family 249
olive family 243
olive tree 17, 121, 243
Omumborombonga 248
Opuntia aurantiaca 216
Opuntia ficus-indica 216
Opuntia vulgaris 216
orange tree 94
Outeniekwageelhout 49
Outeniqua yellowwood 22, 24, 32, 40, 41, 42, 47, 48, 49, 52, 54, 59, 79, 90, 109, 131
Oxytenanthera abyssinica 146
Ozoroa species 219

P

Paarl Arboretum 71
Pachypodium namaquanum 250
Pachypodium saundersii 250
palm family 138
palm park (Makhado) 100
palm-nut vulture 138, 140
Panax species 232
'pancake tree' 44, 190
paperbark false-thorn 193
'paperbark thorn' 190
Papilionoideae 182, 200
Parinari capensis subsp. *capensis* 45
Parinari curatellifolia 179
Parktown Tree 58
patula 231
Paul Roos Trees 56, 225
pea family 200
Peace Garden 91
pear tree 181
Pedaliaceae 254
Pelargonium species 73
Pella date palms 145
Peltophorum africanum 198
pepperbark tree 105, 111, 116
Persea americana 175, 178
Peruvian pepper tree 217, 220
petticoat palm 143
Phalaena venus 202
Philenoptera sutherlandii 203
Philenoptera violacea 202
Phoenix canariensis 94, 143
Phoenix dactylifera 75, 138, 142, 144
Phoenix reclinata 142
Picea smithiana 89
Piet Retief cycad 129
Pinaceae 228
pincushion 165
pine family 228
pine tree emperor moth 229
Pinus aristata var. *longaeva* 17
Pinus coulteri 230
Pinus elliotti 231
Pinus halepensis 56, 230
Pinus lambertiana 17
Pinus montezumae 231
Pinus patula 231
Pinus pinaster 121, 230
Pinus pinea 89, 121, 229
Pinus pseudostrobus 58, 231
Pinus radiata 56, 229
Pinus roxburghii 230
Pinus taeda 27, 58, 231
pioneer species 109, 112
plant taxonomy 117
plantation show blocks 69 *see also* arboreta
Platanus acerifolia 53, 74, 85
Platland baobab 28, 30, 44, 47, 52, 116, 237, 238
Plebina denoita 197

Plettenberg Bay timber storehouse 78
ploughbreaker 45, 202
Poaceae 146
pod mahogany 198
Podocarpaceae 131
Podocarpus elongatus 131
Podocarpus henkelii 131, 133
Podocarpus latifolius 131, 133
Podocarpus species 67, 117
poinsettia 211
poison berry 217
pollution 107, 108, 109
Pondo palm 80, 140
poplar 113
Populus deltoides 58
Populus fremontii 102
Populus nigra 54, 104
porkbush 15, 108, 174
Port Jackson 194
portulaca family 174
Portulaca grandiflora 174
Portulacaceae 174
Portulacaria afra 15, 108, 174
Post Office baobab 28, 31, 237
Post Office Tree (Mossel Bay) 18, 19, 52, 74, 241, 242
Pretoria National Botanical Garden 91
Pretoria National Zoological Garden 94
prickly pear family 215
Pride of Barbados 195
Pride of De Kaap 197
Prince Alfred Park 80
privet 243
protea 92
Protea caffra 164
protea family 161
Protea gaguedi 164
Protea neriifolia 162
Protea nitida 163
Protea Park 92
Protea roupelliae 164
Protea species 161, 162
Protea woodland 164
Proteaceae 72, 161
protected tree 38, 105, 111, 114, 117, 132, 146, 176, 182, 196, 213, 219, 236, 238, 245, 255
protected woodland 186
Protorhus longifolia 219
Prunus africana 48, 79, 180
Prunus species 100, 179, 180
Ptaeroxylaceae 205
Ptaeroxylon obliquum 205
Pteleopsis species 247
Pterocarpus angolensis 203
Pterocarpus rotundifolius 204
purple beech tree 172
purslane family 174
pynbos 91
pyrogenic geoxylic suffrutices 45
Pyrus species 181

Q

Queens Park 81, 102
Queensland kauri 56
Quercus cerris 55
Quercus ilex 172
Quercus nigra 170
Quercus robur 42, 53, 54, 55, 56, 58, 65, 94, 104, 121, 169
Quercus species 168
Quercus suber 55, 60, 172
quince 177
Quisqualis species 247
quiver tree 73, 148, 149
quiver tree forest 150

R

radiata pine 229
Radyn Tree 59

Index

raffia palm 139
'Rain Forest' 126
'rain tree' 197, 198
rainbow leaf 91, 219
Raphia australis 139
Raphia species 139
real date palm 138, 142, 144
real yellowwood 131, 133
'Rebellion Tree' 185
red alder 120
red beech 219
red boekenhout 167
red eye wattle 194
red flowering gum 55
red mahogany 207, 210
red mangrove 109
red quince 177
red stinkwood 48, 79, 180
red-leaved rock fig 155, 259
Reinet House vine 81
Rendsburg Cycad Colony 129
renosterveld 17
resin trees 219
Rhigozum species 251
Rhipsalis baccifera 215
Rhizophora mucronata 109
Rhizophora species 84, 85
Rhizophoraceae 84
rhododendron 67, 68, 89, 100
Rhoicissus tomentosa 233
Rhus species 219
ribbon gum 89
Ricinus communis 211
Rietvlei Natural Heritage Site 174
river red gum 26, 40, 53, 54, 56, 57, 59, 226
robust cabbage palm 144
rock ash 219
rock cabbage tree 232
rock hakea 113
rocket pincushion 166
rooikrans 114, 194
Rosaceae 179
rose family 179
rose gum 37, 58, 59, 85
Rosslyn red-leaved rock fig 259
rough-barked ribbon gum 227
round-leaved teak 204
rubber euphorbia 214
rubber tree 210, 211
Rubiaceae 41, 255
Rumi olive 74
Ruth Fischer Tree 54
Ruth Steer Tree 56
Ryneveld Oaks 54

S

Saasveld Sentinels 58
Sabal palmetto 144
sagewood 257
Sagole baobab 22, 23, 28, 29, 44, 47, 51, 61, 239
saligna gum 26, 37, 52, 53, 57, 58, 60, 61, 225, 259
sap flow measurement 115
sapele mahogany 207
Sapotaceae 240
Satico Giants 59
Satico plantation 37
sausage tree 251
Savannah Biome 15 106, 107
Scanlen's Lane 56
Schefflera species 232
Schinus molle 217, 220
Schinus terebinthifolius 217
Schinziophyton rautanenii 212
'School Tree' 185
Schotia afra var. *angustifolia* 197
Schotia brachypetala 197
Schotia latifolia 197
Schotia species 197

Sclerocarya birrea subsp. *caffra* 74, 107, 217
sea bean 192
'sea oak' 241
Searsia lancea 219
Searsia radicans 217
Searsia species 219
Searsia succedanea 217
Seemannaralia species 232
Segeneiti tree 159
Selati palm 138, 139, 258
Senegalia burkei 189
Senegalia galpinii 23, 48, 57, 187
Senegalia mellifera 107
Senegalia nigrescens 189
Senegalia species 91, 182, 183
Senekal Church Square 83
Senna species 195
Sequoia sempervirens 27, 57, 58, 60, 61, 73, 74, 225
Sequoiadendron giganteum 61, 73
seringa 208
sesame family 254
Sesamothamnus lugardii 254
Sesamum indicum 254
Settlers Park 80
Shakespeare mulberry tree 74
shepherd's tree 44
show blocks 120
Sideroxylon inerme 52, 241
silk cotton tree 234
silver bottlebrush 166
silver sugarbush 164
silver tree 63, 72, 109, 165
Silwerboomkloof Natural Heritage Site 165
Sir Lionel Phillips Park 223
sjambok pod 198
Skyline Arboretum 88
slash pine 231
'Slave Tree' 42, 55, 169
small-leaved Karoo boer-bean 197
Smodingium argutum 217, 219
sneezewood family 205
Sonneratiaceae 84
Sonnertia species 84
Sophiatown Oak 39, 55
sour prickly pear 216
southern mountain bamboo 146
Spanish chestnut 172
Spanish fir 89
Spathodea campanulata 253
spekboom 15, 108, 109, 174
spiny cocklebur 112
Spirostachys africana 211, 212
spotted gum 42, 53
Spring Grove Arboretum 88
Springbok Park 92
St George's Park 80, 144, 155
St John's bread 75, 195
star tree 179
Stellenbosch University Botanical Garden 73
stemfruit 240
Sterboom Natural Heritage Site 180
Sterculiaceae 84
stinkwood 67, 120, 175
stone pine 63, 69, 121, 229
strandveld 17
strangler fig 157
Subtropical Thicket 15, 106, 108
Succulent Karoo 15, 102
succulents 73
sugar pine 229
sugarbushes 162
Suikerbosrant Nature Reserve 164

sun plant 174
Sunland baobab 28, 30, 44, 45, 47, 52
Suurberg cushion bush 257
Suurberg cycad 125
swamp fig 160
Swartwater baobab 59
Swazi lily 249
sweet prickly pear 216
sweet saffron pear 181
sweet thorn 92
Swietenia species 207
sycamore fig 40, 45, 158
Synadenium cupulare 214
syringa 113, 208
Syringa vulgaris 243
Syzygium species 221

T

Tabebuia species 253
Table Mountain 63, 64, 69
Table Mountain Grove 57
Table Mountain National Park 64
taeda pine 27
tallow gum 53
tamboti 211, 212
tambuki thorn 202
tapioca plant 211
Tarchonanthus camphoratus 257
tarwood 219
Taxodium mucronatum 61, 239
Technadria lacsa 217
Tecomaria capensis 251
terblanz beech 167
Terminalia species 247
Thamnocalamus tessellatus 146
thick-stemmed petticoat palm 143
thin-stemmed petticoat palm 143
thorn tree family 182
thorny pomegranate 251
Three Matrons 58, 231
Three Queens 23, 51, 52, 255
tipu 94, 204
tipuana 113
Tipuana tipu 94, 204
Tokai Arboretum 53, 69
tomography 32, 42, 117
'Town under the Trees' 186
'transformer species' 112
transpiration rate measurement 115
Transvaal boekenhout 167
Transvaal milkplum 240
Transvaal sesame bush 254
Transvaal stinkwood 176
Transvaal teak 255
'trassiedoring' 189
'Treaty Tree' 242
tree age 17, 21, 116, 132, 236
tree aloe 73, 148
tree demography 107
tree euphorbias 213
tree fern 100
tree fern family 124
tree measurement 52, 51
'Tree of Assemblage' 171
'Tree of Conspiracy' 245
'Tree of Meeting' 208
tree park (Makhado) 100
tree protea 163
Tree Protection Cooperative Programme 115
tree roots, longest 44
tree size 15, 21, 40, 41, 61
tree size, index 21, 28, 41, 47, 51
tree wistaria 91, 202
Trichilia dregeana 88, 208
Trichilia emetica 89, 208

Trinity vine 74
Triplaris americana 87
troutwood 179
'Truce Tree' 185
true cycad 125
true fynbos 17
true mahogany 207
trumpet trees 253
trumpet-thorn 251
Tsitsikamma Big Tree 32, 33, 42, 54
Tugela bush milkwood 241
Tule tree 61, 239
tulip tree 57, 90
Turkey oak 55
'Twee Eike' 170
Twin Streams 88
Tzaneen 99

U

Ulmaceae 152
'Ultimatum tree' 159
umbrella pine 229
Umfomothi 193
Umgwashu 242
umHlonhlo 214
Umhlume Natural Heritage Site 255
Umtentweni Giant 57
umtiza 196
Umtiza listeriana 196
Umtiza Nature Reserve 196
umzimbeet 203
underground trees 45
urban forest 95

V

Vachellia erioloba 17, 104, 114, 182, 186, 187
Vachellia haematoxylon 187
Vachellia hebeclada 189
Vachellia hebeclada subsp. *hebeclada* 44
Vachellia karroo 92
Vachellia sieberiana var. *woodii* 190
Vachellia species 91, 182, 183
Vachellia xanthophloea 190
Valley Bushveld 15
Valley of Ferns 124
valley-bush euphorbia 255
Van der Stel, Simon 64, 65, 69, 121
Van der Stel, Willem Adriaan 18, 53, 64, 121, 169, 177
Van Riebeeck, Jan 64, 72, 73, 121, 181
Verbenaceae 84
Vergelegen Estate 18, 27, 42, 45, 168, 169, 177
Vergelegen Oak 53
Vhembe Nature Reserve and Natural Heritage Site 159
Victoria Park 80
Virgilia oroboides 109, 202
Vitaceae 233
Vitellariopsis dispar 241
Von Ludwig, Baron 65, 66, 67, 68, 216, 253
Voortrekker Museum tree garden 89
vulturine fish eagle 138
Vygekraal Trees 59

W

wagon tree 163
Walter Sisulu National Botanical Garden 96
Warburgia salutaris 105, 111, 116
Washingtonia filifera 143
Washingtonia robusta 143
water berry 221

water oak 170, 171
Waterberg cycad 126
Waterkloof Giant 59
waterwood 221
watsonia 67
Watsonia ardernei 67
wattles 113, 182, 193, 194
wax palm 138
wax tree 217
weeping boerbean 197
weeping myall 194
weeping pine 231
Welbedacht Tree 60
Welwitschia mirabilis 73
Westfalia Estate 53, 60, 99, 178, 226
white mangrove 84, 109
white milkwood 241
white stinkwood 49, 92, 94, 152, 153
Widdringtonia cedarbergensis 134
Widdringtonia nodiflora 134
Widdringtonia schwarzii 136
Widdringtonia species 117, 134
wild almond 72, 73, 167, 180, 181
wild camphor bush 257
wild camphor tree 177
wild cotton 257
wild currant 219
wild date palm 142
wild elder family 246
wild fig 22, 45
wild laurel 177
wild mango 49, 199
wild myrtle 221
wild oleander 255
wild olive 73, 82, 243, 244, 258
wild plum 207, 219
wild quince 212
wild rice-bushes 179
wild rubber fig 49
wild sage 257
wild silver oak 257
wild teak 203
Wilds, The 96
Wilgenhof Grandfather 57
Willowmore cedar 136
Wits Campus Tree 57
'witteboom' 165
Wolkberg Wilderness Area 32
Wonderboom fig 22, 24, 43, 44, 47, 51, 75, 104, 155
Wonderboom Nature Reserve 22
Wonderwoud 32
Wood's cycad 87, 126, 129
Woodbush saliga gum 259
Woodbush State Forest 26, 37, 180, 225, 231
Woodville Big Tree 34, 54
Working for Water programme 113
World Heritage Site 73, 159

X

Xanthium spinosum 112
Xanthocercis zambesiaca 23, 48, 49, 203
Xanthorrhoea hastilis 89
Xylocarpus species 84

Y

yellow bush 164
yellowwood 17, 67, 79, 116, 117, 120
yellowwood family 131

Z

Zamiaceae 125
Zandvliet Oak 54
Zoo Giant 58